ELEMENTS
of COMPUTER
PROGRAMMING

ELEMENTS
of COMPUTER
PROGRAMMING

KENNETH P. SWALLOW
Late of the College of San Mateo

WILSON T. PRICE
Merritt College

HOLT, RINEHART AND WINSTON

New York   Chicago   San Francisco   Toronto   London

In Memoriam

KENNETH P. SWALLOW
1926–1965

Preface

Undoubtedly the greatest service a basic computer programming course can provide a beginner is to give him a firm foundation in stored program concepts. The degree to which he grasps these basic principles will determine, to a great extent, his success in advanced programming.

The choice of computer, programming language, and exercises for a basic course are important factors in determining the ease with which stored program concepts can be taught. We have used the following principles as guidelines in making our choices:

1. The instructional computer should be a commonly used system, simple to program in its own machine language, usable with an easy symbolic programming language, and readily suited to both alphabetic data manipulation and numeric computation.

2. A beginner should know that many professional programmers are using the same computer language he is studying, and that he can run his own programs on a real computer. Moreover, he should have experience with a computer, for two reasons: first, the computer is an excellent motivating factor; second, the student learns a great deal while "debugging" his programs. In this sense, the computer becomes a teaching machine.

3. Emphasis should be on concepts, approached in the simplest manner. Presenting details of operation unique to a specific computer is not desirable; in fact, it can frequently be confusing and discouraging to a beginner.

In this book the 141 DPS, an abbreviated version of the IBM 1401 DPS, provides the means for fulfilling all the above principles. The 141 was designed as a vehicle solely for teaching basic programming concepts. The instruction set is large enough to code a wide range of programming problems, but small enough to free the student from memorizing a large number of operational rules, thus allowing him to concentrate on understanding programming concepts.

The 141 set of fourteen instructions permits field definition, data movement, input/output operations, comparing, arithmetic operations, and branching. Exercises in 141 programming can illustrate all the basic programming concepts, such as reading, punching, and printing, looping for iterative processes, sequence checking, counted loops, address modification, program switches, and subroutine linkages.

Programs written in the 141 language can be run on the IBM 1401, 1410, 1460, and 7010 systems, and on the IBM System/360. They also can be run on the IBM 1620 system with a special simulator program.

Although a 1401 type of system suggests a business content, the materials in this book are not oriented exclusively in that direction. Examples involve problems of common interest, such as computing grade-point averages, square-root values, and values of pressure and temperature based on the perfect gas law.

The first three chapters introduce the history and fundamental ideas of computation. The basic instructions, in machine language, are described in Chapter 4. The transition to a symbolic programming system is developed in Chapters 5 and 6, so that programming fundamentals may be stressed without becoming bogged down in the "bookkeeping" necessary for a machine language. However, the machine-language equivalents of SPS programs are emphasized, since a thorough understanding of machine language is required throughout the remainder of the book. If an IBM 1620 is readily available, it is desirable for a student to study the appropriate portions of Appendix IV along with Chapters 4 and 6, to permit him to run his machine-language and/or SPS programs. Flowcharting and more sophisticated programming techniques are presented in Chapters 9–14. The final chapters give a brief introduction to the complete IBM 1401 system, and to Fortran and Cobol.

We would like to express our appreciation to Richard E. Gentry of the IBM San Francisco Education Center for his many creative ideas in the development of the 141 simulation on the IBM 1620, and to Libby Hines and Mary Price for their encouragement, understanding, and help. We also wish to thank Neil Rogers, Richard Banks, and William Seney for their time and effort in testing example programs during their course of study at Merritt College.

Oakland, California   Kenneth P. Swallow
January 1965   Wilson T. Price

Contents

PREFACE   vii

CHAPTER 1   HISTORY OF DIGITAL COMPUTERS   1

First Calculating Devices *1*
A Milestone *5*
The Punched Card *9*
Logic Machines *10*
Development of the Modern Digital Computer *11*
Commercially Available Computers *12*
Exercises *12*

CHAPTER 2   PRELIMINARY CONCEPTS   13

An Analogy *13*
The Computer *18*
The 141 Data Processing System *20*
Exercises *24*

CHAPTER 3   INFORMATION STORAGE   25

Card Coding *26*
Coding for Internal Storage *29*
Magnetic Core Storage *32*
Review Questions *36*

ix

CHAPTER 4   BASIC INSTRUCTIONS   37

    Data Movement   37
    Input/Output   49
    Branching   55
    Chapter Summary   56
    Exercises   57

CHAPTER 5   THE SYMBOLIC PROGRAMMING SYSTEM   60

    The Coding Sheet   61
    The SPS Card   63
    Assembling   65
    Pseudo Instructions   65
    Example Programs   67
    Additional SPS Instructions   75
    Chapter Summary   80
    Exercises   80

CHAPTER 6   SYMBOLIC PROGRAMMING SYSTEM
    ASSEMBLY   82

    An Analogy   82
    The Assembly   84
    The Object Deck   87
    Storage Contents   88
    Instructions and Pseudo Instructions   90
    Chapter Summary   91
    Exercises   91

CHAPTER 7   THE COMPUTER AND ARITHMETIC   92

    Addition   92
    Negative Numbers   95
    Subtraction   98
    Example Programs   100
    Chapter Summary   113
    Exercises   113

CHAPTER 8   CONDITIONAL BRANCHING   115

    Compare   116
    Branch If Indicator On   121
    Example Programs   122
    Chapter Summary   132
    Exercises   132

CHAPTER 9   PROGRAM DOCUMENTATION   134

      Comment Cards   *134*
      Program Reports   *136*
      Flowcharting   *136*
      Debugging   *146*
      Additional Examples   *146*
      Chapter Summary   *155*
      Exercises   *155*

CHAPTER 10   ADDITIONAL INSTRUCTION FORMS   157

      Set and Clear Word Mark   *157*
      Branching Forms   *158*
      Clear Storage   *160*
      Arithmetic   *162*
      Branch if Character Equal   *163*
      Remarks   *164*
      Exercises   *164*

CHAPTER 11   SUBROUTINES AND PROGRAM SWITCHES 165

      Address Adjusting   *165*
      Subroutines   *169*
      Subroutine Linkage   *169*
      The "Suppress Zero" Subroutine   *171*
      Subroutine Placement   *174*
      The "Multiply" Subroutine   *175*
      Another Subroutine Linkage   *178*
      The Program Switch   *180*
      Using the NOP   *181*
      Chapter Summary   *186*
      Exercises   *186*

CHAPTER 12   ADDRESS MODIFICATION   188

      Data and Instructions   *188*
      A Simple Program   *189*
      The "Suppress Zero" Subroutine   *192*
      The "Multiply" Subroutine   *193*
      Table Look-up   *200*
      Table Look-up Applications   *203*
      Index Registers   *211*
      Chapter Summary   *212*
      Exercises   *212*

CHAPTER 13   PROBLEMS AND SOLUTIONS   214

        Grade-point Averages   *215*
        Gross to Net   *220*
        Money and Interest   *225*
        Sorting Routines   *231*
        Statistical Computations   *238*
        Prime Numbers   *242*
        Square Root   *245*
        The Perfect Gas Law   *250*
        Remarks   *254*
        Exercises   *256*

CHAPTER 14   THE LOAD ROUTINE   263

        An Additional Instruction   *263*
        Loading the Object Program   *264*
        The "Bootstrap" Card   *268*
        "Clear Storage" Cards   *269*
        Reviewing the Load Operation   *271*
        Processor Control Operations   *272*

CHAPTER 15   THE IBM 1401 DATA PROCESSING SYSTEM   277

        IBM 1401 Addresses   *277*
        Arithmetic Operations   *279*
        Chaining Instructions   *281*
        Input/Output   *282*
        Branching Operations   *285*
        Data Movement   *288*
        Indexing Feature   *290*
        Magnetic Tape   *292*
        Basic Autocoder   *294*
        Full Autocoder   *296*
        Remarks   *298*
        Exercises   *298*

CHAPTER 16   HIGHER-LEVEL LANGUAGES   300

        Assemblers   *300*
        Compilers   *302*
        Fortran   *302*
        Cobol   *314*
        Algol   *319*
        Conclusion   *320*

APPENDIX I   SUMMARY OF INSTRUCTIONS   321

    141 Instructions   *321*
    SPS Pseudo Instructions   *327*

APPENDIX II   THE 141 CHARACTER CODE CHART   330

APPENDIX III   SUBROUTINES   332

    The "Multiply" Subroutine   *333*
    The "Divide" Subroutine   *334*
    The "Suppress Zero" Subroutine   *337*
    The "Edit" Subroutine   *338*

APPENDIX IV   OPERATING PROCEDURES   340

    141 SPS Assembler   *341*
    141 Simulator   *342*

INDEX   347

Chapter One

HISTORY OF DIGITAL COMPUTERS

From the beginning of time man has sought to find better devices to aid him in his computations. Probably the first, and certainly the simplest, device he found was his own fingers. In fact, it is from the word *digit*, meaning finger, that the class of calculating devices known as digital computers received its name. The term *digital* is used to contrast this type computer with the *analog* computer, which solves problems by means of mechanical or electrical analogies. This book deals entirely with digital computers.

Although using ten fingers for a counting device is certainly "handy" in all senses of the word, it is also very limited. One solution of running out of fingers is of course to count on the toes, and indeed, in many warmer areas of the world, early man used a number system based on twenty. The use of ten as a standard number base is a biological rather than a logical choice.

FIRST CALCULATING DEVICES

Early Devices

Probably the first device that man used to extend his counting capabilities beyond his digits was a pile of stones. For example, an early shepherd might have added one stone to a pile as each sheep went out to graze. At the end of the day, when the sheep returned, he would remove one stone as each sheep entered the gate. If, when the last sheep came in, there were no stones left, he could enjoy his supper.

However, if there were any stones left, he had another task, that of finding the strays. This was the basic idea of a *countdown* and the idea of one-to-one correspondence; that is, one stone corresponded to one sheep.

As time went on, the emphasis in man's life shifted from farming to merchandising. The quantities of measure and money became too large to use simple one-to-one correspondence with stones. One method by which the markers, which were originally small stones or pebbles, were given more than simple unit value was to draw a set of lines and spaces on a table top, as shown in Figure 1–1. Here the lines have the values 1, 10, 100, 1000 and 10,000, while the spaces between the lines have the values 5, 50, 500 and 5,000. The x on the 1000 line separates the

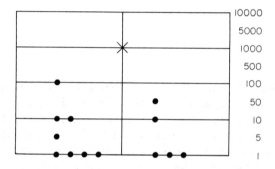

Figure 1–1. Early Merchandising Counter

thousands just as our comma does. In Figure 1–1, 129 is being added to 63. The place values on this counter correspond to the money system that was used at the time.

Note the similarity to our money system. Note also the many terms and phrases that we still hear today—we still call the bargaining table the *counter*, we still ask the customer to "lay it on the line," and we still use the term *carrying* when we do addition, as if we were moving a stone or marker from a space to the next line. In fact, it is from the Latin word *calculus*, meaning *pebble*, that we derive the words *calculate*, *calculation*, and *calculator*.

The early forms of this counter can be traced back to a time when the lines were simply traced in the dirt with a stick. At sometime during the course of history clever craftsmen began to drill holes in the stones, or beads, and mount them on rungs, which in turn they placed in a wooden frame. The resulting portable counting device became known as the *abacus*, from the Latin form of the Greek word *abax*, meaning dirt or dust.

The Abacus

The abacus is the most widely known digital computer. It has appeared all over the world in many forms and with as many different names. Figure 1–2 shows some of the more familiar forms. Notice that

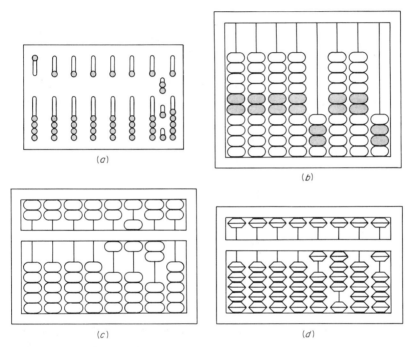

Figure 1–2. (a) *Roman Grooved Abacus* (b) *Russian Schoty*
(c) *Chinese Saun-Pan* (d) *Japanese Soroban*

the principal differences lie in the various coding schemes by which a group of beads represents a digit.

Improved "Carry" Techniques

The abacus was, and still is, a widely used calculating device, but it is limited by its inability to perform a "carry" from one place value to another. This task is left to the operator, who physically returns a group of beads on one rung and then advances one bead on the next rung. It was not until 1617 that any major improvement was made in the method of "carry." In that year, the Scotsman John Napier introduced his multiplication rods, which helped clarify the carrying in multiplication problems. To see how Napier's rods work (also called

Napier's bones, because they were often carved from bone), let us multiply 326 by 6. From the set of rods we would select the ones marked 3, 2, and 6 and place them on the table in that order (Figure 1–3*a*). We would then look only at the numbers on the sixth row and add diagonally (Figure 1–3*b*). Note that once again the carry was not actually performed by the calculating device; its design was such that it accentuated the concept.

Although Napier's rods are well worth mentioning, he is best known for his invention of logarithms. With the use of logarithms, multiplication and division become addition and subtraction. This simplification becomes an important time saver in performing long or complex calculations, such as those required in computing astronomical orbits. The famous astronomer Kepler praised Napier as having "doubled the life

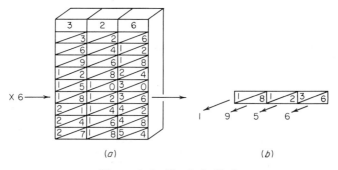

(*a*)   (*b*)

Figure 1–3. Napier's Rods

of the astronomer." Perhaps we can now see that logarithms did for the astronomer what the electronic digital computer is doing for all academic disciplines many times over.

The actual mechanical carry came into being in 1642 when a nineteen-year-old French boy constructed the first true adding machine in hopes of alleviating the tiresome work of his accountant father. The lad, a mathematical genius named Blaise Pascal, marked the digits 0 through 9 around the edges of circular dials. He then connected the dials by gears so that at the end of each revolution of a dial, a tooth would mesh with the gear connected to the next dial on the left and advance it 1/10 revolution. Figure 1–4 shows Pascal's adding machine. The same mechanical carry principle is used in modern adding machines, gas and electrical meters, odometers (automobile mileage gages), and many other devices.

Since the dials in Pascal's machine could be rotated in either direction, it could in principle both add and subtract. In 1671 the German mathematician, Baron Gottfried Wilhelm Von Leibniz, extended the principles of the adding machine to a machine that could also multiply and divide. The Pascal and the Leibniz machines were the forerunners of the modern desk calculator, but neither was mechanically reliable.

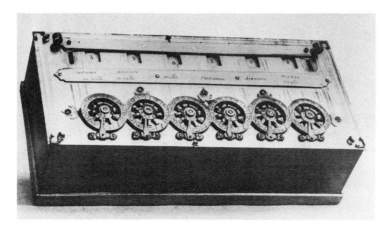

Figure 1–4. Pascal's Adding Machine (Photograph, Bettmann Archive)

A MILESTONE

The Difference Engine

Undoubtedly the most remarkable contributor to the development of the modern digital computer was an Englishman, Charles Babbage, who spent his entire life in the effort to build a powerful computing machine. It began around 1812 when Babbage considered the possibility of expanding the logarithm tables by machine; Napier had spent 25 years preparing the first tables. In Babbage's own words:

> The intolerable labour and fatiguing monotony of a continued repetition of similar arithmetical calculations, first excited the desire, and afterwards suggested the idea, of a machine, which, by the aid of gravity or any other moving power, should become a substitute for one of the lowest operations of the human intellect.

In 1822 Babbage gained the financial support of the British government to build his proposed *difference engine*. This calculating machine is based upon the principle of constant differences, which states that for a first-degree algebraic expression the first differences are constant, for a second-degree expression the second differences are constant, for a third-degree expression the third differences are constant, and so on.

This will be clearer through a simple example. Suppose that we have the equation $y = x^3 + 2x^2 + 3$ and are required to make a table of the values of y for $x = 0, 1, 2, 3, 4$ and so on. The usual method would be to substitute the values of x, one at a time, into the expression and obtain the corresponding value of y, as follows:

$$x = 0 \quad y = (0)^3 + 2(0)^2 + 3 = 0 + 0 + 3 = 3$$
$$x = 1 \quad y = (1)^3 + 2(1)^2 + 3 = 1 + 2 + 3 = 6$$
$$x = 2 \quad y = (2)^3 + 2(2)^2 + 3 = 8 + 8 + 3 = 19$$
$$x = 3 \quad y = (3)^3 + 2(3)^2 + 3 = 27 + 18 + 3 = 48$$
$$x = 4 \quad y = (4)^3 + 2(4)^2 + 3 = 64 + 32 + 3 = 99$$

Having these values, let us look at the differences between various adjacent numbers, as shown in Table 1–1.

Table 1–1

		DIFFERENCES		
x	y	FIRST DIFFERENCE	SECOND DIFFERENCE	THIRD DIFFERENCE
0	3			
		6 − 3 = 3		
1	6		13 − 3 = 10	
		19 − 6 = 13		16 − 10 = 6
2	19		29 − 13 = 16	
		48 − 19 = 29		22 − 16 = 6
3	48		51 − 29 = 22	
		99 − 48 = 51		
4	99			

Note that values for the first difference are obtained by subtracting adjacent values of y, values for the second difference by subtracting adjacent values of the first difference, and so on. Such a difference table is usually made without indicating the arithmetic, as shown in Table 1–2.

Upon examining these tables, we can see that for this third-degree equation, the third differences are a constant 6. If the differences were computed for more values of x, we would find that the third difference would remain unchanged.

Let us now look at another means for determining successive values of y by a simple addition process using the differences. Assume that we have computed values of y for $x = 0, 1, 2, 3$ as shown above the broken line in Table 1–2. We know the third difference entry immediately below the broken line will be 6 since it is constant. Now, adding 6 to 16, the last second difference shown above the broken line, gives 22, which is the next second difference. Proceeding on, 22 + 29 = 51 and 51 + 48 = 99, the value for y when $x = 4$.

Notice in the method of differences that no multiplication is used, and that the sum from the first addition is used as an addend for the next addition, and so on. This gives an indication of the method for constructing Babbage's difference engine; that is, a series of Pascal-type adding machines are connected in cascade fashion such that the output of one becomes the input to the next. Babbage built a working model of the difference engine (shown in Figure 1–5) that could produce a table of squares up to five places, but never finished the proposed machine that was to calculate table values to the sixth order with 20-digit accuracy. In 1833 Babbage ceased work on the difference engine after spending 17,000 pounds of British government funds and about an equal amount of his own money.

Table 1–2

x	y	FIRST DIFFERENCE	SECOND DIFFERENCE	THIRD DIFFERENCE
			DIFFERENCES	
0	3			
		3		
1	6		10	
		13		6
2	19		16	
		29		
3	48			6
			22	
		51		
4	99			

The Analytic Engine

Babbage dropped work on the difference engine when he envisioned an even greater calculating machine. This new machine, which he called the *analytic engine*, would be able to hold 1000 fifty-digit numbers in its "store." In another part of the engine, the "mill," arithmetic operations would take place at the rate of 60 additions or subtractions of 50-digit numbers in one minute, or multiplication of two 50-digit numbers giving a 100-digit product in one minute. Still other parts of the engine would print answers and read and punch holes in pasteboard cards. But probably most unique of all was its ability to hold, execute, and modify its instructions internally.

Babbage drew over 200 masterful engineering drawings of his analytic engine, but existing machine-tool methods could not produce the needed 50,000 parts. Babbage had undertaken to build, this time without government funds, the mechanical equivalent of the modern electronic digital computer. When he died in 1871, his most outstanding work was considered to be a book he wrote in the area now known as industrial engineering. This book, entitled *On the Economy of Manufacture and Machinery*, was published in five languages.

Figure 1–5. Charles Babbage's Difference Engine
(British Crown Copyright. Science Museum, London)

THE PUNCHED CARD

The Jacquard Loom

Another development that took place during this time involved the punched card. Actually, the history of the punched card goes back two centuries, when they were used in France to control patterns on looms. In 1741, Jacques de Vaucouson invented a method by which the patterns were controlled by holes on a metal drum. In 1790, Joseph Marie Jacquard modified the system to employ punched cards in looms such as the one shown in Figure 1–6.

Figure 1–6. The Jacquard Loom
(Engraving, 1877, Bettmann Archive)

A half century later, Charles Babbage, who knew of Jacquard's punched cards, proposed the use of this media for both the input of data and the storage of instructions for his analytic engine. This was the beginning of punched-card data processing.

The Census

Article I, Section 2 of the Constitution of the United States requires that the census be taken every ten years. It had taken seven years to compile the results from the census of 1880, and it was obvious that soon the census results would require more than ten years to complete. The result would be the permanent and hopeless situation of not only never catching up but continuously getting further behind. The solution to the problem was presented by Dr. Herman Hollerith, a statistician and inventor from Buffalo, New York. He developed a system by which the census data was punched into cards with a hand punch and counted on a tabulating machine which he invented. It is often said that when a worker asked Dr. Hollerith what size the card should be, Dr. Hollerith placed a dollar bill on the table and said "that large." Although the size of the dollar bill was changed in 1929, the card has remained the same. With this system the 1890 census was done in one third the time of the 1880 census, in spite of a 25-percent increase in population. Dr. Hollerith's work was material in the development of such companies as IBM and Remington-Rand.

Originally the punched card contained 45 columns of numeric information, punched with circular holes. Later additional punches were added to permit the card to hold 45 columns of alphabetic or numeric information, and in 1928 IBM initiated the use of rectangular holes, which would permit 80 columns of information.

LOGIC MACHINES

While Pascal, Leibniz, and Babbage were creating better calculating devices and Hollerith was developing the punched card, others were attempting to build logic machines. Probably the first noteworthy achievement along this line was the publication, in 1854 by George Boole, of a small book entitled *An Investigation of the Laws of Thought*. In it he outlined the system of symbolic logic now known as Boolean algebra. This subject remained in the area of abstract mathematics until 1938, when Claude Shannon, a graduate student at M.I.T., published a paper entitled "A Symbolic Analysis of Relay and Switching Circuits." By showing the relationships between electrical circuits and Boolean algebra, Shannon opened the way to building electric calculating machines. He showed that simple series and parallel electric circuits had their Boolean equivalents and that these could be combined to perform binary arithmetic. This work also made a major contribution to the development of the dial telephone, which in turn contributed much to the modern computer. Logically, the storage addressing system of a computer is analogous to a city telephone exchange.

DEVELOPMENT OF THE MODERN DIGITAL COMPUTER

History records many instances of parallel yet independent work subsequently brought together and resulting in a single great achievement. One hundred years after Babbage, many men succeeded where he had failed. The building of the electronic digital computer was the culmination of many different technological efforts, requiring the genius of many men.

Electromechanical Machines

During the nineteen forties electronic components were developed on a mass-produced low-cost basis, which made possible giant strides in the computer field. Although a great many computers were built on a one-of-a-kind basis and countless people contributed to their success, four particular machines seem to be the highlights of the story. From 1937 to 1944, Howard Aiken, with the support of IBM, built the Mark I computer at Harvard University. It was the first completely automatic electromechanical (relay) computer. It is felt by some that this was the first realization of Babbage's dream of an analytic engine, although it was not until the Mark I was almost complete that Howard Aiken became aware of Babbage's work.

Electronic Machines

From 1939 to 1946, Dr. John W. Mauchly and J. Presper Eckert, Jr., built the first electronic digital computer. This machine, constructed at the Moore School of Electrical Engineering of the University of Pennsylvania, was given the name Eniac, for Electronic Numerical Integrator and Calculator. It contained 18,000 vacuum tubes and could perform 5000 additions in one second. The purpose of building the Eniac was the same as that which started Babbage working on his two engines, the creation of mathematical tables. This time they were ballistic tables for the Aberdeen Proving Ground in Maryland.

The Stored Program Computer

From 1946 to 1952, the Eniac team, expanded to include A. W. Burks, John von Neumann, and H. H. Goldstine, built another computer for the Ordnance Department of the U. S. Army at Aberdeen. This one was called the Edvac, for Electronic Discrete Variable Automatic Computer. This machine included many new features, the most important of which was an internally stored program—all the instructions for the computer are stored electronically within the machine, and therefore it can operate at electronic speeds without human or mechanical intervention. Credit for the first stored-program computer should probably go to a group at the Mathematical Laboratory of the University of Cambridge, England. Under the direction of M. V. Wilkes, a stored program computer named Edsac, for Electronic Delayed Storage Automatic Computer, was completed in May 1949. It is the stored-program feature that distinguishes the machines called *calculators*, which do not have a stored program, from those called *computers*, which do.

COMMERCIALLY AVAILABLE COMPUTERS

In 1949, the Card Programmed Calculator (CPC), which was the first commercially available general-purpose electronic calculator, was marketed by IBM. This machine consisted of a 402 Alphabetical Accounting Machine, a 604 Electronic Calculating Unit, a 521 Punching Unit, and a 941 Storage Unit, all electrically interconnected. However, it was not a stored program machine, since both the data and the program of instructions were contained externally in IBM cards.

The team at the University of Pennsylvania that built the Eniac and the Edvac saw the commercial value of their stored-program computer and convinced the Remington-Rand Company to produce an Edvac type of computer. In 1951 Remington-Rand sold a large-scale, stored-program computer commercially under the name Univac, for Universal Automatic Computer.

In 1953 IBM entered the stored-program computer race with their 701. Since then a great number of manufacturers have produced scores of different types of computers to meet the market demand. Of particular interest to us in our study of programming fundamentals will be the IBM 1401 and the IBM 1620, both of which were announced in 1959.

■ EXERCISES

1.1 Sketch a block representation of the development of the computer; show events leading to the inventions of the last 25 years.

1.2 What is the advantage of an electrical machine versus a mechanical one for use as a computer?

1.3 Compute a table of squares using the method of differences on the formula $y = x^2$.

Chapter Two

PRELIMINARY CONCEPTS

AN ANALOGY

Before discussing the basic components of the computer, let us consider a simple "pigeon-hole analogy." Assume that the boss of a secretary, who was better known for her appearance than her intelligence, left a job to be completed while he was away. He left chalk, an eraser, a chalk board, and a pigeon-hole box with cards in it, as shown in Figure 2–1. Each pigeon hole was numbered and contained a card with infor-

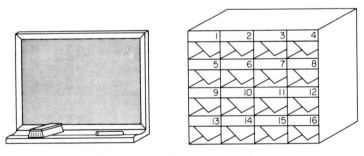

Figure 2–1. Pigeon-hole Analogy

mation on it. The boss had instructed the secretary to start with card number 6, do whatever it said, then proceed to card number 7, and so on. He further indicated that instructions would be found on the cards. The contents of the cards were as follows:

CARD NUMBER	CONTENT
1	200
2	106
3	5
4	1
5	Place new cards in holes 1, 2, and 3
6	Erase slate, write number from card 1
7	Multiply by number on card 2
8	Round off answer two places
9	Replace number on card 1 with number from slate
10	Erase slate, write number from card 3
11	Subtract number on card 4
12	If result is zero go to card 15
13	Write number from slate on card 3
14	Go back to card 6
15	Remove cards 1, 2, and 3 and save for boss
16	Go back to card 5

Performing the Operations

Let us do as the secretary and perform this task to get a better feeling for what is required. Card 6 indicates that we should erase the slate and write the number from card 1, which is 200. After this is done we return cards 1 and 6 to their respective holes and go to card 7, which indicates we should multiply the number 200 on the chalk board by the number on card 2, which is 106, giving 21200. We return cards 2 and 7 to their respective positions and go on to card 8, which tells us to round off two places, leaving 212. Proceeding on to card 9 directs us to write the number from the slate on card 1, giving 212 on this card instead of 200. Card 10 tells us to erase the slate and write the number from card 3, which is 5. By direction of card 11, we subtract the number on card 4, which is 1, from the number on the slate, which leaves 4. Card 12 represents an interesting situation. It says that if the result from the subtraction is zero, go to card 15. However, since the result is not zero, we proceed to card 13, which says to write the number from the slate on card 3, thus replacing the 5 with the 4 from the slate. Card 14 directs us to go back to card 6, which begins the cycle again.

By continuing in this fashion we would find that each time through the cycle the number on card 3 would decrease by one until the cycle had been completed five times and the number would be zero. Then, upon executing the instruction on card 12, we would proceed to card 15, which directs us to remove cards 1, 2, and 3 and save them for the boss. The contents of these cards will be

Card 1, 268—final value
Card 2, 106—unchanged
Card 3,   0—final value

A Flowchart

To obtain a clear and concise picture of the logic and flow of information in this set or *program* of instructions, we will consider a schematic representation of the over-all process, shown in Figure 2-2. This type of diagram, which is called a *flowchart*, will be used extensively in later chapters. In the analogy, the boss had given the secretary verbal instructions to begin with card 6, which in conjunction with 7, 8, and 9 performs the necessary multiplication, rounding off, and storing of the resulting number. Consequently an oblong block labeled *start* feeds into the first rectangle, representing the multiplication function. To illustrate which instruction card each geometric figure depicts, card numbers are included above and to the left of the respective blocks. Proceeding downward, the second rectangle represents the subtraction operation performed to *count* the number of times through the loop. After this is completed, the *decision* card, number 13, is shown, on which the number on the card is tested. If the number is not zero, it is necessary by direction of card 14 to return to card 6; if it is zero, save the cards as directed on the trapezoid figure and return to obtain new cards, as shown on the other trapezoid figure. This flowchart represents a good visual display of the program of instructions given the secretary, and as we will discover is an invaluable technique in writing programs.

What is the Problem?

The question that comes to mind at this point is, "What is the purpose of the program of instructions and what is the meaning of the numbers on the cards?" Before proceeding further, we shall attempt to determine this. It is significant that we need not know the answer to this question, nor need we use the flowchart in order to perform the required operations. By taking the instructions in order as directed, it is possible to perform the function required, since each individual operation is relatively simple and straightforward. In the words of Charles Babbage, these represent ". . . the lowest operations of the human intellect." Once the program of instructions is planned and listed on cards, which would appear to be the difficult part of the problem, the actual execution of them is a menial task. It might be time-consuming but certainly not difficult.

Let us proceed through the program of instructions once again, but this time with an eye toward the process rather than the computations involved. To make the study somewhat more general, we will call the number on card 1 A and the number on card 2 B. The first time through

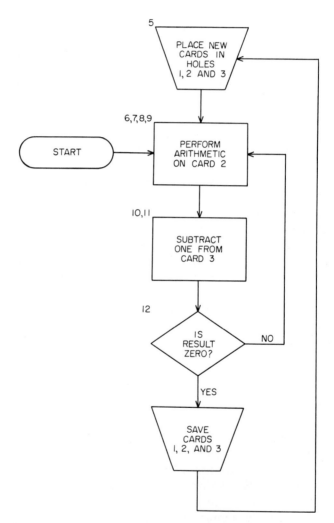

Figure 2–2. Flowchart of Pigeon-hole Analogy

the cycle (or *loop*) yields $A \times B$, or AB with appropriate rounding off. The second time through gives $AB \times B$ or AB^2, and so on, until the fifth (last) time we have AB^5. Perhaps the form and the values for A and B which were used suggest to the student that this is computation of compound interest, from the formula $A = P(1 + i)^t$.

The particular computation illustrated here uses 200 dollars and an interest rate of six percent for five years. Thus the accumulated amount, including interest, would be 268 dollars. Again let us emphasize that knowledge of the problem, computation of compound interest, is not necessary to perform the function; all operations are done under the direction of the set of instructions in the pigeon-hole box. Of course the boss was responsible for writing the instructions and originally placing them in the pigeon-hole boxes. Certainly he understood the problem well enough to break it down into detailed instructions for his secretary. After one set of cards had been processed, the secretary would return to card 5 and place new data cards in holes 1, 2, and 3 and continue.

Categorizing the Cards

The set of instructions that was placed in the pigeon-hole box represents what might be called a *stored program*. It is interesting to note that the program and data were stored side-by-side in a series of storage units comprising a box. The first four cards contained numbers and the remainder of the cards contained instructions. Let us inspect the card contents from the point of view of categorizing them. The first and third cards we could call *variables*, that is, numbers that change as we progress through the program of instructions. Card 2 remains constant for any given set of computations, but after completing one full cycle it is also replaced, so it would also be called a variable. On the other hand, card 4 remains unchanged at all times; consequently, it would be called a *constant*. Card 5 contains the first instruction and directs that new cards be placed in holes 1, 2, and 3. Since the execution of this instruction will place new data in the first holes, we call this an *input* instruction. In a similar fashion, card 15 would contain an *output* instruction. The instruction on card 6, which requires that the number on the slate be replaced, serves the purpose of *moving data*. An inspection of the program indicates that cards 9, 10, and 13 also serve this purpose. The instructions on cards 7 and 8 perform the actual task for which the program was designed, and, along with card 11, are the *arithmetic* instructions. Until card 12 is encountered, instructions are taken in sequence from the numbered boxes. However, card 12 says *if* the number on card 3 is zero, skip to card 15; if *not*, continue on. In other words, under certain conditions, we are to *branch* to a card other than the next one, so this is called a *conditional branch* instruction. Cards 14 and 16 are similar to card 12 since they both require that the sequence of taking the cards in order be broken. On the other hand, there is no condition on either of these, so they are called *unconditional branch* instructions. The summary shown below groups these instructions according to their functions:

Number Fields

Data	1, 2, 3
Program constant	4

Instructions

Input	5
Output	15
Arithmetic	7, 8, 11
Data movement	6, 9, 10, 13
Unconditional branch	14, 16
Conditional branch	12

THE COMPUTER

The analogy given above is simple but it illustrates the fundamental principles of the stored-program computer and suggests the following logical components: (1) input/output; (2) storage; (3) arithmetic; (4) control.

Input/Output

Means for communicating with computers has always been a formidable problem to computer designers since all input/output devices involve some type of mechanical linkage and, in general, mechanical methods are relatively slow. This undoubtedly has contributed to the many and varied means used to get information into and out of a computer. The most common forms for input/output of data are punched cards, magnetic tape, punched paper tape, and the typewriter. Printers capable of printing entire lines at a time are also commonly used for output.

Storage

Computer storage, the single component that is probably most glamorized, is often referred to as a memory analogous to the human memory. This popular representation can be misleading, since the storage unit is better compared to a file cabinet capable of storing vast quantities of information in an orderly fashion. For this reason we will use the term *storage* exclusively. It is interesting to note that Charles Babbage chose to call the comparable portion of his analytic engine the "store." The most widely used type of internal storage is the magnetic core, which will be discussed in the next chapter; also commonly used is the magnetic drum.

Arithmetic Unit

The primary purpose of every digital computer is to perform computations of one type or another with numbers. The arithmetic and logic units of the computer contain the electronic switches, transistors, and so on, necessary for these computations. These are analogous to the wheels and gears of a desk calculator and provide the capability to perform, directly or indirectly, operations of addition, subtraction, multiplication, and division.

Control Unit

The task of directing operations within the computer is the function of the automatic control unit. This portion of the computer can be considered analogous to the combination of a traffic officer and automatic telephone switchboard. It obtains instructions from storage, interprets them, and makes certain that they are carried out as required. These functions require opening and closing appropriate circuits, starting and stopping input/output devices and, in general, directing the flow of information within the computer.

The control unit, storage, and arithmetic units make up what is usually called the *central processing unit* of the computer. Figure 2–3 is a schematic representation of these logical components. In the data processing system which we shall study, as in many other computer systems, information flow is (1) from input through control to storage, (2) from storage through control to the arithmetic section and back to storage through control, (3) from storage through control to output.

These are the elementary concepts and components common to all digital computers. At the present time there are electronic computers in use with the capacity for storing only a few hundred characters of information and with minimal input/output capabilities. On the other hand the newest and largest computer systems store several million pieces of information and utilize many input/output devices, as well as extra equipment including auxiliary storage facilities. The capabilities of the system that we shall discuss are modest by comparison, but are adequate for learning the elements of computer programming.

THE 141 DATA PROCESSING SYSTEM

The 141 concept is an abbreviated version of the IBM 1401 data processing system. Programs written in the 141 language can be run on the IBM 1401, 1410, 1460 and 7010 data processing systems, and on the IBM System/360. They can also be run on the IBM 1620 data processing system when used with a special simulator program, as described in Appendix IV. The 141 system is a stored-program computer concept with the following features:

1. Input—card reader
2. Output—card punch and 100-character-per-line printer
3. Storage—magnetic core, 1000 positions

The 1401 and 1620 systems are shown in Figures 2–4 and 2–5 respectively. The processing units, the card input/output units, and the other peripheral equipment are appropriately indicated.

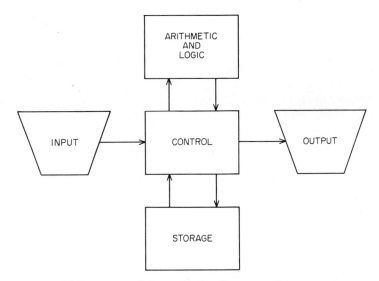

Figure 2–3. Schematic of a Computer System

The 141 Storage

All information read into or out of the 141 system goes to or comes from the computer storage. The 141 has 1000 positions of core storage, addressed 000–999, and at any given time each of them may store one letter or number representing data or instructions.

In order to have a convenient means for representing the entire

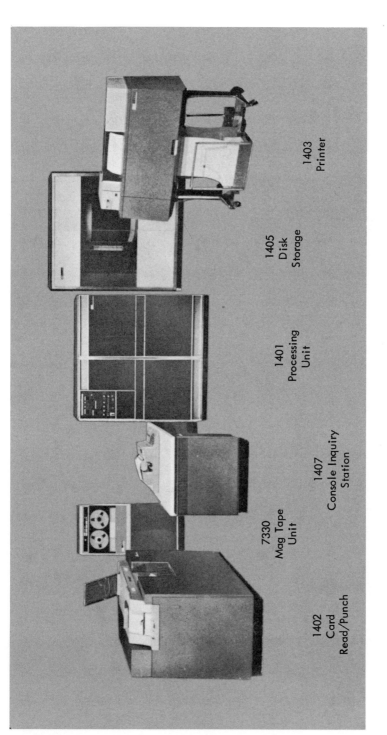

7330
Mag Tape
Unit

1402
Card
Read/Punch

1407
Console Inquiry
Station

1401
Processing
Unit

1405
Disk
Storage

1403
Printer

Figure 2-4. IBM 1401 Data Processing System (Photograph, IBM)

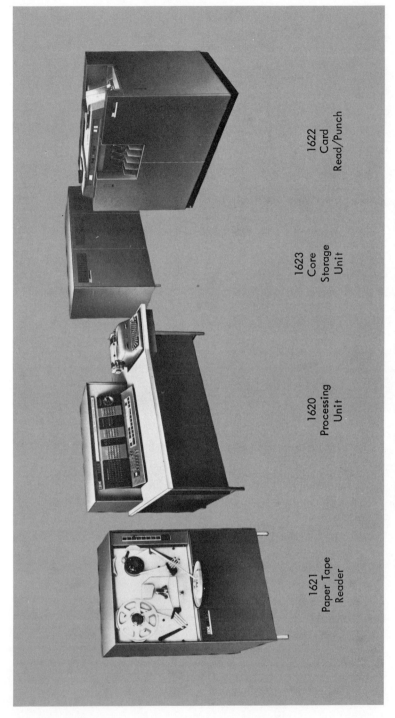

Figure 2–5. IBM 1620 Data Processing System (Photograph, IBM)

storage, we will use a "map" with the format shown in Figure 2–6. As can be seen, the storage areas are shown with 50 positions per line, which are in turn grouped in blocks of five. On the first line, the first location is 000 and the last is 049; the last location in the entire storage is 999. For convenience, addresses are printed to the left of each line signifying the range in that given line. The storage can be thought of as a large housing project with 1000 identical houses. Their addresses, which range 000–999, are the only means for distinguishing among them. Moreover, the occupants of any given house are independent of the address; in fact, occupants come and go without changing the house or its address. In the computer storage, the address of a given position remains unchanged but its contents are easily changed.

We will find, on the one hand, that 1000-position storage capability is relatively small by modern standards. On the other hand, we will

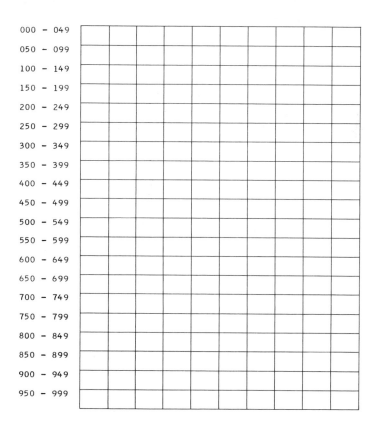

Figure 2–6. Storage Map

discover that this system provides a powerful computation tool and learning device. It is interesting to note that many early computers were designed with capacities equivalent to that of the 141 yet, in many cases, extremely complex problems were solved on them. We will study some of the many and varied types of problems that can be solved with this system.

■ EXERCISES

2.1 Think of a simple, everyday task which you perform and then write a detailed list of instructions that could be used by someone else to perform that task.

2.2 Name the logical "blocks" of a computer and describe their functions.

2.3 Do the corresponding five logical blocks exist in the desk calculator? If so, describe them.

2.4 What devices are used for input and output in the 141 system?

2.5 How many positions of storage are in the 141 system?

2.6 Point out the input and output devices in Figures 2–4 and 2–5.

2.7 Does the magnetic tape unit in Figure 2–4 represent an input device, an output device, a storage device, or some combination of these?

Chapter Three

INFORMATION STORAGE

A definition frequently used for the term *communication* is "a process by which meanings are exchanged between individuals through a common system of symbols." The English-language symbols on this page convey information about computer programming to the reader. The symbols themselves are not the information; they are simply a means for representing it. On the other hand, our English-language symbols are not always the best for a given situation nor are they sometimes even usable.

For instance, during the early days of our country, much overland communication was by telegraph wire. Neither characters printed on a page nor speech could be transmitted over the wires, so it was necessary to devise a code. In 1844 the first message was sent over a telegraph wire using the code developed by Samuel F. B. Morse. This code consisted of a series of long and short sounds separated by varying increments of time. It was later revised to the form shown in Table 3–1 and

Table 3–1
INTERNATIONAL CODE

A	·—	J	·———	S	···
B	—···	K	—·—	T	—
C	—·—·	L	·—··	U	··—
D	—··	M	——	V	···—
E	·	N	—·	W	·——
F	··—·	O	———	X	—··—
G	——·	P	·——·	Y	—·——
H	····	Q	——·—	Z	——··
I	··	R	·—·		

is now known as the International code. These coding symbols were a means for communicating with individuals via a medium through which only pulses could be transmitted. Therefore, a convention compatible to the medium was adopted.

CARD CODING

In many respects, the International code is similar to the ways we present information to the computer. The machine cannot read this book directly; the text must be reduced to a set of coded symbols and fed into the computer through the appropriate devices. For the 141 system this is the card reader, which utilizes 80-position Hollerith cards (now commonly known as IBM cards). The coding system used for the Hollerith card, as in the Morse code system, must be capable of representing the alphabet, the numbers 0–9, and certain special characters (for instance, the comma and the period). Information is represented as small rectangular holes punched in specific locations on a standard-size card. This card is a piece of light cardboard $7\frac{3}{8}$ in. long and $3\frac{1}{4}$ in. wide. It contains 80 vertical columns; each of these columns contains 12 punching positions, which form 12 horizontal rows across the card. One or more punches in a single column represents a character. The card is often called the *unit record*, because the information is restricted to the 80 columns and the card is read by the computer as a complete unit of information. It may, as we will see later, consist of one or more instructions to the computer or of data to be used in computations.

The Code

As shown in Figure 3–1, the card uses the 12 possible punch positions of a vertical column to represent the required symbol. These 12 positions are divided into two portions called the *digit area* and *zone area*. Beginning from the bottom of the card, the 9, 8, 7, 6, 5, 4, 3, 2, 1 and 0 positions constitute the digit areas; the three rows 0, 11, and 12 are zone positions. Note that zero is both a digit and a zone. Each number from 0 through 9 is represented by a single punch in the required column. For instance, in Figure 3–1, three is punched in column 18 and zero in column 15 (note that in this instance, the zero position is considered to be a numeric punch).

The alphabetic characters are represented by a combination of two punches in a single column, one is a digit punch and the other is a zone punch. Thus, using zero as a zone punch, we have 27 different combinations with which to represent the 26 letters. The coding, apparent in Figure 3–1, uses the 12 zone and 1–9 digit punches to represent *A* through *I*, the 11 zone and 1–9 digit punches to represent *J* through *R*, and the 0 zone and 2–9 digit punches to represent *S* through *Z*. This alphabetic card code is summarized in Table 3–2.

Table 3–2
CARD CODING

	ZONE		
DIGIT	12	11	0
1	A	J	
2	B	K	S
3	C	L	T
4	D	M	U
5	E	N	V
6	F	O	W
7	G	P	X
8	H	Q	Y
9	I	R	Z

Since there are 27 combinations but only 26 letters in the alphabet, one combination of a zone and digit, the 0–1, is not used for an alphabetic character. A simple aid to remembering just how the letters are divided is that the first and last letters using the 11 zone are *J* and *R* or *JR* respectively. In addition to the numbers and the alphabet, special characters using one, two, or three punches may be coded.

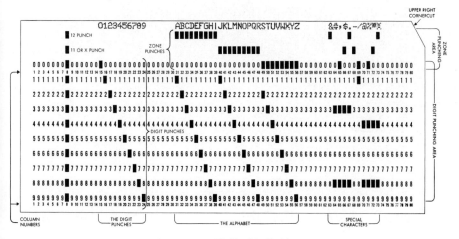

Figure 3–1. Hollerith Coding

The Key Punch

Although it is useful to know this coding system, it need not be memorized in order to put coded information on cards. The key-operated card-punch machine shown in Figure 3-2 is designed for this purpose. One model of this machine will print the character which has been punched across the top of the card in the manner shown in Figure 3-1. The machine has a keyboard (Figure 3-3) similar to that of a typewriter; depressing the desired key automatically punches the appropriate coding into the card. The complete coding system is summarized in Appendix II, which also includes additional symbols for which there are no individual keys on the keyboard. They may be punched by special methods, however.

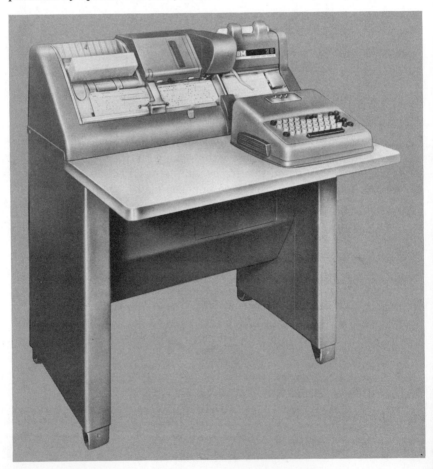

Figure 3-2. IBM 26 Printing Card Punch (Photograph, IBM)

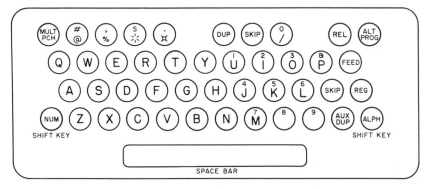

Figure 3–3. Keyboard for Card-Punch Machine

CODING FOR INTERNAL STORAGE

If we carefully consider the punched-card method of storing information, we see that character storage is accomplished by an indicator which can be *yes* or *no;* in other words, a binary indication which, in the case of a card, takes the form *punch* or *no punch.* For instance, if 9 is to be stored in column 70 of a card, a hole is punched in that position of the card; otherwise there is no hole punched.

Since computer storage devices are best suited to coding methods using the *on-off* principle, the Hollerith code appears to be an attractive means for internal storage coding also. The coding system used in the 141 system is, in its essentials, the same as the Hollerith code, although differences do exist because of practical considerations in designing the computer. The card column uses 12 rows, one for each of the 10 digits and all 12 for letters and special characters. The use of 12 positions on the card is no problem, since cardboard is relatively inexpensive. On the other hand, the 141 system core storage consists of thousands of very expensive components. As a consequence, it is desirable to use the most efficient coding method possible in order to get the most out of the given equipment.

First let us consider the nine digits represented on the card. By using multiple indication, as was done with letters on card coding, it is possible to represent them by using the digits 8, 4, 2 and 1; that is,

$$1 = 1 \qquad 4 = 4 \qquad 7 = 4 + 2 + 1$$
$$2 = 2 \qquad 5 = 4 + 1 \qquad 8 = 8$$
$$3 = 2 + 1 \qquad 6 = 4 + 2 \qquad 9 = 8 + 1$$

This can also be represented as shown in Table 3–3 if the x is considered equivalent to a punch on a card or to an *on* state.

Table 3–3

	BIT			
DIGIT	*8*	*4*	*2*	*1*
1				x
2			x	
3			x	x
4		x		
5		x		x
6		x	x	
7		x	x	x
8	x			
9	x			x
0	x		x	

The term commonly given to each of the characters 8, 4, 2, 1 is *bit*, denoting *bi*nary dig*it*. Thus 1 is represented by an *on bit* in the 1 position, 2 by an on bit in the 2 position, 3 by on bits in the 2 and 1 positions, and so on. In contrast to the card code, zero is expressed by on bits in the 8 and 2 positions since the *blank* (which is important for input/output) is represented by no on bits.

Here we have accomplished a substantial saving by using only four bits for coding the 10 digits. This method for storing numbers, commonly used in computers, is the basis for character coding in the 141 system. However, all possible combinations, from using no on bits to four on bits, gives only 16 different codes, which is insufficient for representing all of the letters. The Hollerith code uses three zone positions; this is accomplished in the 141 storage with the two zone positions called the A bit and the B bit. Table 3–4 summarizes the equivalence between these two methods for representing the zone positions.

Table 3–4

	ON BIT	
ZONE	*B*	*A*
12	x	x
11	x	
0		x

Now, by combining Tables 3–2, 3–3, and 3–4, we can easily convert from card to core-storage coding. For instance, in Table 3–2, the letter *A* is represented by the 12–1 punches. In Table 3–3, 1 is represented in storage by 1, and the 12 zone by the BA bits, as summarized in Table 3–4. Thus the letter *A* is represented in storage by on bits B, A, and 1 as shown in Table 3–5.

Table 3–5

	ZONE		DIGIT			
LETTER	B	A	8	4	2	1
A	x	x				x
B	x	x			x	
C	x	x			x	x
D	x	x		x		
.	.	.	.	.	.	.
.	.	.	.	.	.	.
.	.	.	.	.	.	.

Thus the entire coding task is completed by using only six bits instead of twelve. In the 141 system, two additional bits are included in the coding system, to make a total of eight indicators for each character. One is the *word-mark* bit, which will be discussed later, and the other is the *parity-check* bit. The sole purpose of the check (C) bit is to aid in detecting machine errors. Whenever a character is placed in storage— whether it is a letter, number, or special character—the number of on bits is checked. If there are an even number of them, the computer automatically turns on the parity bit to give an odd number of them in the on state; if an odd number is already on, the parity bit is left off.

Whenever any characters are moved or operated upon, the number of on bits is checked to make certain there are an odd number of them. If by chance there is an even number, something has gone wrong and the machine can be required to stop. If there is an odd number of on bits, the computer will continue. This method of checking for internal errors in the computer is called *parity checking*. Table 3–5 has been modified, as shown in Table 3–6, to include the parity position. Note that the parity indicator is on for the letter *C* in order to give an odd number of on bits in the coding. The complete coding system for all characters is shown in Appendix II.

Table 3-6

LETTER	PARITY C	ZONE B	A	DIGIT 8	4	2	1	
A		x	x				x	(3 on bits)
B		x	x			x		(3 on bits)
C	x	x	x			x	x	(5 on bits)
D		x	x		x			(3 on bits)
.	.	.	.		.	.	.	
.	.	.	.		.	.	.	
.	.	.	.		.	.	.	

MAGNETIC CORE STORAGE

In the short history of electronic computers, advances and new inventions have been many and varied but the basic principle of the magnetic core has proved to be simple, economical, and relatively long-lived in a field where equipment is often obsolete within a few years.

Discovery of Magnetism

In the year 1820, a Danish scientist named Hans Christian Oersted completed one of many lectures on magnetism at the University of Copenhagen. During the discussion following, he accidentally placed a small compass near a wire carrying electricity, and, much to his amazement, the compass needle deflected. He quickly recognized the implications, and after considerable experimentation and study, he found that the electrical current flow produced a magnetic field whose direction depended on the direction of current flow. Sparked by this discovery, many scientists pressed further, and after several years of intense study both Michael Faraday and John Henry discovered that, under certain conditions, a magnetic field can cause an electric current to flow through a wire (Faraday later became director of the Royal Institute in London and Henry director of the Smithsonian Institution in Washington, D.C.).

The Magnetic Core

These principles are fundamental to nearly every type of electrical and electronic equipment today and are the basis for the design of modern computer storage units. It is now well known that if the current within a wire is shut off, the magnetic field will disappear. However, the effects of it will remain if the wire is near a piece of iron, since the field caused by the current will produce magnetism within the iron. The effect is even more pronounced if the material is a small core made from a ferromagnetic material through which the wire has been threaded. Such a magnetic core is now commonly used as a storage device for electronic digital computers, principally because of its following properties and characteristics:

1. It can easily be magnetized in either of two directions.
2. It will retain its magnetism indefinitely if not disturbed.
3. A minimum or "threshold" current will change magnetization.
4. It can be manufactured in extremely small sizes (some the size of the period at the end of this sentence).

The concept of the magnetic core is shown in Figure 3–4. In (*a*) the current is being applied and a magnetic field results according to the conventional laws of physics. After the current flow has ceased the field remains as shown in (*b*). Reversal of the current flow causes reversal of the field, which again is retained after the current is stopped, as illustrated in (*c*) and (*d*).

In large computer systems, millions of such cores are used to store data and instructions. To use one wire for each core would be nearly impossible, so the cores are strung on wires like beads. (See Figure 3–5.)

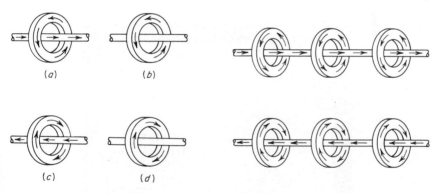

Figure 3–4. Magnetic Cores   *Figure 3–5. Cores Strung on a Wire*

However, if a core were to be set to the *on* state, then all of the cores on the wire would also be set, which would probably not be desirable. To accomplish the selection of any individual core, a second wire is run through each core at right angles to the others (Figure 3–6). Now the desired core can be set by sending one half the current through one wire and one half through the other wire.

In this manner only the core at their intersection will experience sufficient field to change its setting. All of the other cores on both wires would experience only one half of the required current, leaving

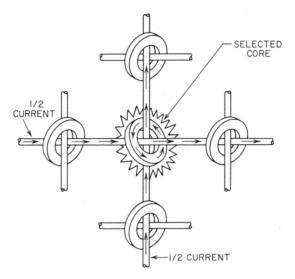

Figure 3–6. Core Selection

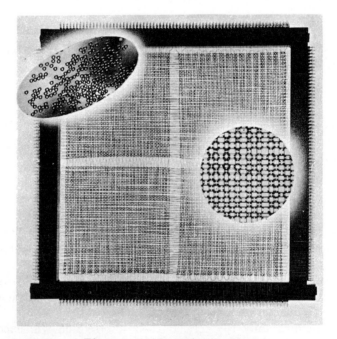

Figure 3–7. Magnetic-core Plane

them unaffected. This is the reason that the threshold current property is important. Using this principle, a large number of cores can be strung in a screen of wires, which represents a *core plane* (Figure 3–7).

In order to conform to the coding system for the 141, seven positions are required, so seven of these planes are stacked one above the other. To illustrate this, Figure 3–8 shows a complete array of seven planes, which are labeled C, B, A, 8, 4, 2, 1. We will assume that it is desired to store the letter *A* (recall that *A* uses *on* bits B, A, and 1). The letter *A* is shown by the imaginary line drawn vertically through the cores representing a single storage position.

The pair of wires which pass through each core obviously serves the need for placing information in storage; additional wires are used to read it out again. The basic knowledge of how core storage works is helpful in understanding the operation of data processing systems that use this type of storage.

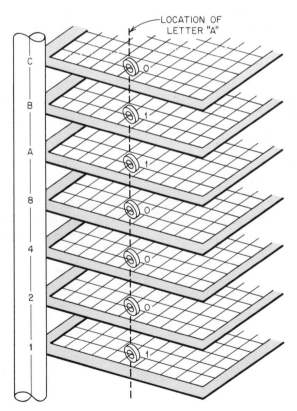

Figure 3–8. Core-plane Character Storage

■ REVIEW QUESTIONS

3.1 Describe several situations where communication by using code is necessary because of conditions or circumstances.

3.2 Why must two holes be used to represent alphabetic information on cards?

3.3 Name the punching positions on a card (from top to bottom of the card).

3.4 How many characters of information may be stored on a single punched card?

3.5 Why is the exact Hollerith code not used for storing information in the computer storage?

3.6 What is a *parity check?*

3.7 If every possible coding combination were used (from all *on* through all *off*), what is the minimum number of bits that could possibly be used to represent all of the characters in Table 3–2?

3.8 What are the characteristics of magnetic cores that make them useful as computer storage devices?

3.9 How many individual cores are required for the 141 storage? (Remember that a word-mark core is also included for each storage position in addition to those that were described.)

3.10 Describe the process of magnetizing only a given core on a string and not affecting the others.

3.11 The binary system that uses 1, 2, 4, and 8 to represent all ten digits is one of several. Find a set of four digits which when combined would give all of the digits without summing more than two of the four.

Chapter Four

BASIC
INSTRUCTIONS

In order to process data with a computer, it is necessary to provide the computer with a set of instructions similar to the instructions provided the secretary in the pigeon hole example. The 141 system is designed around fourteen basic instructions and their variations, which are fundamental to computers in general. We will first study these instructions in *machine language*, and then later in a symbolic language that relieves the programmer of much routine work.

DATA MOVEMENT

The MOVE Instruction

The first instruction to be considered is the one which commands the computer to move data within the storage. Since the MOVE instruction tells the machine to move information from one storage location to another, a three-part instruction seems logical. That is, the MOVE instruction is composed of an *operation code* which tells the computer that it is to move information, a FROM address which tells the computer where to find the data, and a TO address which tells the computer where to place the data. The operation code for the MOVE instruction could logically be the word MOVE itself, but for reasons we will explore soon, the coding M is used. The first address, the FROM address, is more generally called the *A address* and will always consist of a three-digit storage address. The second address, the TO address, is commonly called the *B address* and will also consist of a three-digit storage address. To illustrate this let us consider the following instruction, by which we wish to move a character from storage location 076 to location 154. The instruction would take the following form:

Operation code	A address	B address
M̲	076	154

In order to see what the instruction will do, assume that prior to the execution of the instruction the content of location 076, or the A field, is a 5, and the content of location 154, or the B field, is an H.

The following method for visual representation of the instruction will be used throughout the text in illustrating examples. The addressed areas of storage will be shown in their relative positions according to the storage map previously discussed, and the character stored will be indicated in its appropriate position. The contents of storage *before* execution of the instruction are:

$$\overline{\qquad\quad |\,5\,|\qquad\quad}$$
$$^0{}_7$$
$$_6$$

$$\overline{\qquad\quad |\,H\,|\qquad\quad}$$
$$^1{}_5$$
$$_4$$

Instruction: M̲076154

Following execution of the instruction, which will move the digit 5 from location 076 to location 154, the storage will contain the following:

$$\overline{\qquad\quad |\,5\,|\qquad\quad}$$
$$^0{}_7$$
$$_6$$

$$\overline{\qquad\quad |\,5\,|\qquad\quad}$$
$$^1{}_5$$
$$_4$$

Note that, after the instruction has been executed, there is a 5 in location 154 and also a 5 in location 076; that is, the A field is unchanged by the MOVE instruction. For this reason the MOVE instruction is frequently thought of as a COPY AND MOVE instruction.

Groups of Characters

Normally there will be not one character but a whole field of characters to be moved. In the above example the desired operation could have been to move a yearly income from one area to another. Here the 5 might have been the last digit of the yearly income 13865, with the *high-order* digit 1 located in storage position 072 and the low-order digit 5 in position 076 as shown.

$$| 1 | 3 | 8 | 6 | 5 |$$

0$_{72}$ 0$_{76}$

The MOVE instruction, instead of transferring only single characters, will transfer whole *fields*. Of course a question arises concerning the addressing of a several-position field that occupies several storage locations. Referring to the example, we can ask the question, "Is the field specified by 072, which is the leftmost or high-order position, or by 076, which is the rightmost or low-order position?" Consistent with the processes of addition and subtraction, a field, whether it is alphabetic or numeric, is addressed by its rightmost position. Thus the instruction M076154 would move the field 13865 character by character from its storage area, 076 down through 072, to the storage area 154 through 150. That is, first the 5 would be moved from 076 to 154, then the 6 from 075 to 153, and similarly through each digit until the 1 was moved from 072 to 150. The machine would then have achieved the desired result, that of moving the A field, representing a yearly income, to the B address.

Now it remains to be shown how the computer will know when it has completed the move after reaching the high-order 1 in the field. We know, but the computer is no mind reader, and the number of characters in the field is nowhere described in the instruction. Just as a row of dominos falls piece by piece when nothing exists to halt any given domino, the computer will continue moving characters. To the computer, one character is like another so it will move the character at 071 to 149, that in 070 to 148 and so on without stopping. The answer to this is some means to mark the left end of the field. The device used in the 141 system is called the *word mark*. Briefly then, every storage position can store any alphameric character *and* a word mark to indicate the left end of a field. A word mark is also used to indicate the operation code of an instruction. In this text a word mark accompanying an alphameric character will be represented by a dash

(—) or by a one (1) directly beneath that character. This complete moving operation can be summarized as shown in Example 4–1.

EXAMPLE 4-1

Contents of storage *before* execution of the MOVE instruction:

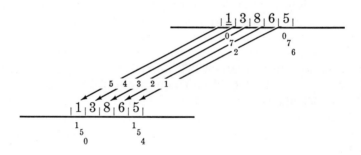

Instruction: M076154

Contents of storage *after* execution of the MOVE instruction:

1. The A field is not changed.
2. The last character moved was that character which included a word mark.
3. Word marks in the A and B fields were not disturbed. The word mark at 072 was not lost and no word mark was placed at 150 since none existed there prior to execution of the instruction. The word mark affects the MOVE instruction but the MOVE instruction does not affect the word mark.

In this example numbered arrows have been included to indicate the order in which individual characters are moved. Another feature of the MOVE instruction which will be illustrated in Example 4–3 and 4–5 is that the MOVE instruction is terminated when the first word mark in *either* field is encountered. Had the B field contained a word mark at position 153, only the two digits 6 and 5 would have been moved. The complete name which is given this instruction is MOVE CHARACTERS TO A OR B WORD MARK (MCW), and its formal definition is

MOVE CHARACTERS TO A OR B WORD MARK (MCW)

Op code	A address	B address
M̲	aaa	bbb

Description. The MOVE CHARACTERS TO A OR B WORD MARK instruction causes the field specified by the A address (A field) to be moved to corresponding positions of the B field. The A field remains undisturbed but the B field is lost.

Word Marks. The first word mark encountered in either field stops the transmission of data. Existing word marks in neither field are disturbed. The MOVE CHARACTERS TO A OR B WORD MARK has the mnemonic (meaning aiding the memory) abbreviation MCW.

The Field

Up to this point, a collection of characters meaningful as a group has been identified as a *field*, which is consistent with the terminology A field and B field. However, since the left end of a given collection of characters is indicated by a word mark, frequently the term *word* is used. Historically, a word is associated with a fixed number of characters, whereas the 141 field length is variable. Consequently we shall use the term *field* and define it in the following way:

Field (synonymous with *word*): A character or set of characters treated as a single unit of information.

Note that numbers and special characters are not excluded in this definition. Fields may contain numbers, alphabetic characters, special characters, or combinations of them. In the 141 system a field will be designated or addressed by its low-order position (rightmost) and terminated by a word mark at its high-order position (leftmost).

Examples Demonstrating the MCW Instruction

Several points of significance which have not been considered explicitly are illustrated with the following examples:

EXAMPLE 4-2

Contents of the storage *before* execution of the MCW instruction:

$$| 6 | 5 | 4 | 3 | 2 | 1 |$$

$$1_2 \quad\quad\quad 1_2$$
$$2 \quad\quad\quad\quad\quad 7$$

$$| \underline{M} | O | N | D | A | Y |$$

$$2_7 \quad\quad\quad 2_8$$
$$9 \quad\quad\quad\quad\quad 4$$

Instruction: $\underline{M}284127$

Contents of the storage *after* execution of the MCW instruction:

$$| M | O | N | D | A | Y |$$

$$1_2 \quad\quad\quad 1_2$$
$$2 \quad\quad\quad\quad\quad 7$$

$$| \underline{M} | O | N | D | A | Y |$$

$$2_7 \quad\quad\quad 2_8$$
$$9 \quad\quad\quad\quad\quad 4$$

1. This field is moved to a lower address in the storage. Fields can be moved in either direction.
2. This field is purely alphabetic. Fields may be composed of alphabetic, numeric, or special characters, or any combination.
3. The A field is unchanged.
4. The word mark in the A field is undisturbed. No word mark existed in the B field before the operation, so this condition is unchanged.

EXAMPLE 4-3

Contents of storage *before* execution of the MCW instruction:

$$| 3 | A | B | 4 |$$

$$0_6 \quad\quad\quad 0_6$$
$$6 \quad\quad\quad\quad 9$$

$$| \underline{5} | 5 | 5 | 5 |$$

$$6_8 \quad\quad\quad 6_8$$
$$0 \quad\quad\quad\quad 3$$

Instruction: <u>M</u>069683

Contents of storage *after* execution of the MCW instruction:

<pre>
      |3|A|B|4|
       0   0
        6   6
         6   9
</pre>

<pre>
                    |<u>3</u>|A|B|4|
                     6   6
                      8   8
                       0   3
</pre>

1. The word mark terminating the MCW instruction was in the B field.

EXAMPLE 4-4

Contents of storage *before* execution of the MCW instruction:

<pre>
                    |P|
                     1
                      8
                       2
</pre>

<pre>
          |<u>5</u>|
           7
            6
             3
</pre>

Instruction: <u>M</u>763182

Contents of storage *after* execution of the MCW instruction:

<pre>
                    |5|
                     1
                      8
                       2
</pre>

<pre>
          |<u>5</u>|
           7
            6
             3
</pre>

1. The length of the field transferred here is one character, which is the minimum number of characters in a field. The maximum length could be, in theory, the entire 1000 characters in the storage.
2. Notice, that, as always, the MCW instruction does not disturb word marks.

EXAMPLE 4-5

Contents of storage *before* execution of the MCW instruction:

E	C	O	N		1	5
090					096	

G	E	O	L	O	G	Y
292				288		

Instruction: M096288

Contents of storage *after* execution of the MCW instruction:

E	C	O	N		1	5
292					096	

E	C	O	N		1	5
282				288		

1. The blank in storage location 094 was moved to location 286 in the same manner as any other character.

EXAMPLE 4-6

Contents of storage *before* execution of the MCW instruction:

X	Y	G	R	A	D	E
006	008				012	

9	8	7	2	3	4	5
119					125	

Instruction: M012125

Contents of storage *after* execution of the MCW instruction:

|X|Y|<u>G</u>|R|A|D|E|
$\begin{matrix}0\\0\\6\end{matrix}$ $\begin{matrix}0\\0\\8\end{matrix}$

|9|8|7|<u>R</u>|A|D|E|
$\begin{matrix}1\\1\\9\end{matrix}$ $\begin{matrix}1\\2\\5\end{matrix}$

1. The move has been terminated by the first word mark reached and only RADE has been moved. If the word GRADE were to be moved, this instruction would be incorrect because of the word mark in the B field.
2. The characters preceding the word mark are undisturbed.
3. Neither word mark is disturbed.

EXAMPLE 4-7

Contents of storage *before* execution of the MCW instruction:

|<u>X</u>|Y|G|R|A|D|E|
$\begin{matrix}0\\0\\6\end{matrix}$ $\begin{matrix}0\\1\\2\end{matrix}$

|9|8|7|2|3|4|5|
$\begin{matrix}1\\1\\9\end{matrix}$ $\begin{matrix}1\\2\\5\end{matrix}$

Instruction: <u>M</u>012125

Contents of storage *after* execution of the MCW instruction:

|<u>X</u>|Y|G|R|A|D|E|
$\begin{matrix}0\\0\\6\end{matrix}$ $\begin{matrix}0\\1\\2\end{matrix}$

|X|Y|G|R|A|D|E|
$\begin{matrix}1\\1\\9\end{matrix}$ $\begin{matrix}1\\2\\5\end{matrix}$

1. This example is identical to 4–6 except that the word marks in the data fields are located differently. If only the word GRADE were to be moved, a word mark under either the G in the A field or the 7 in the B field (or both) would be required.

Setting and Clearing Word Marks

As was noted in Example 4–6, the whole word GRADE was not moved; the operation was terminated by the word mark in position 122, allowing only the move of RADE. Had it been desired to move the entire five letters GRADE with the one MCW instruction, then it would have been necessary to remove the word mark from location 122. In the slightly different situation of Example 4–7, too many characters were moved, assuming again that it was desired to move only the letters GRADE. The word mark at 006 does no harm but a word mark at either location 008 or location 121 is required to terminate the MOVE instruction at the proper point.

To satisfy these needs, instructions to set and clear word marks at desired locations are needed. The instructions which perform these functions are SET WORD MARK (SW) and CLEAR WORD MARK (CW). In setting (or clearing) a word mark, it is necessary to specify only a single address, that is, the address of the word mark. Hence it is not necessary to use both the A and B addresses for these instructions; the A address specifies the address at which a word mark is to be set (or cleared). The formal definitions are:

SET WORD MARK (SW)

Op code	A address
$\underline{,}$	aaa

Description. The SET WORD MARK instruction causes a word mark to be set at the location specified by the A address. Existing word marks are undisturbed. Data at the location will not be disturbed.

CLEAR WORD MARK (CW)

Op code	A address
$\underline{\square}$ or $\underline{)}$	aaa

Description. The CLEAR WORD MARK instruction causes a word mark to be cleared from the location specified by the A address. If no word mark existed prior to the instruction, there will be no change at that location. Data will not be disturbed.

Note that the two forms $\underline{\square}$ and $\underline{)}$ are given for the operation code of the CLEAR WORD MARK instruction. The coding for both of these is the 12, 4, and 8 punches on a card and the B, A, 8, and 4 bits in storage. Some machines interpret it as a lozenge and some as closing parenthesis. The following examples illustrate the SET WORD MARK and CLEAR WORD MARK instructions.

EXAMPLE 4-8

Contents of storage *before* execution of the sw instruction:

$$\underline{\quad\quad _|4_|7_|8_|6_|3_| \quad\quad\quad}$$
$$^{0}_{\ 7}_{\ \ 6}$$

Instruction: ‚076

Contents of storage *after* execution of the sw instruction:

$$\underline{\quad\quad _|4_|7_|\underline{8}_|6_|3_| \quad\quad\quad}$$
$$^{0}_{\ 7}_{\ \ 6}$$

1. The instruction does not contain a B address.
2. The digit at storage location 076 is unchanged by the instruction.
3. The word mark is placed only at position 076.

EXAMPLE 4-9

Contents of storage *before* execution of the sw instruction:

$$\underline{\quad\quad _|4_|7_|\underline{8}_|6_|3_| \quad\quad\quad}$$
$$^{0}_{\ 7}_{\ \ 6}$$

Instruction: ‚076

Contents of storage *after* execution of the sw instruction:

$$\underline{\quad\quad _|4_|7_|\underline{8}_|6_|3_| \quad\quad\quad}$$
$$^{0}_{\ 7}_{\ \ 6}$$

1. There is no change since location 076 already contained a word mark.

EXAMPLE 4-10

Contents of storage *before* execution of the cw instruction:

$$\underline{\quad\quad _|\underline{T}_|\underline{O}_|\underline{D}_|\underline{A}_|Y_| \quad\quad\quad}$$
$$^{3}_{\ 5}_{\ \ 2}$$

Instruction:)352

Contents of storage *after* execution of the cw instruction:

$$\underline{\;|\,\text{T}\,|\,\underline{\text{O}}\,|\,\text{D}\,|\,\underline{\text{A}}\,|\,\text{Y}\,|\;}$$
$$\overset{3}{_{5}}$$
$$_{2}$$

1. Although each of the characters in locations 350–354 contain word marks, only that word mark designated by the A address is removed.
2. In all three examples, data is unchanged.

Now it is possible to return to Examples 4–6 and 4–7 armed with the CLEAR WORD MARK and SET WORD MARK instructions and move the field GRADE as desired. In Example 4–6 we first clear the word mark from position 122 and then move the field, as follows:

EXAMPLE 4-11

Contents of storage *before* execution of cw and mcw instructions:

$$\underline{\;|\,\text{X}\,|\,\text{Y}\,|\,\underline{\text{G}}\,|\,\text{R}\,|\,\text{A}\,|\,\text{D}\,|\,\text{E}\,|\;}$$
$$\overset{0}{_{0}}\qquad\qquad\overset{0}{_{1}}$$
$$_{6}\qquad\qquad\qquad_{2}$$

$$\underline{\;|\,9\,|\,8\,|\,7\,|\,\underline{2}\,|\,3\,|\,4\,|\,5\,|\;}$$
$$\overset{1}{_{1}}\qquad\qquad\overset{1}{_{2}}$$
$$_{9}\qquad\qquad\qquad_{5}$$

Instruction:)122M̲012125

Contents of storage *after* execution of cw and mcw instructions:

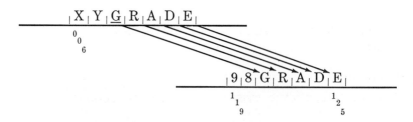

$$\underline{\;|\,\text{X}\,|\,\text{Y}\,|\,\underline{\text{G}}\,|\,\text{R}\,|\,\text{A}\,|\,\text{D}\,|\,\text{E}\,|\;}$$
$$\overset{0}{_{0}}$$
$$_{6}$$

$$\underline{\;|\,9\,|\,8\,|\,\text{G}\,|\,\text{R}\,|\,\text{A}\,|\,\text{D}\,|\,\text{E}\,|\;}$$
$$\overset{1}{_{1}}\qquad\qquad\overset{1}{_{2}}$$
$$_{9}\qquad\qquad\qquad_{5}$$

1. The word mark at storage location 122 was cleared.
2. The MOVE instruction was terminated by the word mark in loca-

tion 008 of the A field since the word mark in location 122 was cleared prior to the MOVE instruction.

3. The order of instructions is important. It is necessary to clear the word mark before attempting to move the field.

In Example 4–7, it is necessary to set a word mark in either location 008 or 121 in order to limit the move operation to the five characters GRADE. Writing instructions to accomplish this is left as an exercise.

INPUT/OUTPUT

The READ Instruction

Now that means have been provided to move data within storage, we shall consider how to communicate with the machine and how it communicates with us. The importance of this is typified by the internal organization of the storage unit itself. As previously described, the computer storage has 1000 positions, each identical to the other; the only means for distinguishing one location from another is by its address. Moreover, any location may be addressed as required in writing a program. However, in the 141 system, certain storage locations have been assigned the additional functions of serving as input and output areas. That is, whenever information is read into the machine it is read into storage locations 001 through 080; information which is punched from the storage onto cards is punched from locations 101 through 180; finally, information from the storage which is to be printed is obtained from locations 201 through 300. Figure 4–1 is a storage map in which each of the input/output areas has been appropriately labeled.

In order to read a card into the READ area of storage, the READ A CARD (R) instruction is used. Upon execution of this instruction, the computer will place the entire contents of a card in positions 001–080. When the card is read into the machine, the character in card column 1 is placed in position 001, the character in column 2 in position 002, and so on, through column 80, which is placed in position 080. Each READ instruction that is executed will cause a single card to be read into this area of storage; the previous contents of the READ area will be lost unless they are moved. It is not possible to read only part of a card; the entire 80 characters are always read. Since the information is always read into a predetermined area, no address is required.

A question frequently asked is, "What happened to location 000?" The answer is simply, "Nothing; it is not used as part of the READ area." Computer designers recognized the simplicity of having the

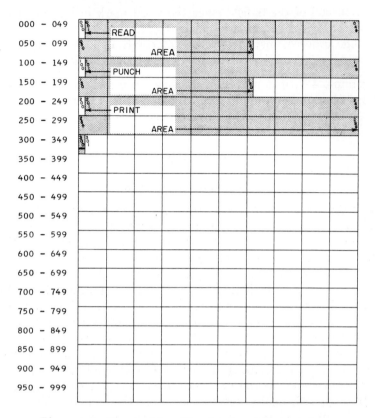

000 - 049									
050 - 099									
100 - 149									
150 - 199									
200 - 249									
250 - 299									
300 - 349									
350 - 399									
400 - 449									
450 - 499									
500 - 549									
550 - 599									
600 - 649									
650 - 699									
700 - 749									
750 - 799									
800 - 849									
850 - 899									
900 - 949									
950 - 999									

Figure 4–1. Storage Map Showing Input/Output Areas

storage address correspond to card column number. It is strictly a matter of convenience and simplicity. The formal definition for the READ A CARD instruction is

READ A CARD *(R)*

Op code

1

Description. The READ A CARD instruction causes the information in columns 1–80 of a Hollerith-coded card to be read into storage positions 001–080 respectively. The Hollerith code from each column is converted to the appropriate computer coding as it is read into the computer. The READ A CARD instruction *always* reads into positions 001–080 (the READ area).

Word Marks. Word marks that exist in the READ area prior to execution of the instruction are not disturbed nor do they affect the reading of information.

The following example illustrates the READ A CARD instruction:

EXAMPLE 4-12

A card has the name F JONES punched in columns 74–80 with a blank in column 75; all other columns are blank.

Contents of storage *before* execution of the READ instruction:

$$\underline{\;|1|2|3|4|5|6|\underline{7}|8|9|0|A|B|C|\;}$$

$$\underset{4}{\underset{7}{0}} \qquad \underset{0}{\underset{8}{0}}$$

Contents of storage (and card) *after* execution of READ instruction:

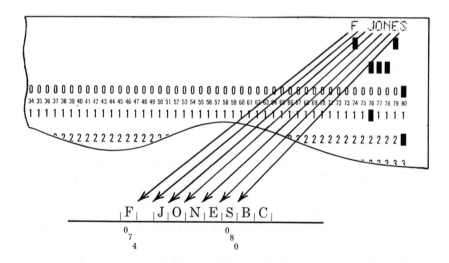

$$\underline{\;|F|\;|J|O|N|E|S|B|C|\;}$$

$$\underset{4}{\underset{7}{0}} \qquad \underset{0}{\underset{8}{0}}$$

1. The contents of locations 001–080, that is, the entire READ area, were replaced by the contents of the card. It is significant that in position 075 the 6 was replaced by a blank; in a similar fashion blanks were placed in each position of 001–073.
2. The word mark in location 076 was not disturbed; the READ A CARD instruction does not affect word marks.

3. The contents of storage locations 081 and higher were not affected by this instruction. Cards are read into the READ area, locations 001–080, and nowhere else.

The Output Instructions

To satisfy output needs the PUNCH and WRITE areas are available. Information stored in positions 101–180 can be transferred to a punched card by execution of the PUNCH A CARD (P) instruction. This instruction will cause the computer to punch the entire contents of locations 101–180 into card columns 1–80 of a Hollerith card. The contents of the PUNCH area are not changed. It is not possible to punch only part of the 80 columns; all 80 positions will be punched. If it is desired to leave blank columns in the card, the corresponding storage locations must contain blanks. The following is the formal definition:

PUNCH A CARD (P)

Op code

<u>4</u>

Description. The PUNCH A CARD instruction causes information in storage locations 101–180 (PUNCH area) to be punched in columns 1–80 respectively of a Hollerith coded card. The machine coding is converted to Hollerith coding prior to punching. The information stored in the PUNCH area is undisturbed. This instruction punches only information from the PUNCH area of storage onto the card.

Word Marks. Word marks are not punched, are not affected by the PUNCH instruction, and do not affect punching in any manner.

The other storage positions used for output are locations 201–300, which represent the PRINT area. The instruction WRITE A LINE (W) will cause the computer to print out the entire contents of storage locations 201–300 with a printer or typewriter, whichever is used. In a manner similar to the PUNCH instruction, all 100 positions will be printed. If it is desired to refrain from printing part of a line, then appropriate storage locations must contain blanks. The formal definition is

WRITE A LINE (W)

Op code

<u>2</u>

Description. The WRITE A LINE instruction causes the information in storage locations 201–300 (the WRITE area) to be printed out by the printer (or the typewriter). The information will remain in the PRINT area of storage after execution of the instruction. This instruction *always* prints information from all 100 positions of the WRITE area.

Word Marks. Word marks are not printed, are not affected by the instruction, and do not affect printing in any manner.

We have now discussed sufficient instructions to consider the following program to reproduce a card.

EXAMPLE 4-13

The procedure is reasonably simple; it is only necessary to read the card, move the contents and punch a new one. The program instruction would be

$$,0011\,M0801804$$

1. It is necessary to set a word mark at either 001 or 101 in order to terminate the MOVE operation. The sequence of instructions is important, except for the R instruction, which could have been written before the SW instruction. Otherwise none of them may be interchanged. For reasons which will soon become apparent, we will normally write most of the SET WORD MARK instructions at the beginning of the program.
2. This program will reproduce one card and no more.

Instruction Length

Before proceeding with further examples we shall pause and consider a few particulars of how the computer functions. The instructions studied thus far vary from one to seven characters in length; the data fields also vary in length since they are set by the programmer using the SET WORD MARK instruction. As a consequence, the 141 system is a *variable instruction length* and *variable word length* machine. This is in contrast to some computers, which have fixed instruction and/or word length features. Because of the variable instruction length, it is necessary to signal the end of a given instruction to the computer during execution of the program. Referring to the program of Example 4-13, we observe that the end of an instruction can be determined by placing a word mark on the operation code of the next instruction. This is a simple and obvious method and, in fact, is the means used by the computer.

Additional Needs

There are two further observations that we can make concerning Example 4-13. First is that the computer will find no word mark after the PUNCH instruction and thus will not be able to execute it. Further, even if the machine were to punch a new card, there is no instruction commanding it to halt. This leads us to two additional instructions, HALT (H) and NO OPERATION (NOP).

HALT *(H)*

Op code

$\stackrel{\bullet}{\bullet}$

Description. The HALT instruction causes the computer to stop. Depressing the start key will cause the program to proceed to the next instruction in sequence.

NO OPERATION *(NOP)*

Op code

$\underline{N}$

Description. The only purpose of the NO OPERATION instruction is to cause the program to proceed to the next instruction in sequence. The instruction may have the format of any allowable instruction; that is, it may have an A address, an A address and a B address, and so on.

As described, the NOP can consist of only an operation code, or of an op code and an A address, and so on. It is commonly used to replace the operation code of an instruction that is no longer required in a program. We will use it in this chapter to provide the extra word mark required at the end of the program.

EXAMPLE 4-14

A card has the full 80 columns punched. We wish to punch a new card with columns 41–80 containing the information punched in columns 1–40 of the old card, and columns 1–40 of the new card containing information from columns 41–80 of the old card.

As in Example 4–13, it will be necessary to read the card, but in this case two word marks will be required, since the card field is to be split in two and each half moved separately. The following program instruction will accomplish the required function:

$$\underline{,001}\underline{,0411}\ \underline{M040180}\underline{M0801404}\ .\ \underline{N}$$

1. The two SET WORD MARK instructions divide the READ area into two fields of equal length consistent with the problem requirements.
2. The first MCW instruction moves the information obtained from

the first 40 card columns to the last 40 positions of the PUNCH
area.

3. The second MCW instruction moves the information obtained
   from the last 40 card columns to the first 40 positions of the
   PUNCH area.

4. The computer halts after punching a card.

5. The NOP instruction is never executed. Its sole purpose is to provide a word mark that signals to the computer the end of the
   preceding instruction.

As we will discover, special provisions are made in the 141 system so
that three important instructions do not require the terminating word
mark. However, the reason for this special treatment will not become
apparent until Chapter 14 in which the loading routine is discussed.
The first of these three instructions represents our next topic.

BRANCHING

The programs of Examples 4–13 and 4–14 will each process one card
and no more. However, the normal need is to process not one but a
whole deck of cards. Thus means are required to instruct the computer
to return to the beginning of the program and start over again. In other
words, we wish the computer to operate in a READ-MOVE-PUNCH *loop*
once it has set the word mark.

Let us refer back to the pigeon-hole example once again and note
that the employer numbered the cards and on card 14 told the secretary
to "go back to card 6" and on card 16 to "go back to card 5." In
other words, she was directed to break from her sequence of proceeding
in order and *branch* to another portion of the program. In the computer,
this function is performed in much the same manner; the 141 system
is provided with a BRANCH (B) instruction that will cause the computer
to transfer to a designated instruction and continue from that point.

In the 141 system, each character of every instruction is placed in
one storage position. If we wish to address an instruction, we must
refer to the location of the operation code of that instruction. This is
in contrast to data fields, which are referred to by their low-order positions. Thus, whenever we wish to use a BRANCH instruction in a program, it is necessary to know the address of the instruction which we
wish the computer to execute next. Of the instructions considered thus
far, the A address and the B address when used have specified the
location of data. On the other hand, the BRANCH instruction will specify
the location of another instruction. In order to make a distinction between data addresses and instruction addresses, we will refer to the A

(or B) address when dealing with data, and the I address (instruction address) when dealing with instructions. The formal definition of the BRANCH instruction is as follows:

BRANCH (B)

Op code	I address
<u>B</u>	iii

Description. The BRANCH instruction causes the program to branch to the instruction specified by the I address.

Referring once again to the program for reproducing a card, we can now insert a BRANCH instruction and reproduce a deck of cards. By arbitrarily placing the program beginning at location 400, we cause it to appear as shown in the following example:

EXAMPLE 4-15

1. The READ instruction is located at 404, which is used as the I address of the BRANCH instruction.
2. In executing this program, the computer will set the word mark, read a card, move the card contents to the PUNCH area, punch a card, and branch back to the instruction at 404; read another card, move, punch, branch; and so on. The operation will continue until the last card is processed.

The BRANCH instruction in this program is not followed by a word mark. As was discussed previously, the unconditional BRANCH does not require a terminating word mark if the storage location immediately following the last character of the I address is blank. In this case, nothing is stored beyond 416 so 417 is blank, satisfying the requirement.

■ CHAPTER SUMMARY

One and only one character can be stored in each of the 1000 positions of storage at any given time.

A field, which is a group of characters, is specified in storage by the location of its low-order (rightmost) position. The left end is indicated by the presence of a word mark.

An instruction is specified in storage by the location of its operation code (high-order position).

Of the 1000 identical positions in storage the following have been assigned input/output functions:

Function	*Storage positions*
READ	001–080
PUNCH	101–180
PRINT	201–300

The following nine instructions have been studied:

MOVE CHARACTERS TO A OR B WORD MARK
SET WORD MARK
CLEAR WORD MARK
READ A CARD
PUNCH A CARD
WRITE A LINE
BRANCH
HALT
NO OPERATION

■ EXERCISES

4.1 If the storage contents include

$$\underline{1}|4|1|\underline{A}|D|D|\underline{1}|2|4|8|\underline{A}|1|X|5$$

$$0\,7\,3 \qquad\qquad 0\,8\,6$$

what are the fields specified by the addresses (*a*) 075, (*b*) 076, (*c*) 086?

4.2 If the MOVE instruction $\underline{M}999663$ were executed, what would be the resulting contents of the two storage areas indicated below?

$$1|2|3|A|B|C$$

$$6\,5\,8 \qquad\qquad 6\,6\,3$$

$$\underline{R}|E|P|O|R|T$$

$$9\,9\,4 \qquad\qquad 9\,9\,9$$

4.3 If the MOVE instruction $\underline{M}$099180 were executed, what would be the resulting contents of the two storage areas indicated below?

$$|\underline{1}|0|\ |\ |\ |S|$$

positions: $0\,9\,4$ ... $0\,9\,9$

$$|A|B|C|D|E|F|$$

positions: $1\,7\,5$ ... $1\,8\,0$

4.4 If the instruction $\underline{M}$899898 were executed, what would be the result in storage? Assume that the storage contents include

$$|\underline{5}|6|7|8|9|0|$$

positions: $8\,9\,4$ ... $8\,9\,9$

4.5 The contents of two portions of the storage is shown below. Without using the SW or CW instructions, demonstrate how the entire word GRADE may be moved from 080 to 291. Show the contents of both areas after execution.

$$|\underline{G}|R|\underline{A}|D|E|$$

positions: $0\,7\,6$ ... $0\,8\,0$

$$|4|3|2|1|0|$$

positions: $2\,8\,7$ ... $2\,9\,1$

4.6 In Example 4–7 what instructions are necessary to move only the word GRADE? Indicate storage contents before and after execution of the instruction.

4.7 Assume that a student name and number are stored as indicated. Write a program which will move the name and number to the storage area with the first letter of the name at 281. The number must immediately follow the name. Show the storage before and after execution of the instruction.

$$|1|2|3|5|J|O|N|E|S|$$

positions: $0\,7\,1$ ... $0\,7\,9$

4.8 A card with 1 2 3 4 5 6 7 8 9 0 in columns 1–10 (the others blank) is read into the computer. What will be the contents of the storage locations 001–080?

4.9 A card with the name W J O H N S O N punched in columns 28–35 is read into the computer. A new card is to be punched with the name as J O H N S O N W in card columns 15–23. Column 22 must be blank. Assume that the PUNCH area is blank. Write a program which will perform the required function.

4.10 Write a program that will read a deck of cards and punch a new deck, with the information from columns 1–40 of the card read in columns 41–80 of the card punched, and the information from columns 41–80 of the card read in columns 1–40 of the card punched. Use only one SET WORD MARK instruction.

4.11 A deck of student grade cards contain the name of the student in columns 2–17 and other information in the remainder of the card. The names are to be repunched, four to a card. The new cards will be divided into four sections, columns 5–20, 25–40, and so on. Write a program which will perform this function.

4.12 Distinguish between the A address and I address.

Chapter Five

THE SYMBOLIC
PROGRAMMING SYSTEM

In the early days of computers, all programs where written in the basic computer languages and determination of instruction and data addresses was left to the programmer. One can imagine that this detailed bookkeeping could amount to a considerable chore in the case of a long and involved program. A partial solution to this was to give names or *labels* to instructions which would later be specified in a BRANCH instruction. Then after the program had been completed and carefully checked, each position would be counted and actual addresses determined and substituted for the labels. Of course, if the program did not run, it was frequently necessary to change part of the instructions, thus resulting in changes of addresses for BRANCH instructions. Because of this and many other problems inherent with coding in the machine language, symbolic languages were developed which allowed the programmer to use labels which were assigned storage positions by the computer itself. A more detailed development of such programming languages is given in Chapter 16. One such "programmer-oriented" language is the 141 Symbolic Programming System (SPS), which we shall use almost exclusively in our programming. This language is designed to use mnemonics as extensively as possible and to facilitate the correction of the errors that almost always occur in writing extensive programs.

THE CODING SHEET

Figure 5–1 is the program from Example 4–15 written on the standard SPS coding form. Each line contains one instruction and will be punched one to a card. The meaning of each coding sheet position (that is, card column) is as follows:

1. Positions 1 and 2, which appear in the upper right-hand corner of the coding sheet, identifies the page number. Since our program is short it requires only one coding sheet and is numbered accordingly.
2. Positions 3–5 are reserved for the line number (that is, the card number) for identification purposes. Positions 1–5 are for programmer convenience and do not affect the program.
3. Use of the COUNT area, positions 6 and 7, will be described later in this chapter.
4. Positions 8–13 are used for the names or *labels* that must be given to an instruction. Since we must specify the READ instruction in the I address of the BRANCH, the READ is labeled INPUT.
5. The symbolic operation code for each instruction is placed in positions 14–16. Now we can use the more easily remembered codes such as SW instead of ‚ .
6. Positions 17–22 are reserved for the A (or I) address. Whenever actual storage addresses are used, we will write a leading zero in position 17, followed by the three-digit address. The purpose of this is to insure compatibility with the larger 1401 system. Sufficient positions are provided to accommodate the address when written in symbolic form.
7. Whenever a B address is required in an instruction, it is written in positions 28–33 similar to the A address.
8. For the present we will ignore positions 23–27 and 34–39.
9. Positions 40–55 are provided for comments as a reminder to the programmer and do not affect the program in any manner.
10. Finally, positions 76–80 are used only for identification and do not affect the program.

In this program the label, the symbolic operation codes, and both the A and B addresses are left-justified; that is, they are written in the leftmost positions of their respective areas. This is an important rule to follow in writing SPS programs.

IBM 1401 SYMBOLIC PROGRAMMING SYSTEM
CODING SHEET

Program CARD REPRODUCER

Programmed by ____________

Date 10/29

Page No. 01 of 1

Identification REPO (76–80)

LINE (3–5)	COUNT (6–7)	LABEL (8–13)	OPERATION (14–16)	(A) OPERAND ADDRESS (17)	(A) ± (23)	(A) CHAR. ADJ.	(A) IND. (27)	(B) OPERAND ADDRESS (28)	(B) ± (34)	(B) CHAR. ADJ.	(B) IND. (38)	d (39)	COMMENTS (40–55)
010			SW	0001									DEFINE FIELD
020		INPUT	R										READ A CARD
030			MCW	0080				0180					MOVE CRD TO PNCH
040			P										PUNCH NEW CARD
050			B	INPUT									RETURN TO READ
060													
070													
080													
090													
100													
110													
120													
130													
140													
150													
160													
170													
180													
190													
200													

AREA-DEFINITION CHARACTER COUNT → 1 5 10 15 20 25 30 32

Figure 5–1. Symbolic Programming System Coding Sheet

Labels

The choice of a label is usually made so that the label is descriptive and thus also functions as a mnemonic device. However, any labels are acceptable so long as they satisfy the following criterion:

1. The label may be 1–6 characters in length.
2. The characters may be letters (alphabetic) or numbers (numeric).
3. The first character of the label must be alphabetic.
4. No blanks are permitted within the label field.

By these criterion, the following would be acceptable labels:

A	GEORGE
A12345	GO
A12344	PROCES

The second and third labels, even though differing in only the last character, are different. The last label is the word *process*, with the final "s" left off because the correct spelling contains too many characters. As previously indicated, it is normal practice to use labels as mnemonic devices, that is, to choose them so that they are descriptive of the instruction or operation.

Examples of invalid labels are:

PROCESS	Too many characters; six is the maximum.
2517	The first character is not a letter.
DATA 1	Contains a blank between the A and the 1.

THE SPS CARD

The position numbers on the coding sheet correspond to card columns on a card. Each instruction or line on the coding sheet will be one card in the SPS language deck of cards. Thus the label is punched in columns 8–13, the operation in columns 14–16, the A (or I) address in columns 17–22, and the B address in columns 28–33. The additional columns, used as programming aids, are columns 1–5, 40–55, and 76–80. Again it is emphasized that these additional columns contain information helpful to the programmer and are *not* used by the computer. The significance of the remaining positions will be discussed later. The entire program from the coding sheet is shown punched on SPS cards in Figure 5–2. Note the correspondence between the position numbers on the coding sheet and the card columns.

LINE	COUNT	LABEL	OPERATION	(A) OPERAND ADDRESS	±	CHAR. ADJ.	ZONE	(B) OPERAND ADDRESS	±	CHAR. ADJ.	d ZONE	COMMENTS
0 1 0		INPUT	SW	0001								DEFINE FIELD
0 2 0			R									READ A CARD
0 3 0			MCW	0080				0180				MOVE CRD TO PNCH
0 4 0			P									PUNCH NEW CARD
0 5 0			B	INPUT								RETURN TO READ

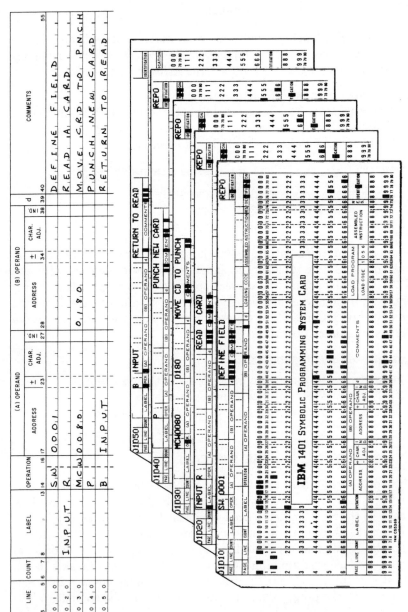

Figure 5–2. Symbolic Programming System Cards

ASSEMBLING

The five-instruction program of Example 4–15 can be punched into an SPS deck of cards by punching one line from the coding sheet on each card. This deck, called the *source* deck, will then represent the SPS version of a program deck to reproduce a deck of cards.

However, before the set of instructions can be loaded into the computer and executed, it must be translated to an equivalent machine language program such as that described in Example 4–15. The process of converting a program from SPS to machine language is termed *assembling*, and it is done by the computer using a special program called the *assembler*. Our SPS deck will then be assembled in the computer and the machine will punch out a machine-language or *object* deck which will contain cards with our original SPS program plus the machine-language equivalent. However, before assembling, it is necessary to provide the assembler with instructions concerning the proper handling of the source program. Frequently called *pseudo instructions*, these are merely instructions to the assembler. *They are not translated to equivalent machine-language instructions;* their sole function is to aid in the assembling function.

PSEUDO INSTRUCTIONS

Of the several pseudo instructions in the 141 system, the one which signals the end of the source deck to the assembler will be considered first. All SPS source decks must contain a last card with the pseudo instruction END punched in columns 14, 15, and 16 to specify to the assembler that the end of the program has been reached so that the assembler may complete the production of the object program. It is again stressed that the END instruction is not translated to an equivalent machine-language instruction. In fact, there is none. One other piece of information which the END card conveys is the location of the first instruction that we wish the computer to execute after the object deck is loaded into the computer and execution is ultimately begun; that location is specified by a symbol in the I address of the appropriate card (that is, line of the coding sheet). The complete SPS program is shown in Figure 5–3. Line 060 contains the END pseudo instruction and indicates the location of the first instruction of the program by the symbol BEGIN.

A formal definition for the pseudo instruction END is as follows:

IBM 1401 SYMBOLIC PROGRAMMING SYSTEM
CODING SHEET

Program CARD REPRODUCER

Programmed by ______

Date 10/29

Page No. 01 of 1

Identification REPO

LINE (3–5)	COUNT (6–7)	LABEL (8–13)	OPERATION (14–16)	(A) OPERAND ADDRESS (17)	(A) ± (23)	(A) CHAR. ADJ.	(A) IND. (27)	(B) OPERAND ADDRESS (28)	(B) ± (34)	(B) CHAR. ADJ.	(B) IND. (38)	d (39)	COMMENTS (40–55)
010		BEGIN	SW	0001									DEFINE FIELD
020		INPUT	R										READ A CARD
030			MCW	0080				0180					MOVE CRD TO PNCH
040			P										PUNCH NEW CARD
050			B	INPUT									RETURN TO READ
060			END	BEGIN									
070													
080													
090													
100													
110													
120													
130													
140													
150													
160													
170													
180													
190													
200													

AREA-DEFINITION CHARACTER COUNT → 1 5 10 15 20 25 30 32

Figure 5–3. The Complete Symbolic Programming System Program

END *(END)*

Description. The END statement is an indication to the assembler that the last card of the source program has been processed. The symbolic operation code END must be placed in the operation field and the address of the first instruction, either actual or symbolic, must be placed in the A operand area of the coding sheet.

The SPS source program to reproduce a deck of cards is now complete. In order ultimately to reproduce a deck of cards using the program, the following steps are necessary:

1. Punch the SPS program on cards according to the required format.
2. Assemble the source deck. The outcome will be an object program punched in another deck of cards.
3. Load and execute the object program.

Constants

Another pseudo instruction available with the 141 allows us to specify constants (either letters or numbers) which are loaded with the object deck and stored for subsequent use. It is the DCW or DEFINE CONSTANT WITH WORD MARK instruction. Five examples illustrating its description and use are shown in Figure 5–4 and described in Example 5–1.

EXAMPLE PROGRAMS

EXAMPLE 5-1

1. The symbolic operation code DCW is written in the operation area.
2. The specified constants, consisting of numbers, letters or special characters, begin in position 24 and may extend through column 55.
3. The number of characters in each constant field is specified in the COUNT area of the coding sheet.
4. In each case the constant is given a label by which it may be addressed for future use.
5. Referring to the examples of Figure 5–4, we see that
    (*a*) the first three are alphabetic; the second consists of four blanks,
    (*b*) the fourth and fifth are numeric; the fifth is a negative number so the minus sign has been placed in column 23. The sign is not included in the COUNT,

LINE 3–5	COUNT 6–7	LABEL 8–13	OPERATION 14–16	(A) OPERAND ADDRESS 17	± 23	CHAR. ADJ.	IND. 27	(B) OPERAND ADDRESS 28	± 34	CHAR. ADJ.	IND. 38	d 39	COMMENTS 40–55
010	20	HEAD	DCW	*		GRA	D	E POIN	T	AV	E	R	AGES
020													
030	04	BLANKS	DCW	*									
040													
050	06	HEAD1	DCW	0280		OUT	P	UT					
060													
070	03	CONST1	DCW	*		314							
080													
090	03	CONST2	DCW	*	-	500							
100													
110													
120													
130													
140													
150													
160													
170													
180													
190													
200													

AREA-DEFINITION CHARACTER COUNT → 1 5 10 15 20 25 30 32

Figure 5–4. Use of the DCW Pseudo Instruction

(c) the third is assigned the actual address 280; the others will be assigned storage locations as determined by the assembler.

The formal definition of the DCW pseudo instruction is as follows:

DEFINE CONSTANT WITH WORD MARK (DCW)

Description. The symbolic operation code DCW causes a constant to be loaded into storage and sets a word mark in the high-order (leftmost) position of the constant field. The number of characters in the constant field is specified in the COUNT portion of the coding sheet (columns 6 and 7). The symbolic label by which the constant is referenced is placed in the LABEL area (columns 8–13). The code DCW is placed in columns 14–16. Column 17 may contain an asterisk to indicate to the assembler that it may choose the location of the constant field, or columns 17–20 must contain the desired storage location of the low-order position (rightmost) of the constant field. In using an actual address, care must be taken that nothing else is assigned to that area. Constants *cannot* be defined in the READ area. The constant itself begins in column 24 and may extend through 55, giving a maximum of 32 characters. If the constant is to be signed number, the sign may be placed in column 23.

EXAMPLE 5-2

A deck of student master cards contains the information shown in Figure 5–5. Write a program that will take the student name from columns 7–26 and the student file number from columns 2–6, and print a complete list with the names in print positions 20–39 and the file numbers in positions 45–49. The heading at the top of the page should be STUDENT FILE NUMBERS, with the first letter of STUDENT in print position 20.

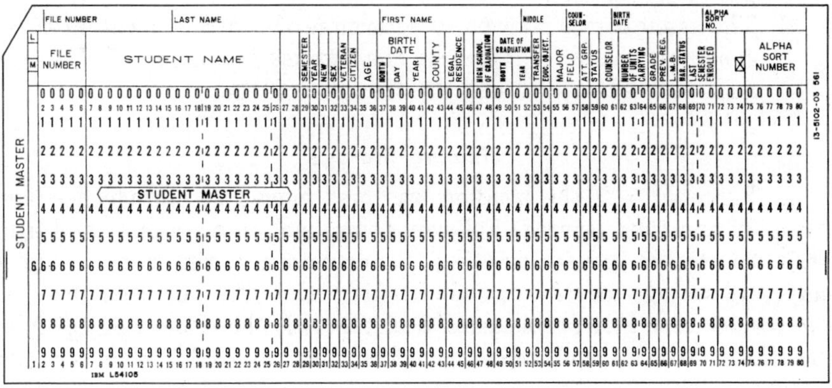

Figure 5–5. The Student Master Card of Example 5–2

Program Planning

To clarify the order in which various operations will be performed in executing this program, it will be helpful to outline the over-all steps that must be contained in the program.

1. Set the necessary word marks.
2. Print out the heading.
3. Read a card.
4. Move the appropriate fields.
5. Write.
6. Return to the third step.

The Program

The program of Figure 5–6 is consistent with the preceding outline. We can make the following observations concerning this program:

1. The END statement is the last one in the program. The location specified by the I address of the END statement is the location of the first instruction.
2. Immediately preceding the END statement is the DCW instruction. The DCW will cause a program constant to be stored along with the instructions but will not result in a machine-language instruction. On the other hand, the END statement will result in no equivalent field in the object program. All DCW's are most frequently placed at the end of the program immediately preceding the END statement.
3. The heading STUDENT FILE NUMBERS is addressed as a field and as such is moved to PRINT area locations 220–239. The address 239 is determined by counting.
4. The assembler is allowed to determine the storage location of the constant; this is indicated by the asterisk in column 17. We need address the constant only by the label HEAD.

Clearing Storage

In Example 5–2, the heading was first moved to storage positions 220–239 and then printed. Following this, each name was moved from 007–026 to 220–239 for printing. By coincidence, the name occupied as many storage locations as the heading. Had this not been the case, we would have had problems. For instance, if the name had occupied positions 007–024 and been moved to 239, it would have occupied locations 222–239. Thus ST, the first two letters from the heading, would have been printed out each time a name and number were

IBM 1401 SYMBOLIC PROGRAMMING SYSTEM
CODING SHEET

Program: EXAMPLE 5-2 | Page No. 01 of 1
Programmed by: ______ | Date: 10/29 | Identification: FILE (76–80)

LINE (3–5)	COUNT (6–7)	LABEL (8–13)	OPERATION (14–16)	(A) OPERAND ADDRESS (17)	± (23)	CHAR. ADJ.	IND. (27)	(B) OPERAND ADDRESS (28)	± (34)	CHAR. ADJ.	IND. (38)	d (39)	COMMENTS (40–55)
010		BEGIN	SW	0002									DEFINE FILE AND
020			SW	0007									NAME FIELDS
030			MCW	HEAD				0239					MOVE AND
040			W										PRINT HEADING
050		READ	R										READ A CARD
060			MCW	0006				0249					MOVE FILE NUMBER
070			MCW	0026				0239					AND NAME
080			W										THEN PRINT
090			B	READ									BRANCH TO READ
100	20	HEAD	DCW	*		STUDENT FILE NUMBERS							
110			END	BEGIN									
120													
130													
140													
150													
160													
170													
180													
190													
200													

AREA-DEFINITION CHARACTER COUNT → 1 5 10 15 20 25 30 32

Figure 5–6. Program to Print Student File Numbers

printed. There are two methods by which we could eliminate these characters. First, we could define a two-position DCW containing blanks; that is, put nothing in columns 24 and 25 of the coding sheet, then move them to 221 (and 220) after printing the heading. This method would be satisfactory here but would be cumbersome if it were necessary to clear a larger portion of the WRITE area. In order to clear large portions of storage at a time, the 141 system is provided with the CLEAR STORAGE (CS) instruction. This instruction consists of an operation code and an A address, and will cause the contents of storage, including word marks, to be cleared from the location specified by the A address down to the nearest hundreds position. The formal definition is as follows:

CLEAR STORAGE (CS)

Op code	A address
/̲	aaa

Description. The CLEAR STORAGE instruction causes the storage to be cleared to blanks beginning at the location specified by the A address and continuing downward through the nearest hundreds position.

Word Marks. Both word marks and data are cleared by this instruction.

EXAMPLE 5-3

Write a program that will reproduce the student master deck of the preceding example without the alpha sort numbers (columns 75–80), and print a listing with the heading COUNSELOR ASSIGNMENTS beginning in print position 10, followed by

FIELD	PRINT POSITIONS
File number	4–8
Name	12–31
Counselor	36–37

The Program

The logical steps and their ordering is shown in the flowchart of Figure 5–7; the program follows as Figure 5–8. The following comments are appropriate:

1. Word marks for file number, name, and counselor were set in the PRINT area rather than the READ area. This way they did not interfere with moving the card contents to the PUNCH area.
2. The CLEAR STORAGE instruction will clear from 230 down to 200.
3. The heading was printed before setting word marks for two reasons. First, word marks would interfere with moving the heading, and second, execution of the CLEAR STORAGE instruction would clear them.

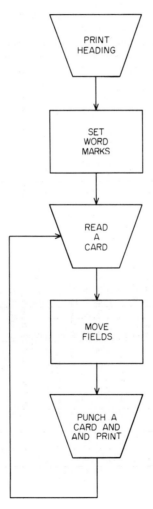

Figure 5-7. Flowchart for Example 5-3

IBM 1401 SYMBOLIC PROGRAMMING SYSTEM
CODING SHEET

Program EXAMPLE 5-3   Page No. 0 1 of 1

Programmed by ______   Date 10/29   Identification COUNS

LINE (3–5)	COUNT (6–7)	LABEL (8–13)	OPERATION (14–16)	(A) OPERAND ADDRESS (17)	± (23)	CHAR. ADJ.	IND. (27)	(B) OPERAND ADDRESS (28)	± (34)	CHAR. ADJ.	IND. (38)	d (39)	COMMENTS (40–55)
010		BEGIN	MCW	HEADG				0230					SET UP AND
020			W										PRINT HEADING
030			CS	0230									CLEAR PRINT AREA
040			SW	0001									SET
050			SW	0204									WORD
060			SW	0212									MARKS
070			SW	0236									
080		READ	R										READ A CARD
090			MCW	0074				0174					MOVE CRD TO PNCH
100			MCW	0006				0208					MOVE FILE NUM,
110			MCW	0026				0231					NAME AND COUNS
120			MCW	0061				0237					TO PRINT AREA
130			P										PUNCH NEW CARD
140			W										PRINT
150			B	READ									NEW CARD
160	21	HEADG	DCW	*		COU	N	SELOR	A	SSI	G	N	MENTS
170			END	BEGIN									
180													
190													
200													

AREA-DEFINITION CHARACTER COUNT → 1 5 10 15 20 25 30 32

Figure 5–8. Student Counselor Assignments

ADDITIONAL SPS INSTRUCTIONS

The heading COUNSELOR ASSIGNMENTS occupied 21 positions; what if COUNSELOR ASSIGNMENTS FOR FALL SEMESTER, needing 39 positions, had been required? Since it is greater than 32 characters in length, it cannot be defined with one DCW. However, COUNSELOR ASSIGNMENTS could be defined with a 21-position DCW and FOR FALL SEMESTER with a 17-position DCW. However, two MOVE instructions would be required to place the entire heading in the PRINT area. A useful method of avoiding this is to define the second constant without the word mark. For this purpose, the DEFINE CONSTANT (DC) pseudo instruction is provided. The DC functions the same as the DCW except the constant is placed in storage without a word mark. The formal definition is as follows:

DEFINE CONSTANT (DC)

Description. The symbolic operation code DC causes a constant to be loaded into storage without a word mark. The number of characters in the constant field is specified in the COUNT portion of the coding sheet (columns 6 and 7). The symbolic label by which the constant is referenced is placed in the LABEL area (columns 8–13). The code DC is placed in columns 14–16. Column 17 may contain an asterisk to indicate to the assembler that it may choose the location of the constant field, or columns 17–20 must contain the desired storage location of the low-order position (rightmost) of the constant field. The constant itself begins in column 24 and may extend through 55, giving a maximum of 32 characters. If the constant is to be a signed number, the sign may be placed in column 23.

It is of utmost importance that constants not be defined in the READ area of storage, or they will be lost when the program is loaded into the machine, and occasionally will not allow the program to be loaded at all. Often we desire to refer to an input quantity by a mnemonic rather than its actual location in the READ area. This is especially true if the quantity is referred to several times in the program. To satisfy this need we can use the following DEFINE SYMBOL instruction:

DEFINE SYMBOL (DS)

Description. The operation code DS causes the processor to assign equivalent addresses to labels or to assign storage for work areas. The DS differs from DC and DCW statements in that neither data nor word marks are included during loading. The number of positions to be reserved in storage is specified in the COUNT portion of the coding sheet.

If we wish to refer symbolically to the low-order position of the field reserved, then a label must be placed in the LABEL field. If the assembler is to assign the address, an asterisk must be placed in column 17 of the coding sheet. If we wish to equate the label with an actual address, that address is written beginning in column 17, and the COUNT field of the coding sheet is left blank.

EXAMPLE 5-4

Rewrite the program of Example 5–3 using the heading COUNSELOR ASSIGNMENTS FOR FALL SEMESTER.

The Program

A program reflecting this modification is shown in Figure 5–9, and the following comments clarify what has been done:

1. The three quantities to be moved from the READ area are given mnemonic labels and referred to by these symbols in the MOVE instructions.
2. The heading, which exceeds 32 positions, is formed using a 30-position DCW without a label. This sets up the COUNSELOR ASSIGNMENTS FOR FALL with a word mark under the first position. The word SEMESTER is defined immediately following by using a DC with an asterisk in column 17. Since it is given a label, the label will refer to the field from the last character (R in SEMESTER) proceeding downward until the word mark is sensed (at the C in COUNSELOR); in other words, the field will consist of the entire 39 positions.

Extensive use of mnemonics can be useful to the programmer both in writing his program and in getting it to function properly (*debugging*). Convenience and ease of error correction is a significant factor in programming. The following example illustrates how the coding sheet has been designed to make life easier for the programmer when making corrections.

EXAMPLE 5-5

Rewrite the program of Example 5–3 so that two identical cards are punched for each input card.

The Program

The answer here is merely to insert another card containing the PUNCH instruction either preceding or following the existing one in the source program, and then reassemble to obtain a new object program.

IBM 1401 SYMBOLIC PROGRAMMING SYSTEM
CODING SHEET

Program EXAMPLE 5-4 | Page No. 0 1 of 1
Programmed by ______ | Date 10/30 | Identification COUN2 (76–80)

LINE (3–5)	COUNT (6–7)	LABEL (8–13)	OPERATION (14–16)	(A) OPERAND ADDRESS (17)	± (23)	CHAR. ADJ.	IND. (27)	(B) OPERAND ADDRESS (28)	± (34)	CHAR. ADJ.	IND. (38)	d (39)	COMMENTS (40–55)
010		BEGIN	MCW	HEADG				0240					SET UP AND PRINT
020			W										HEADING
030			CS	0240									CLEAR PRINT AREA
040			SW	0001									SET
050			SW	0204									WORD
060			SW	0212									MARKS
070			SW	0236									
080		READ	R										READ A CARD
090			MCW	0074				0174					MOVE CRD TO PNCH
100			MCW	FILE				0208					MOVE FILE NUMBER
110			MCW	NAME				0231					NAME AND COUNS
120			MCW	COUNS				0237					TO PRINT AREA
130			P										PUNCH NEW CARD
140			W										PRINT
150			B	READ									NEW CARD
160	30		DCW	*		COU	N	SELOR	A	SSI	G	N	MENTS FOR FALL
170	09	HEADG	DC	*		SE	M	ESTER					
180		FILE	DS	0006									
190		NAME	DS	0026									
200		COUNS	DS	0061									
210			END	BEGIN									

AREA-DEFINITION CHARACTER COUNT → 1 5 10 15 20 25 30 32

Figure 5–9. Student Counselor Assignments

Rather than rewrite the coding sheet, the extra instruction can be added as shown in Figure 5–10.

The PUNCH instruction *must* be inserted in the proper sequence in the source deck. The line (or card) number coded in columns 3–5 is designated accordingly.

To incorporate such changes in a source program is usually a simple task, whereas the same change in a machine-language program could be a major revision. When writing a new program or rewriting existing ones, it is frequently necessary to add instructions after the program has been roughed out. Consistent with this need is the organization of the coding sheet and the card numbering system. Note that a feature of the preprinted line numbers on the coding sheet is that they all end in zero. This means that up to nine additional instructions may be inserted between any two original instructions without destroying the sequence.

In this example the extra instruction was inserted between lines 130 and 140 and called 135, which maintains the desired sequencing. The absence of cards numbered 131, and so on, is of no consequence. Use of the line number in addition to the page number in columns 1 and 2 provides an unambiguous method for handling the cards, thereby minimizing the possibility of misordering cards. Line 130 on page 01 would be identified in the sequence by the number 01130 in columns 1–5. A card punched from the same line but on page 02 (for a program consisting of two pages) would be numbered 02130. To further protect against mixups between programs, necessary program identification information may be punched in columns 76–80.

Although DCW and DC instructions may be placed at either the beginning or end of a program (but not between instructions), it is considered good practice to put them all at the end, preceding the END card. In a similar fashion all SET WORD MARK instructions are placed at the beginning of the program whenever possible. In writing a program we will normally have several word marks to be set, several DCW's, and so on. However, the exact needs are not always obvious when the programmer first starts coding. A convenient method to avoid confusion is to use three separate coding sheets, one for SET WORD MARK instructions, one for the main program, and one for pseudo instructions and the END card.

Whenever it is found in writing a program that a word mark must be set or a constant defined, it can be accomplished without continual erasing and changing. Then, when the coding is completed, the sheets can be placed one on top of the other and cards punched.

Perhaps it may seem that overemphasis has been placed on correct-

IBM 1401 SYMBOLIC PROGRAMMING SYSTEM
CODING SHEET

Program __EXAMPLE 5-5__

Programmed by _____

Date __11/1__

Page No. |0|1| of |1|

Identification |C|O|U|N|3| (76-80)

LINE	COUNT	LABEL	OPERATION	(A) OPERAND ADDRESS	±	CHAR. ADJ.	±IND	(B) OPERAND ADDRESS	±	CHAR. ADJ.	±IND	d	COMMENTS
0 1 0		BEGIN	MCW	HEADG				0230					SET UP AND
0 2 0			W										PRINT HEADING
0 3 0			CS	0230									CLEAR PRINT AREA
0 4 0			SW	0001									SET
0 5 0			SW	0204									WORD
0 6 0			SW	0212									MARKS
0 7 0			SW	0236									
0 8 0		READ	R										READ A CARD
0 9 0			MCW	0074				0174					MOVE CRD TO PNCH
1 0 0			MCW	00006				0208					MOVE FILE NUM ;
1 1 0			MCW	00026				0231					NAME AND COUNS
1 2 0			MCW	0061				0237					TO PRINT AREA
1 3 0			P										PUNCH NEW CARD
1 4 0			W										PRINT
1 5 0			B	READ									NEW CARD
1 6 0	21	HEADG	DCW	*			COUNSELOR ASSIG					N	MENTS
1 7 0			END	BEGIN									
1 8 0													
1 9 0													
2 0 0													
1 3 5			P										ADDITIONAL CARD

AREA - DEFINITION CHARACTER COUNT → 1

Figure 5-10. Student Counselor Assignments

ing and modifying programs, and that programmers must be "mistake prone." It is extremely difficult and tedious to write a long and involved program without making errors, and virtually all programs are constantly being revised with use in order to increase efficiency and/or flexibility. The whole concept of the Symbolic Programming System is to provide a more efficient programming tool so that the programmer's time may be most effectively used.

■ CHAPTER SUMMARY

The Symbolic Programming System (SPS) language is the language in which most programming is done on the 141 system. It is an easy-to-read, easy-to-write, easy-to-understand programming language. The computer, however, operates in absolute language.

The process of translating the source (SPS) program to the object (absolute) program may be done by the computer under the control of a prewritten assembly program. The end product is an object deck, which may then be loaded into the computer.

Four pseudo instructions have been introduced:

END — Signals the end of the source program to the assembler and designates the location of the first instruction.

DCW — DEFINE CONSTANT WITH WORD MARK

DC — DEFINE CONSTANT (no word mark)

DS — DEFINE SYMBOL

■ EXERCISES

5.1 Which of the following are invalid labels? Why?

ABCDEF   X432
2START   A
START   RETURN2
READ 2

5.2 What is the purpose of the assembler?

5.3 What is the difference between a source deck and an object deck?

5.4 What is the function of the END card in an SPS deck?

5.5 How do SPS pseudo instructions differ from machine instructions (for example, MCW, and so on)?

5.6 How does END differ from DCW and DC?

5.7 Describe the format for the DCW instruction.

5.8 A deck of student master cards contains the information shown in the card of Example 5–2. Reproduce the deck with the identifying information STMACD (*ST*udent *MA*ster *Car*D) in columns 75–80 of each card.

5.9 A deck of student master cards contains the information shown in the card of Example 5–2. Print a listing of names and birthdates. The name should begin in print position 3 and the birthdate begin in position 26. At the top of the page print STUDENT BIRTHDATES beginning in position 9.

5.10 A deck of student master cards contains the information shown in the card of Example 5–2. Print a listing with the following information:

> File number
> Student name
> High school of graduation
> Date of graduation

The headings FILE, NAME, HIGH SCHOOL and GRAD DATE should appear above the respective positions. Format planning is left to the student.

5.11 A deck of cards contains the following information:

FIELD	*CARD COLUMN*
Name	7–26
Address	31–49
City	50–60
State	61–65

Write a program that will print an address tag for each card. The first line must contain the name; the second line, the address; and the third line, the city and state with a comma between them. Begin each line in print position 10. Skip two lines between each address.

Chapter Six

SYMBOLIC PROGRAMMING SYSTEM ASSEMBLY

So far we have discussed the writing of simple computer programs in both machine language and SPS. Details of the assembly process to obtain a machine-language program from one written in SPS have been omitted thus far. We shall now concentrate on the process of assembling and the resulting machine-language program.

AN ANALOGY

The process of converting SPS language to machine language can best be explained by use of an analogy. Suppose we had a book on programming written in German which we wished to read. The only problem is that we cannot read German. If the need were sufficient, we could hire a person to translate the book from German to English for us. The function of the translator would be to convert the descriptions and accounts written in German into like descriptions and accounts in English, and record them in a programming book written in English. Whether or not the translator had an extensive background in computer programming would be unimportant. The primary requirement would be that he have the capability to translate from German to English. We need only refer to the book written in English. This idea can be represented by diagrams, as shown in Figure 6–1. In this analogy the following points are significant:

1. The material was originally written in German by an author who was presumably German. It was written in the language easiest for him to use.

2. The contents of the text were converted to English and recorded by a translator expert in translating from German to English. He need not have known anything about computer programming.
3. The translator did not read the book for us, he merely changed it to a form which was easy for us to read.
4. Once the translation was complete, the need for the original text in German and for the translator no longer existed. Both could have been dispensed with.

The idea of changing from a language which is easy for the writer to one which is easy for the user cannot be overemphasized, since this is precisely the relationship between SPS language and machine language. The SPS language is easy for us to use and understand, but the computer operates in machine language, which is considerably more difficult to program.

The process of translating an SPS program could be accomplished in a number of ways. The programmer himself could first write the program in SPS and then translate it to machine language, but this would be little better than writing the original program in machine language. An alternative would be to submit the SPS program to an individual who is an expert in translating and allow him to do it. This would be very similar to the analogy, and probably would be an improvement over the preceding method. However, the most attractive possibility is to allow the computer to perform this task, thus relieving the programmer of it. Before the translating can be accomplished in this fashion it is necessary to "educate" the computer in the art of translating, much the same as the translator in the analogy had to know how to change German to English.

(a)   (b)   (c)

Figure 6–1. Analogy for Symbolic Programming System Assembly

This is accomplished by using a prewritten program called a *processor* or an *assembler*. The assembler is a program that has been prepared by programmers trained in machine language and that can be fed into the machine. The computer, under control of the assembler program, can efficiently serve to assemble or process the SPS program into a machine-language program. As in the analogy, *the assembler will not execute the program, it will only translate from SPS language to machine language.* At all times during assembly the assembler has complete control of the computer and no instructions designated in the source program will be executed.

THE ASSEMBLY

The First Pass

To illustrate the problems involved in assembling a program, we refer to the program of Example 5–4, which is repeated here in Figure 6–2. If we were to perform the translation to machine language manually, we would not proceed very far without encountering problems, since the A address of the first instruction is not known. In the SPS program it is designated by the symbol HEADG. In the machine-language program, the program constant specified by the symbol HEADG is stored at the end of the program, that is, at an address yet to be determined. Thus it is necessary for us either to leave the A address blank and return to it later, or, preliminary to translating the instructions, to compile a list of labels in which the storage location synonymous with each label is determined. The latter method is the one used by the assembly program. Thus the process of assembling consists of two very distinct portions, or *passes*. The purpose of the first pass is merely to establish a meaning for each of the labels in terms of machine-storage locations and to set up a table of labels for use in the second pass.

In the cited example, the first instruction is designated by the label BEGIN. Since machine-language programs are stored by the assembler beginning in location 333, the assembler will assign 333 to the symbolic location BEGIN and place both the symbolic and the absolute addresses in a label table. To determine the equivalent absolute location of the label READ is a little more difficult. In order to do this, the machine will inspect each SPS instruction and keep a check on the storage space required. The process thus involves inspecting the first instruction, which requires seven storage locations; the second, which requires one; the third, which requires four; and so on. Summing these up to the READ instruction gives a storage location of 361 for this instruction. The symbol READ would then be entered in the label table along with

IBM 1401 SYMBOLIC PROGRAMMING SYSTEM
CODING SHEET

Program ____FROM EXAMPLE 5-4____   Page No. |0|1| of __1__

Programmed by _____   Date __11/2__   Identification |C|O|U|N|S|

LINE	COUNT	LABEL	OPERATION	(A) OPERAND ADDRESS	±	CHAR. ADJ.	(B) OPERAND ADDRESS	±	CHAR. ADJ.	d	COMMENTS
0 1 0		BEGIN	MCW	HEADG			0240				SET UP AND
0 2 0			W								PRINT HEADING
0 3 0			CS	0240							CLEAR PRINT AREA
0 4 0			SW	0001							SET
0 5 0			SW	0204							WORD
0 6 0			SW	0212							MARKS
0 7 0			SW	0236							
0 8 0		READ	R								READ A CARD
0 9 0			MCW	00074			0174				MOVE CRD TO PNCH
1 0 0			MCW	FILE			0208				MOVE FILE NUMBER
1 1 0			MCW	NAME			0231				NAME AND COUNS
1 2 0			MCW	COUNS			0237				TO PRINT AREA
1 3 0			P								PUNCH NEW CARD
1 4 0			W								PRINT
1 5 0			B	READ							NEW CARD
1 6 0	30		DCW	*		COUNSELOR	ASSIGNMENTS FOR FALL				
1 7 0	09	HEADG	DC	*		SEMESTER					
1 8 0		FILE	DS	0006							
1 9 0		NAME	DS	0026							
2 0 0		COUNS	DS	0061							
2 1 0			END	BEGIN							

AREA—DEFINITION CHARACTER COUNT →

Figure 6-2. Source Program for Example 5-4

its absolute equivalent of 361. Continuing the counting process, a slightly different situation is encountered with the DC. Up to this point, all of the fields have been instructions and, as such, are addressed by their leftmost positions. On the other hand, the program constant that results from a combination of the DCW and DC is not an executable instruction and it is addressed by its rightmost character. The purpose of 30 and 09 in the COUNT portion of the SPS instructions is to specify the number of characters in the program constant and to specify to the assembler how many storage positions should be reserved for the constant. Since the BRANCH instruction will occupy locations 392–395, the program constant will be stored in 396–434, with an address as a field of 434. The symbol HEADG and its machine-language equivalent 434 would then be placed in the label table. Proceeding on, the assembler would place FILE, NAME, and COUNS in the label table with their equivalent address 006, 026, and 061 respectively as defined in the A address portions of the instructions. The assembler would then detect the END card, which signals the end of the first pass. As indicated previously, the completion of the first pass means only that the label table has been set up. It is necessary that this be done prior to the actual translation of the program in order to have available the machine-language equivalents of symbolic addresses.

The Second Pass

During the second pass the assembler will first punch three utility cards, then assemble machine language instructions one at a time, in much the same manner we had attempted. As each SPS instruction is translated, it is punched into a card, along with appropriate descriptive information indicating, among other things, where the instruction is to be stored when the program is eventually loaded. Upon encountering the first instruction in this example, that is,

MCWHEADG   0240

the assembler will translate the operation code to M; upon encountering the symbolic address HEADG, it will substitute the absolute address 434, as indicated in the label table. Determination of the B address is a simple matter in this case, after which the assembler punches the object card with the seven-character instruction M434240. The assembly program proceeds with the second pass and translates all instructions until END is encountered. The assembler then completes the second pass by punching an extra card called the *transition card*. This card is the last one read in when the program is loaded and causes the object program to assume control of the computer and begin execution of the program, beginning with the instruction specified by the I address of the END instruction.

As emphasized previously, the assembly process is merely the translation of the SPS program to the machine-language program. Control of the computer is under the assembly program at all times during the assembly. Once the assembly is complete, the object program can be loaded into storage; once loaded, it can be executed.

THE OBJECT DECK

First Three Cards

An 80-column listing of the object deck from Example 5–4 is shown in Figure 6–3. We will not study the details of the deck and loading procedures until Chapter 14, but a cursory study now will be useful. Most of the listing appears to be familiar; however, the first three cards are unlike anything from the source deck. These cards are the same on all object decks assembled by the computer, and contain instructions both for clearing the entire storage prior to loading, and loading the program. They are automatically punched by the assembly program.

Columns 1–55 of the remaining cards are identical to the source program, but columns 56–75 contain information not punched in the source deck. These characters represent loading instructions and the corresponding machine-language instruction, which is to be placed in storage. By comparing columns 67–74 of each card with the SPS instruction on that card, it is apparent that the machine-language op code

```
,008015,022026,030034,041,045,053,0570731026
L072116,110106,105117B101/999,027A074028)027B00102708026/0991,001/00111710
,008015,022029,056063/056029                            ,0240671056
01010 7BEGIN  MCWHEADG        0240        SET UP AND      L0733391056M434240
01020 1       W                           PRINT HEADINGSL06734010562
01030 4       CS 0240                     CLEAR PRINT AREAL0703441056/240
01040 4       SW 0001                     SET             L0703481056,001
01050 4       SW 0204                     WORD            L0703521056,204
01060 4       SW 0212                     MARKS           L0703561056,212
01070 4       SW 0236                                     L0703601056,236
01080 1READ   R                           READ A CARD     L06736110561
01090 7       MCW0074        0174         MOVE CD TO PUNCHL0733681056M074174
01100 7       MCWFILE        0208         MOVE FILE NUMBERL0733751056M006208
01110 7       MCWNAME        0231         NAME AND COUNS  L0733821056M026231
01120 7       MCWCOUNS       0237           TO PRINT AREA L0733891056M061237
01130 1       P                           PUNCH NEW CARD  L06739010564
01140 1       W                           PRINT           L06739110562
01150 4       B    READ                   NEW CARD        L07039510568361
0116030       DCW*          COUNSELOR ASSIGNMENTS FOR FALL L0534251056
0117009HEADG  DC  *          SEMESTER                      M0324341056
01180  FILE   DS 0006                                      N00105610560006
01190  NAME   DS 0026                                      N00105610560026
01200  COUNS  DS 0061                                      N00105610560061
01210         ENDBEGIN                                     /333080
```

Figure 6–3. Object Listing for Example 5–4

is punched in column 67 and the remainder of the instruction follows. The storage address to which the last character of the instruction will be assigned is punched in columns 60–62. For example, let us refer to the fourth card, which contains the first instruction in our program. Columns 67–73 contain the machine-language equivalent, which is

M̲434240

Columns 60–62 contain 339, the address of the last character of the B address; thus the instruction will occupy positions 333–339. The op code will be in 333, as previously described. Each of the other instructions is similar to the first.

Pseudo Instructions

Card columns 60–62 for both the DCW and DC pseudo-instruction cards contain the storage address to which each constant will be assigned (addressing them as fields). However, columns 67–73 are blank, since program constants are loaded directly from their positions in columns 24–55. On the other hand, the DS instructions are treated differently. Since their purpose is either to reserve storage space or define symbols, their function is completed once the label table has been compiled and the assembly finished. As a consequence, the instructions punched beginning in column 56 cause the computer to ignore that card and continue to the next one. Finally, the END or transition card contains an instruction to signal the end of loading. The address of the first instruction in the program to be executed is punched in columns 57–59. This instruction will never appear in storage once the program loading is completed, however.

It is noteworthy that the complete program is loaded into storage before a single instruction is executed. During the loading process, control of the computer is under the loading routine, which is described in detail in Chapter 14.

STORAGE CONTENTS

To complete our discussion of the SPS-to-machine-language process, we will now consider the appearance of a processor-assembled program once it is loaded into storage. Furthermore, we will assume that a deck of cards has been processed. Thus, the contents of the last card (shown in Figure 6–4) will remain in the READ area and the PUNCH area (less the alpha sort number in the latter). Also, we would expect to find the name, file number, and counselor number in the PRINT area.

A printout of the complete storage contents, usually referred to as a storage *dump*, is shown in Figure 6–5. As was anticipated, the input/

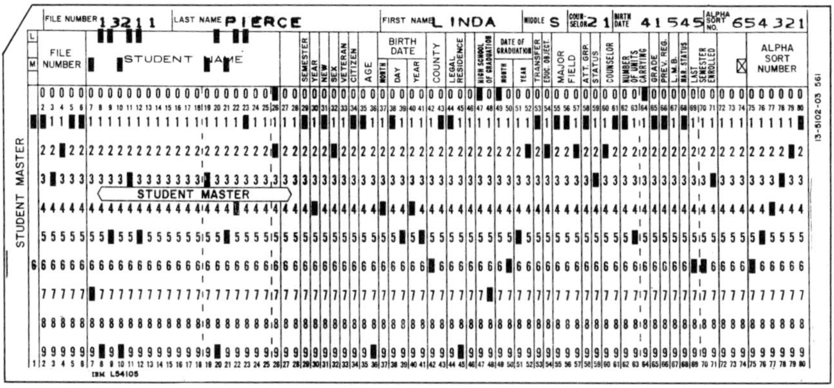

Figure 6-4. Last Card in Assembled Deck

```
I-REG    OP-REG
 362       1

000 - 049   │1132│11PIERCE    L│INDA   S  1│412  1│19415│45611│9 070│
            │1   │
050 - 099   │65212│11213│2115011  1663   654321│
100 - 149   │1132│11PIERCE    L│INDA   S  1│412  1│19415│45611│9 070│
150 - 199   │65212│11213│2115011  1663│
200 - 249   │   13211      PI│ERCE    L│INDA   S   21│
250 - 299   │   1                                   1│
300 - 349   │                              M4│342402│/240,│001,│
            │                               1        11    1    1│
350 - 399   │204,2│12,23│61M07│4174M│00620│8M026│231M0│6123742B361COUN│
            │  1    1    11         1         1          1    111     1│
400 - 449   │SELOR│ ASSI│GNMEN│TS FO│R FAL│L SEM│ESTER│
450 - 499
500 - 549
550 - 599
600 - 649
650 - 699
700 - 749
750 - 799
800 - 849
850 - 899
900 - 949
950 - 999
```

Figure 6-5. Storage Dump for Example 5-4

output areas contain information from the last card that was processed. The machine-language instructions are shown in storage positions 333–395, and the program constant in positions 396–434. It is left to the student to verify that each instruction location is consistent with the addresses given in the object deck.

Registers

A final point concerning the storage dump is the information in the upper left-hand portion of Figure 6–5. Under I REG is the address 362, and under OP REG is the operation code 1. The address 362 was contained in the computer's I register, and the op code 1 was contained in the operation register at the time of the dump. Since execution of the program was terminated when the card supply was exhausted, the op code of the instruction it was attempting to execute (the current instruction) was placed in the op register, and the address of the next instruction was stored in the instruction register. These are always printed with a dump and are useful in debugging.

INSTRUCTIONS AND PSEUDO INSTRUCTIONS

With our present knowledge of machine instructions, the SPS instructions, and the assembly process, the distinction between machine instructions and SPS pseudo instructions is apparent. Perhaps the student has also recognized the difference between various pseudo instructions. This leads us to the following three major categories:

Imperative Statements (Instructions). These statements represent the directives to the computer for performing the required function. They are translated by the assembler into their machine-language equivalents in the object program.

Declarative Statements (Area Definition). These statements assign sections of storage for program constants and work areas. Area-definition statements generally do not result in instructions to be executed as part of the object program. However, the assembler program does produce, for these statements, cards containing program constants and their assigned machine addresses. These constants are loaded with the object program each time the program is used and therefore are considered a part of the machine-language program. The DCW, DC, and DS are declarative statements.

Processor Control Statement (Control). Special information to the assembler is provided by these statements. They allow the programmer to adjust certain portions of the assembly process but are never executed in the object program. The END is a control statement.

The list of imperatives will be expanded considerably over those we have discussed. The four pseudo instructions we have considered are sufficient for the majority of our studies, although we will add one declarative and two control statements in later chapters.

■ CHAPTER SUMMARY

The assembly process is a two-pass procedure. The purpose of the first pass is to compile a table of labels to determine storage addresses equivalent to the symbolic addresses used in the SPS program. Actual translation from SPS to machine language is accomplished by the second pass.

A machine-language program that has been assembled by the computer will normally be loaded into storage beginning at location 333.

Instructions and pseudo instructions may be considered in three categories. They are (*a*) imperative statements, the instructions; (*b*) declarative statements, which serve to define storage areas; (*c*) processor control statements, which serve to give directives to the assembler.

■ EXERCISES

6.1 A common yet serious error that the beginning programmer frequently makes is to place the constant defining DCW's immediately preceding the instructions in which they are used. The assumption is that they must be defined before they are used. What is the basic misunderstanding and why is this reasoning invalid?

6.2 In the program of Figure 5–6 (Example 5–2) assume that the programmer has made the above described error and has placed the DCW immediately following the second SET WORD MARK instruction. Manually assemble this program and show the machine-language program as it will appear in storage. Will the program function properly when executed?

6.3 Manually assemble the program in Figure 6–2, placing *all* of the declarative statements at the beginning of the program. If the END statement still references the MOVE instruction, will the program function properly when executed? How does this modification to the program differ from that of Exercise 6.2?

6.4 Distinguish between imperative, declarative, and control statements and give examples of each.

Chapter Seven

THE COMPUTER
AND ARITHMETIC

Previous chapters have dealt primarily with input/output functions; none of the programs considered have performed computations. For the purpose of actually computing, we will now add arithmetic instructions to our list.

ADDITION

Preliminary to a discussion of the ADD instruction, it will be fruitful to review Chapter 4. In introducing the idea of moving data from one storage location to another, we talked of a FROM address and a TO address; that is, a location from which the data is obtained and a location to which it is moved. These, of course, are properly termed the A address and B address respectively. The ADD instruction, which has the symbolic operation code A and the absolute operation code $\underline{A}$, is very much similar to the MOVE instruction in this respect. In adding, it is necessary to specify the addresses of each of the two fields to be added. With the ADD instruction, as in the case of the MOVE instruction, the A address specifies one of the fields and the B address specifies the other; however, unlike the MCW, the sum replaces the B field. In a fashion somewhat similar to that of the MOVE instruction, the ADD is terminated by a word mark, but the process is more involved and will be explained in detail by the use of the following examples.

EXAMPLE 7-1

Contents of storage *before* execution of the ADD instruction:

$$|1|5|\underline{3}|3|5|$$

$$\begin{matrix} 0 & & 0 \\ & 6 & & 6 \\ & & 0 & & 2 \end{matrix}$$

$$|2|3|\underline{1}|5|9|$$

$$\begin{matrix} 1 & & 1 \\ & 7 & & 8 \\ & & 8 & & 0 \end{matrix}$$

Instruction: $\underline{A}062180$

Contents of storage *after* execution of the ADD instruction:

$$|1|5|\underline{3}|3|5|$$

$$\begin{matrix} 0 & & 0 \\ & 6 & & 6 \\ & & 0 & & 2 \end{matrix}$$

$$|2|3|\underline{4}|9|4|$$

$$\begin{matrix} 1 & & 1 \\ & 7 & & 8 \\ & & 8 & & 0 \end{matrix}$$

1. The field specified by the A address is added to the field specified by the B address, and the sum has replaced the B field.
2. The addition is terminated by a word mark in the B field. Here there is no difficulty since both fields are the same length.
3. Characters to the left of the word marks are not affected.
4. The A field is left unchanged.
5. Word marks are not disturbed.

In Example 7–1, two 3-digit numbers were added together; their lengths were the same and were indicated by word marks. At this point we might consider in a little detail the process of adding in the machine. If we were to take a pencil and piece of paper and add two numbers, the result would appear as follows:

$$\begin{array}{r} 335 \\ \underline{159} \\ 494 \end{array}$$

In performing the addition, the digits in the units positions are first added to obtain 14, but this is recorded as 4 in the units position of the sum with a carry of 1 to the tens position. Addition of the tens digits plus the carry produces 9 for the tens position of the sum. Addition of the hundreds digits yields 4, thus completing the addition. Addition of two numeric fields within the computer is accomplished in exactly the same manner; that is, digits are added from right to left. With this in mind, let us consider some other examples that illustrate other characteristics of the ADD instruction.

EXAMPLE 7-2

Contents of storage *before* execution of ADD instruction:

$$3\,|\,2\,|\,\underline{4}\,|\,7\,|\,9\,|\,3\,|\,2\,|\,9$$

175   180

$$2\,|\,\underline{8}\,|\,5\,|\,3$$

509   511

Instruction: A511180

Contents of storage *after* execution of the ADD instruction:

$$3\,|\,2\,|\,\underline{4}\,|\,8\,|\,0\,|\,1\,|\,8\,|\,2$$

175   180

$$2\,|\,\underline{8}\,|\,5\,|\,3$$

509   511

1. The A field is shorter than the B field.
2. Only the three digits located in 509–511 are added to the B field.
3. Although the A field contains only three digits, the thousands and the ten thousands positions of the B field are affected by the carries of the addition.
4. The above comments can be summarized by pointing out that when the A field is shorter than the B field, the word mark in the A field stops transmission of data from the A field, but carries are propagated in the B field.

Whenever two numbers are added together, there exists the possibility that the sum may contain more characters then either of the two original numbers because of carries. This is a problem to which a programmer must pay particular heed in writing programs. In a computer the result can frequently be an overflow, thus producing an incorrect answer. The following example represents an overflow situation.

EXAMPLE 7-3

We wish to add 557 to 694, which are stored as shown. In this example an overflow results.

Contents of storage *before* execution of the ADD instruction:

$$\underline{|4|\underline{6}|9|4|}$$
$$^{1}{}_{9}{}_{0}$$

$$\underline{|3|\underline{5}|5|7|}$$
$$^{2}{}_{0}{}_{5}$$

Instruction: $\underline{A}190205$

Contents of storage *after* execution of the ADD instruction:

$$\underline{|4|\underline{6}|9|4|}$$
$$^{1}{}_{9}{}_{0}$$

$$\underline{|3|\underline{2}|5|1|}$$
$$^{2}{}_{0}{}_{5}$$

1. The addition was terminated by the word mark in the B field.
2. The carry that should have resulted in a sum of 1251 was lost.

An overflow condition when a 141 program is run on a 1620 will simply be lost, but on a 1401 the result will be a zone bit in the high-order position of the B field. This is discussed in more detail in Chapter 15.

NEGATIVE NUMBERS

These first examples have all used positive numbers in the addition process. In programming most problems, the arithmetic operations are planned so that input data and internal computations normally involve positive numbers. For instance, if we wrote a program to compute our bank balance, we would add deposits to the balance and subtract withdrawals. Thus both deposits and withdrawals would be read into the computer as positive fields.

However, we should anticipate that at some time we might have the misfortune to overdraw our account; thus it is necessary to provide for negative fields. In math and science the need to use both positive and negative numbers is even more frequent. Although the 141 system is oriented more toward business applications than scientific uses, means are provided for distinguishing between a positive and a negative number.

From Chapter 3 we recall that the Hollerith code for any digit is a punch in that digit of the required column. For example, the card in Figure 7-1 has an 8 punched in column 10. Further, a minus sign is

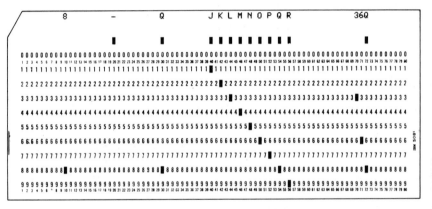

Figure 7-1. Card Coding of Negative Numbers

represented by an 11 punch, shown in column 20. A logical choice for −8 (minus eight) is a combination of these, that is, an 11-8 punch, shown in column 30. Columns 40, 42, 44, 46, 48, 50, 52, 54, and 56 show the negative numbers −1, −2, −3, −4, −5, −6, −7, −8, and −9 respectively.

Unfortunately, however, these card codings also represent the letters *J* through *R*. Internally, this is no problem to the machine because of the manner in which it is designed. However, when we receive output, punched on cards or typed, it is up to us to recognize from context what is meant. When the number to be coded consists of several digits rather than just one, only the units position will be punched with the 11 punch. The negative number −368 will be punched as shown in columns 70–72. If this were interpreted according to the Hollerith code shown in Chapter 3, it would appear as 36Q. Similarly, if it were typed from storage, it would be typed as 36Q; it would be up to us to recognize it as -368 by context. Whenever an addition takes place in which one of the fields is negative, the fields are added algebraically and the sign is determined by the relative magnitudes of the two fields. The following two examples demonstrate the ADD instruction with fields of opposite sign.

EXAMPLE 7-4

Contents of storage *before* execution of the ADD instruction:

$$|\,4\,|\,\underline{7}\,|\,8\,|\,3\,|\,2\,|_{205} \qquad\qquad |\,5\,|\,7\,|\,\underline{6}\,|\,3\,|\,Q\,|_{249}$$

Instruction: A249205

Contents of storage *after* execution of the ADD instruction:

$$|\,4\,|\,\underline{7}\,|\,1\,|\,9\,|\,4\,|_{205} \qquad\qquad |\,5\,|\,7\,|\,\underline{6}\,|\,3\,|\,Q\,|_{249}$$

1. The fields are of opposite sign, so the resulting ADD involves finding the difference between the two and using the sign of the larger for the required sum.
2. Word marks are not disturbed.
3. The A field is unchanged.

EXAMPLE 7-5

Contents of storage *before* execution of the ADD instruction:

$$|\,1\,|\,7\,|\,\underline{3}\,|\,8\,|\,N\,|_{075}$$

$$|\,6\,|\,2\,|\,\underline{4}\,|\,7\,|\,3\,|_{106}$$

Instruction: <u>A</u>106075

Contents of storage *after* execution of the ADD instruction:

$$\underline{\;|1|7|\underline{0}|8|8|\;}$$
$$0\atop7\atop5$$

$$\underline{\;|6|2|\underline{4}|7|3|\;}$$
$$1\atop0\atop6$$

1. The A field, which is positive, is larger in magnitude than the B field, which is negative. The result is a positive field that is the difference between the magnitudes of the two numbers.
2. The minus sign in position 075 does not appear after execution of the instruction because the field is now positive.

The principal points illustrated in the preceding examples of the ADD instruction are summarized in the following formal definition:

ADD *(A)*

Op code	A address	B address
<u>A</u>	aaa	bbb

Description. The ADD instruction causes the data in the A field to be added algebraically to the data in the B field. The A field is not disturbed, and the resulting sum is stored in the B field.

Word Marks. The defining word mark of the B field terminates the operation. If the A field is shorter than the B field, the A-field word mark will halt transmission of data from the A field, but any resulting carries will be added to the B field until the B-field word mark is sensed. If a carry results beyond the B-field word mark, it is lost, or if the A field is longer, the high-order positions of the A field that exceed the limits imposed by the B-field word mark are lost. These both represent overflow conditions.

SUBTRACTION

As might be expected, the process of subtraction is very similar to that of addition except that the A field is subtracted algebraically from the B field and the difference stored in the B field. The formal definition of the SUBTRACT instruction is as follows:

SUBTRACT *(S)*

Op code	A address	B address
S̲	aaa	bbb

Description. The SUBTRACT instruction causes the data in the A field to be subtracted algebraically from the data in the B field. The A field is not disturbed, and the resulting difference is stored in the B field.

Word Marks. Word marks control the SUBTRACT operation in the same manner as they control the ADD instruction.

EXAMPLE 7-6

Contents of storage *before* execution of the SUBTRACT instruction:

$$\overline{ |5|\underline{9}|8|P| }$$
$$^0_2$$
$$_4$$

$$\overline{ |2|\underline{4}|6|3|1| }$$
$$^2_0$$
$$_5$$

Instruction: S̲024205

Contents of storage *after* execution of the SUBTRACT instruction:

$$\overline{ |5|\underline{9}|8|P| }$$
$$^0_2$$
$$_4$$

$$\overline{ |2|\underline{5}|6|1|8| }$$
$$^2_0$$
$$_5$$

1. The A field is negative, so the algebraic subtraction results in a summing process. Here, we must recall the rule for subtraction, which is "Change the sign of the subtrahend and proceed as in addition."
2. The A field is unchanged.
3. Word marks are not disturbed.

EXAMPLE 7-7

Contents of storage *before* execution of the SUBTRACT instruction:

$$| 3 | \underline{4} | 2 | 7 |$$
$${}^5 {}_2 {}_8$$

Instruction: $\underline{S}528528$

Contents of storage *after* execution of the SUBTRACT instruction:

$$| 3 | \underline{0} | 0 | 0 |$$
$${}^5 {}_2 {}_8$$

1. In this example a field is subtracted from itself; the difference, of course, is zero. This is a valid and useful operation. Again, as described in Chapter 15, the 1401 will function in a slightly different manner.
2. The operation was terminated when it reached the (common) word mark.
3. The word mark was not disturbed.

EXAMPLE PROGRAMS

Using the Input/Output Areas

Many applications require that both the A and B fields be retained in storage. In all of the examples thus far, the B field is replaced by the sum and the original contents of the B field are lost. The logical need is either to move the B field or define a "working area" in which arithmetic may be performed. In many programs, particularly those which are input/output oriented, much of the arithmetic can be done by using the input/output areas. More specifically, it is often convenient to perform arithmetic directly in that portion of the storage from which the eventual output is to be obtained. When setting up these work areas, it is essential that the programmer determine the necessary sizes of the working areas so that overflow will not occur and invalidate results. These points are illustrated by Example 7–8.

EXAMPLE 7-8

Write a program that will read a deck of cards containing numeric fields M and N and will punch a new deck that will contain the fields M, N, and P where P = 2M − N. All input and output quantities will be positive. The card format is as follows:

FIELD	CARD COLUMNS	CARD
M	2– 7	Input and output
N	8–13	Input and output
P	ending in 80	Output only

Program Planning

It is important to make a preliminary inspection of the problem in order to set up the P-field size to avoid overflows. Since M is six digits in size, the largest value it may assume is 999,999, and the maximum value for 2M is 1,999,998. Since N is also six digits but is subtracted from 2M to obtain P, the maximum value for P will occur when M = 999999 and N = 0, which will give P = 1999998. Thus it will be necessary to provide seven positions for P, punched in card columns 74–80.

The Program

A completed program is shown in Figure 7–2. The first three instructions set word marks to define the fields M, N, and P respectively. The DS declaratives at the end of the program serve to define mnemonics by which these fields may be referenced. Instruction 050 initializes the work area (that is, sets all characters equal to zero). If this were not done, a high-order carry in location 174 resulting from the previous card could produce erroneous results.

Constants for Work Areas

Frequently a situation will arise in which it is not desirable to use the input/output areas as arithmetic working areas. In particular, we must exercise care when performing the input/output functions in long and involved programs so as not to wipe out accumulated figures being saved in the input/output areas. It is apparent that the choice of location 180 was not the only one which could have been made. Aside from the input/output areas, any storage location could have been chosen that would not overlap the instructions. The simplest way to avoid such overlap is to use the SPS language and allow the assembler to

IBM 1401 SYMBOLIC PROGRAMMING SYSTEM
CODING SHEET

Program: EXAMPLE 7-8 | Programmed by: ______ | Date: 11/2 | Page No. 01 of 1 | Identification: 2M-N

LINE	COUNT	LABEL	OPERATION	(A) OPERAND ADDRESS	±	CHAR. ADJ.	IND.	(B) OPERAND ADDRESS	±	CHAR. ADJ.	IND.	d	COMMENTS
010		BEGIN	SW	0002									DEFINE FIELDS
020			SW	0008									FOR M, N
030			SW	0174									AND P
040		READ	R										
050			MCW	ZERO				P					INITIALIZE P
060			MCW	N				0113					MOVE N AND M TO
070			MCW	M				0107					PUNCH AREA
080			MCW	M				P					THEN
090			A	M				P					COMPUTE
100			S	N				P					P
110			P										
120			B	READ									
130	07	ZERO	DCW	*		000	0	000					
140		M	DS	0007									
150		N	DS	0013									
160		P	DS	0180									
170			END	BEGIN									
180													
190													
200													

AREA-DEFINITION CHARACTER COUNT → 1 5 10 15 20 25 30 32

Figure 7-2. Program to Compute P = 2M − N

determine the location. The means provided the programmer for such area definitions is the declarative statement discussed in a previous section. In the 141 system, a convenient declarative is the DCW, DEFINE CONSTANT WITH WORD MARK.

The use of the word *constant* is misleading because the DCW causes a specified field to be placed in storage. Once the field is in storage, it can be moved or another field can be moved in to replace it. If it is numeric it can be added to any other numeric field in storage and any other numeric field can be added to it, thus replacing the original constant in storage with the resultant sum. The significant point here is that the constant is not really a constant at all, it is just another field in the storage. In place of calling it a program constant, perhaps the term *program data* would be more appropriate.

A second program that will perform the function required in Example 7–8 is shown in Figure 7–3. In this program, the word mark in the working area is obtained automatically when the area is defined with the DCW. Other than that, this SPS program is virtually the same as the previous one.

In order to illustrate the effect on the program constant of executing the instructions, Figures 7–4 and 7–5 illustrate two storage dumps. Figure 7–4 shows the contents after the program has been loaded but not executed; Figure 7–5 shows the contents after the program has been loaded and executed. In the last card processed, M and N had the following values:

$$M = 783000$$
$$N = 27500$$

Table of Squares

In Chapter 1 we studied how Charles Babbage's difference engine used the method of differences to compute values of polynomial equations. Applying this method to the equation $y = x^2$, we have

x	y	FIRST DIFFERENCE	SECOND DIFFERENCE
0	0		
		1	
1	1		2
		3	
2	4		

IBM 1401 SYMBOLIC PROGRAMMING SYSTEM
CODING SHEET

Program: EXAMPLE 7-8 (ALTERNATE) — Page No. 01 of 1

Programmed by: ______ — Date: 11/2 — Identification: 2M-N

LINE (3–5)	COUNT (6–7)	LABEL (8–13)	OPERATION (14–16)	(A) OPERAND ADDRESS (17)	± (23)	CHAR. ADJ.	IND. (27)	(B) OPERAND ADDRESS (28)	± (34)	CHAR. ADJ.	IND. (38)	d (39)	COMMENTS (40–55)
010		BEGIN	SW	0002									DEFINE FIELDS
020			SW	0008									FOR M AND N
030		READ	R										
040			MCW	ZERO				P					INITIALIZE P
050			MCW	N				0113					MOVE N AND M TO
060			MCW	M				0107					PUNCH AREA
070			MCW	M				P					THEN
080			A	M				P					COMPUTE
090			S	N				P					P
100			MCW	P				0180					
110			P										
120			B	READ									
130	07	ZERO	DCW	*		000	0	000					
140	07	P	DCW	*									
150		M	DS	0007									
160		N	DS	0013									
170			END	BEGIN									
180													
190													
200													

AREA-DEFINITION CHARACTER COUNT → 1 5 10 15 20 25 30 32

Figure 7–3. Constants for Work Areas

Note that the first difference 3 could have been obtained by adding the constant second difference 2 to the preceding first difference 1. Then adding 3 to the preceding value of y, which is 1, gives the next value for y of 4. The next square is $2 + 3 + 4 = 9$.

This method for computing squares is programmed in Figure 7–6 for values of x up to three digits in length. A detailed study is left to the student; note that extensive use has been made of mnemonics.

Decimal Alignment

In Example 7–8, it was assumed that decimals of both fields were at the extreme right. If this were not the case provisions for decimal alignment would have to be made. Had the card columns and decimal form of each field been as follows, the problem would have been somewhat more complex.

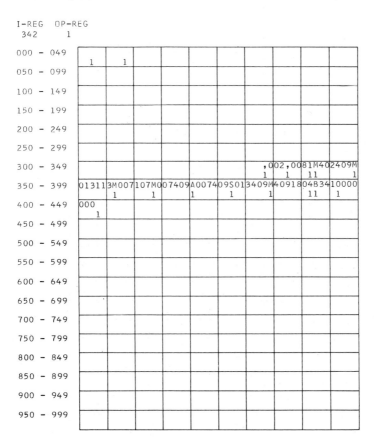

Figure 7–4. Storage Dump Prior to Execution

EXAMPLE 7-9

Write a program that will compute $P = 2M - N$ and punch a new card as in Example 7–8. Provide for decimal alignment and truncation of the answer.

	CARD COLUMN	DECIMAL FORM
Input Card		
M	2– 7	XXXX$_\wedge$XX
N	9–13	XXXX$_\wedge$X
Output Card		
P	71–75	XXXXX$_\wedge$

xx$_\wedge$x indicates a three-digit number with the decimal understood to be between the second and third digits.

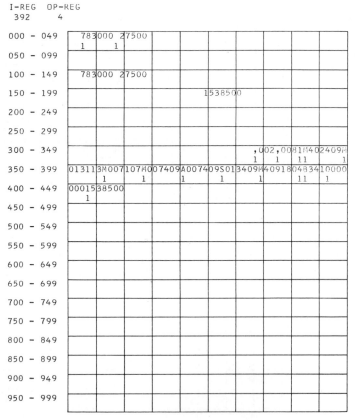

Figure 7–5. Storage Dump after Execution

IBM 1401 SYMBOLIC PROGRAMMING SYSTEM
CODING SHEET

Program: TABLE OF SQUARES — Page No. 01 of 1
Programmed by: ______ — Date: 11/2 — Identification: SQUAR (76–80)

LINE (3–5)	COUNT (6–7)	LABEL (8–13)	OPERATION (14–16)	(A) OPERAND ADDRESS (17)	± (23)	CHAR. ADJ.	IND. (27)	(B) OPERAND ADDRESS (28)	± (34)	CHAR. ADJ.	IND. (38)	d (39)	COMMENTS (40–55)
010		BEGIN	MCW	TITLE				0252					SET
020			W										UP
030			MCW	HEADNG				0252					TITLE
040			W										AND
050			CS	0252									HEADING
060			W										
070			SW	0239									
080			SW	0247									
090			MCW	ZERO				NUMBER					SET NUMBER AND
100			MCW	ZERO				SQUARE					SQUARE TO ZERO
110		WRITE	W										
120			A	ONE				NUMBER					CALCULATE SQUARE
130			A	DIF				SQUARE					BY METHOD OF
140			A	TWO				DIF					DIFFERENCES
150			B	WRITE									
160	16	TITLE	DCW	*		TABLE OF SQUARES							
170	16	HEADNG	DCW	*		NUMBER SQUARE							
180	06	ZERO	DCW	*		000000							
190	06	DIF	DCW	*		000001							
200	01	ONE	DCW	*		1							
210	01	TWO	DCW	*		2							
220		NUMBER	DS	0241									
230		SQUARE	DS	0252									
240			END	BEGIN									

AREA-DEFINITION CHARACTER COUNT → 1 5 10 15 20 25 30 32

Figure 7–6. Squaring by the Method of Differences

Program Planning

In ordinary arithmetic we could accomplish an addition of two decimals, say 273.9 and 45.67, by two different methods, which are fundamentally the same. First we could merely align the decimals on the paper and add:

$$273.9$$
$$\underline{45.67}$$
$$319.57$$

On the other hand, in the interests of bookkeeping we might add a zero to the right of 273.9 so that both numbers contain two decimal places; that is

$$273.90$$
$$\underline{45.67}$$
$$319.57$$

In order to obtain the answer to no decimals, the simplest procedure would be to drop the .57 and call the answer 319. This is called *truncating*. The mathematician will undoubtedly wince at such a practice but we will accept it for now and attempt to pacify him to a limited extent later. With this refresher in mathematics, let us study the program.

The Program

A program that will serve the purpose is shown in Figure 7–7. In essence, this program uses the first method described for obtaining decimal alignment. The comments on the coding sheet describe the functioning of the program reasonably well. A detailed study is left to the student. Figure 7–8 is the storage dump after the program has been executed and has processed a card containing

$$M = 9748.62$$
$$N = 3541.4$$

Half Adjusting

In mathematics, several more sophisticated methods are used to "democratically" reduce the number of significant places in a number. In other words, there are methods for "rounding off" much more palatable than truncating. The rule probably most commonly used is:

> If the highest-order digit to be dropped is less than 5, truncate; if the highest-order digit is 5 or greater, increase the next higher-order digit by one.

IBM 1401 SYMBOLIC PROGRAMMING SYSTEM
CODING SHEET

Program EXAMPLE 7-9 Page No. 01 of 1

Programmed by ______ Date 11/2 Identification 2M-N

LINE (3–5)	COUNT (6–7)	LABEL (8–13)	OPERATION (14–16)	(A) OPERAND ADDRESS (17)	± (23)	CHAR. ADJ.	IND. (27)	(B) OPERAND ADDRESS (28)	± (34)	CHAR. ADJ.	IND. (38)	d (39)	COMMENTS (40–55)
010		START	SW	0002									DEFINE
020			SW	0009									M, N
030			SW	0171									AND P
040		READ	R										
050			S	0175				0175					INITIALIZE
060			MCW	M				0177					COMPUTE
070			A	M				0177					P = 2M - N
080			S	N				0176					
090			MCW	BLANKS				0177					TRUNCATE P
100			P										
110			B	READ									
120	02	BLANKS	DCW	*									
130		M	DS	0007									
140		N	DS	0013									
150			END	START									
160													
170													
180													
190													
200													

AREA-DEFINITION CHARACTER COUNT → 1 5 10 15 20 25 30 32

Figure 7–7. Decimal Alignment and Truncation

To illustrate, the following numbers are rounded off to one decimal:

$$237.63 \rightarrow 237.6$$
$$64.975 \rightarrow 65.0$$
$$97.851 \rightarrow 97.9$$

With the instructions we have at our disposal, programming the computer to round off or truncate by inspecting a given digit would be impossible. However, by a simple trick of mathematics, the computer can perform the task of truncation in every instance. Consider the three numbers we have just rounded off. Since we wish to round them off to one decimal place, let us add 0.05 to each of them and *then* truncate.

$$237.63 + 0.05 = 237.68 \rightarrow 237.6$$
$$64.975 + 0.05 = 65.025 \rightarrow 65.0$$
$$97.851 + 0.05 = 97.901 \rightarrow 97.9$$

```
I-REG   OP-REG
 375       4
```

000 - 049	974	862	3	5414				
	1		1					
050 - 099								
100 - 149								
150 - 199					15955			
					1			
200 - 249								
250 - 299								
300 - 349							,002,009,171	1M007
							1 1 1	11
350 - 399	177A0	07177	S0131	76M38	71774	S1751	75B345	
	1	1	1	1	11	1	1	
400 - 449								
450 - 499								
500 - 549								
550 - 599								
600 - 649								
650 - 699								
700 - 749								
750 - 799								
800 - 849								
850 - 899								
900 - 949								
950 - 999								

Figure 7-8. Storage Dump for Example 7-9

The student should study this method of *half adjustment* in the above examples and determine why the process works and what the general procedure is.

Figure 7–9 is a program written for Example 7–9 to illustrate the use of half adjustment, where the final answer is rounded off rather than truncated. In this program, the first seven instructions do not differ from the program shown in Figure 7–7 in which the value for P was truncated. The instruction

A   POINT5   0176

in this program does not have a counterpart in the previous program, however. Let us carefully inspect what will occur when this instruction is executed. As before, we will let the last values processed for M and N be M = 9748.62 and N = 3541.4. Before rounding off, P will appear in storage as

| 1 | 5 | 9 | 5 | 5 | 8 | 4 |

$1 \atop 7 \atop 1$ $1 \atop 7 \atop 7$

The ADD instruction will add 5 (as defined by the DCW for POINT5) to this field, addressed as 176. The result in storage will be

| 1 | 5 | 9 | 5 | 6 | 3 | 4 |

$1 \atop 7 \atop 1$ $1 \atop 7 \atop 7$

After execution of the subsequent MCW, in which two blanks are moved to 176 and 177, the storage contents will be

| 1 | 5 | 9 | 5 | 6 | | |

$1 \atop 7 \atop 1$ $1 \atop 7 \atop 7$

thus the rounding off has been completed.

The student should give careful study to the placement of fields in the working areas and to the means of addressing in these examples.

Simple mathematical techniques such as these can be very useful to the programmer. However, discretion should be exercised in using them since problems can arise with negative numbers. Since sign indication

IBM 1401 SYMBOLIC PROGRAMMING SYSTEM
CODING SHEET

Program EXAMPLE 7-9 (ALTERNATE)

Programmed by ______

Date 11/2

Page No. 01 of 1

Identification 2M-N

LINE	COUNT	LABEL	OPERATION	(A) OPERAND ADDRESS	±	CHAR. ADJ.	IND.	(B) OPERAND ADDRESS	±	CHAR. ADJ.	IND.	d	COMMENTS
010		START	SW	0002									DEFINE
020			SW	0009									M , N
030			SW	0171									AND P
040		READ	R										
050			S	0175				0175					INITIALIZE
060			MCW	M				0177					COMPUTE
070			A	M				0177					P = 2M - N
080			S	N				0176					
090			A	POINT5				0176					HALF ADJUST
100			MCW	BLANKS				0177					VALUE OF P
110			P										
120			B	READ									
130	02	BLANKS	DCW	*									
140	01	POINT5	DCW	*		5							
150		M	DS	0007									
160		N	DS	0013									
170			END	START									
180													
190													
200													

AREA-DEFINITION CHARACTER COUNT → 1 5 10 15 20 25 30 32

Figure 7–9. Half Adjusting

for a numeric field in the 141 system is on the units digit of a field, indiscriminate truncation can easily change a negative field to a positive one. The illustration of this is left as an exercise for the student.

■ CHAPTER SUMMARY

Numeric fields may be positive or negative. Negative value is indicated in the low-order position.

Two instructions, the ADD and SUBTRACT, have been introduced. The ADD instruction adds the A field to the B field and the SUBTRACT instruction subtracts the A field from the B field. In both cases the process is algebraic (takes sign into account) and the result remains in the B field.

Care should be taken when adding fractional numbers to insure that decimals are aligned, and when working with negative fields—the sign may be lost if the field is referred by other than its low-order position.

■ EXERCISES

7.1 Add the following pairs of fields as the computer would, and indicate the placement of the word mark in the sum and whether or not the addition is valid, assuming a normal arithmetic process:

PAIRS	A FIELD	B FIELD
(1)	2̲374	5̲87
(2)	1̲0	9̲9990
(3)	3̲75	2̲895
(4)	3̲62	5̲91
(5)	2̲3	1̲J

7.2 Repeat Exercise 7.1 but reverse the fields.

7.3 Subtract the following pairs of fields as the computer would, and indicate the placement of the word mark in the difference and whether or not the subtraction is valid:

PAIRS	A FIELD	B FIELD
(1)	2̲374	5̲87
(2)	9̲321	9̲9321
(3)	6̲5K	6̲5K

7.4 In Example 7–8 it is pointed out that erroneous results could occur if the field at 175 is not initialized properly. To illustrate what would happen if this is omitted, step through the program (Figure 7–2), computing P if M = 618382, N = 75 for the first card and M = 575, N = 91 for the second card. Do not execute instruction 050. What will be the contents of 180 after processing the second card? What should the contents be?

7.5 Describe how decimal alignment and truncation are accomplished in Example 7–9

7.6 Truncate the following numbers to one decimal place:
(a) 276.53
(b) 75.955
(c) 29.68

7.7 Half adjust the numbers in Exercise 7.6 to one decimal place.

7.8 Write a program that will process a deck of cards, each card containing P and Q, and compute

$$M = 3P - 2Q$$

then print the answer. The format is

FIELD	CARD COLUMNS OR PRINT POSITIONS	DECIMAL ALIGNMENT
Input		
P	21–26	XXX∧XXX
Q	31–34	XX∧XX
Output		
P	21–27	XXX.XXX
Q	31–35	XX.XX
M	41–47	XXXX.XX

The output for M must be half adjusted to two decimal places. Print the decimal.

7.9 In Chapter 1 the equation

$$y = x^3 + 2x^2 + 3$$

was used to illustrate the method of differences. Using this method, calculate a table of values for x and y beginning with $x = 0$.

Chapter Eight

CONDITIONAL BRANCHING

Normally instructions in the 141 are executed in order, beginning with the one designated by the END card and proceeding to successively higher locations in storage to obtain the next instruction. The exception to this sequence occurs when a BRANCH instruction is encountered that directs the computer to a location designated by the I address for the next instruction. In all of the programs using a BRANCH that we have studied, the computer found itself in a never-ending loop; that is, it became locked in a loop that was terminated only when the supply of cards was exhausted.

It is certainly easy to imagine situations in which we might desire the ability to branch only under certain conditions. For example, the pigeon-hole analogy discussed in Chapter 2 required a conditional BRANCH on card number 12. That is, "If the result is zero, go to card 15; if not, continue on to card 13." A simple flowchart accompanied the example. The instruction on card 12 told the secretary to compare the number on the slate to the number zero; if they were the same she was to execute the BRANCH (but not if they were different).

Two of the elements that help to make the digital computer a very powerful tool are first, the conditional BRANCH, and second, a means to determine the condition that will be used as the criterion for branching. The second of the two will be considered first. In the pigeon-hole analogy the secretary broke her normal sequence by comparing two numbers. In the 141 system, a conditional BRANCH is also controlled by comparing two fields.

115

COMPARE

The COMPARE (C) instruction performs the function of comparing the contents of the A field to the contents of the B field and then setting appropriate indicators, which may be tested later by the conditional BRANCH. If the B field is larger than the A field, the HIGH indicator is turned on; if it is smaller, the LOW indicator is turned on; if the two fields are equal, the EQUAL indicator is turned on. Perhaps the easiest means for remembering which is which, is to think of the COMPARE instruction as a subtraction, in which neither field is disturbed. If the resulting difference is positive, the HIGH indicator is turned on, and so on. Consequently, if any two fields are compared, only one of these indicators will be turned on.

In addition, there is the UNEQUAL indicator, which will be turned on in addition to either the HIGH or LOW indicator whenever the fields being compared are not the same; when they are equal, it is turned off. The following examples illustrate use of the COMPARE instruction and the resulting effect on the indicators.

EXAMPLE 8-1

Contents of storage:

$$|\underline{6}|7|5|6|$$

$$0 \atop 6 \atop 0$$

$$|\underline{5}|6|8|7|$$

$$1 \atop 8 \atop 2$$

Instruction: $\underline{C}060182$

Indicator settings *after* execution of the COMPARE instruction:

| On | UNEQUAL indicator |

| Off | HIGH indicator |

| Off | EQUAL indicator |

| On | LOW indicator |

1. The B field is compared to the A field and is smaller. As a result the UNEQUAL indicator is turned on.
2. In addition, only one of the other three, the LOW indicator, is turned on.
3. Neither field is disturbed.

EXAMPLE 8-2

Contents of storage:

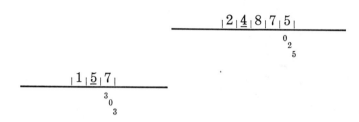

Instruction: <u>C</u>303025

Indicator settings *after* execution of the COMPARE instruction:

On	UNEQUAL indicator
On	HIGH indicator
Off	EQUAL indicator
Off	LOW indicator

1. The B field is compared to the A field and is longer, so the UNEQUAL indicator and the HIGH indicator are turned on.
2. Neither field is disturbed.

EXAMPLE 8-3

Contents of storage:

Instruction: C305030

Indicator settings *after* execution of the COMPARE instruction:

| Off | UNEQUAL indicator |

| Off | HIGH indicator |

| On | EQUAL indicator |

| Off | LOW indicator |

1. The two fields are equal so the EQUAL indicator is turned on.
2. The UNEQUAL indicator is off.
3. Neither field is disturbed.

EXAMPLE 8-4

Contents of storage:

$$|5|7|8|\underline{9}|2|$$
$$5$$
$$1$$
$$2$$

$$|\underline{6}|9|7|8|5|$$
$$8$$
$$9$$
$$6$$

Instruction: C896512

Indicator settings *after* execution of the COMPARE instruction:

| On | UNEQUAL indicator |

| On | HIGH indicator |

| Off | EQUAL indicator |

| Off | LOW indicator |

1. The A field is longer than the B field. When this occurs, extra A field positions beyond the length of the B field are not com-

pared. As a result these two fields were compared as if there had been a word mark at 895.

2. Under these conditions, the B field is larger than the A field to which it was compared so the UNEQUAL indicator and the HIGH indicator are turned on.

3. Neither field is disturbed.

These examples suggest the following definition for the COMPARE instruction:

COMPARE (C)

Op code	A address	B address
C̲	aaa	bbb

Description. The COMPARE instruction causes the information in the B field to be compared with an equal number of characters in the A field. The bit configuration of each character of the two fields is compared and appropriate indicators are set as described below.

Word Marks. The first word mark encountered terminates the operation. If the A field is longer than the B field, extra A-field positions beyond the length of the B field will not be compared.

Indicators. If the two fields are identical character by character, an equal COMPARE results and the EQUAL indicator is turned on. If the fields are not equal, an unequal COMPARE results and the UNEQUAL indicator is turned on. In addition, the HIGH indicator is turned on if the B field is greater than the A field, and the LOW indicator if the A field is greater than the B field. If the B field is longer than the A field, the UNEQUAL and HIGH indicators are turned on regardless of their contents. All indicators are reset *only* by another COMPARE instruction.

Alphabetic Fields

For the sake of simplicity, the preceding examples all used purely numeric fields in illustrating the COMPARE instruction. This does not imply that fields must be numeric in order to be compared. Either or both fields may contain numeric, alphabetic, and/or special characters. To make a comparison of fields that are not pure numeric, the order of the collating sequence discussed in Chapter 3 and summarized in Appendix II is used. Recall that this sequence runs from the "smallest" character, which is a blank, through the letters of the alphabet and the digits to 9, which is the largest. That the COMPARE treats non-numeric (or mixed) fields in exactly the same fashion as numeric fields is shown by the following examples:

EXAMPLE 8-5

Contents of storage:

$$\underline{|\underline{A}_||B_|2_|C_|3_|D_|}$$

0
2
5

$$\underline{|\underline{A}_|1_|B_|2_|C_|3_|D_|}$$

3
4
5

Instruction: $\underline{C}$345025

Indicator settings *after* execution of the COMPARE instruction:

| On | UNEQUAL indicator |

| Off | HIGH indicator |

| Off | EQUAL indicator |

| On | LOW indicator |

1. The UNEQUAL indicator and the LOW indicator are on.
2. These fields are identical except the B field has a blank where the A field has a 1. Referring to the collating list, the 1 is the larger of the two. This is analogous to two nearly identical numbers 675321 and 675021, where the former is larger.

EXAMPLE 8-6

Contents of storage:

$$\underline{|5_|\underline{J}_|O_|H_|N_|S_|O_|N_|||}$$

3
9
9

$$\underline{|C_|J_|O_|H_|N_|S_|O_|N_|||}$$

4
2
5

Instruction: C̲425399

Indicator settings *after* execution of the COMPARE instruction:

| Off | UNEQUAL indicator |

| Off | HIGH indicator |

| On | EQUAL indicator |

| Off | LOW indicator |

1. The fields are identical in every way, so the EQUAL indicator is turned on.
2. A word mark is not required in the A field.

BRANCH IF INDICATOR ON

Whenever indicators have been set by a COMPARE instruction, they remain in their respective settings until reset by another COMPARE. In the meantime, they can be used for a conditional BRANCH instruction. Available in the 141 system is the BRANCH IF INDICATOR ON, instruction in which the indicator specified by appropriate coding is tested. If that indicator is on, the machine will take the next instruction from the location designated in the I address of the BRANCH IF INDICATOR ON instruction. If the indicator is off, the next instruction in the sequence will be executed. The indicator to be tested is specified by the *d char-acter* of the instruction. On the SPS coding sheet, the *d* character is entered in column 39. In machine language, the *d* character is a single-character code immediately following the I address. The formal defi-nition of the BRANCH IF INDICATOR ON is as follows:

BRANCH IF INDICATOR ON *(B)*

| Op code | I address | *d* character |
| B | iii | d |

Description. The BRANCH IF INDICATOR ON instruction is a condi-tional branch. The *d* character specifies the indicator to be tested as a criterion for the branch. If the indicator is on, the program branches to the instruction specified by the I address. If the indicator is off, the next sequential instruction is executed. The indicators to be tested and their *d* character codings are

INDICATOR	d CHARACTER	
EQUAL COMPARE	(B = A)	S
UNEQUAL COMPARE	(B ≠ A)	/
HIGH COMPARE	(B > A)	U
LOW COMPARE	(B < A)	T

Testing of an indicator does not affect its setting.

Note the similarity between this instruction and the unconditional BRANCH instruction. In both SPS and the absolute language, they use the same operation code and both specify an I address. However, only the conditional BRANCH uses the d character. Thus, in machine language, the BRANCH instruction is four characters in length and the BRANCH IF INDICATOR ON consists of five characters. These points are illustrated by the following example problems.

EXAMPLE PROGRAMS

EXAMPLE 8-7

A deck of student master cards has the student file numbers in columns 2–6. The cards should be in ascending order of student file numbers (that is, the lowest number first and highest last). Write a program that will read the deck and check the sequence to verify the ordering. If a card is found out of sequence or if two cards contain the same number, halt the computer.

Program Planning

This program will involve reading a card and comparing the student file numbers. If the file number on the card read is larger than the file number on the preceding card, the cards are in their proper sequence and another card can be read. If this is not true, the cards are out of sequence and the computer should be halted. We must keep in mind that to compare the number from the latest card to number of the preceding card, it will be necessary to save the student number just processed until a new card is read. The flowchart in Figure 8–1 illustrates the over-all logic involved. The diamond symbol represents a decision.

The Program

A source program to perform the function of this example is shown in Figure 8–2. In this program two word marks are set; the first defines the field which will be read from a card and the second defines the area to which the field will eventually be moved prior to reading the next card. With a little ingenuity the second instruction can be eliminated; this is left to the student as an exercise.

The third instruction represents the beginning of the loop. The first time through the program, word marks will be set and blanks will be moved from 006 to 106 (which is already blank). Once the first card is processed, the MOVE instruction will then move the file number prior to reading the next card. After the card is read, the fifth instruction will compare the file number of the previous card (B field) to the file number of the current card (A field). If the sequence is correct, the A field will exceed the B field and the LOW indicator will be turned on.

The BRANCH IF INDICATOR ON instruction tests the LOW indicator, since a *T* is coded in the *d* character column. As a consequence, a BRANCH TO MOVE will be made, the file number retained, a new card

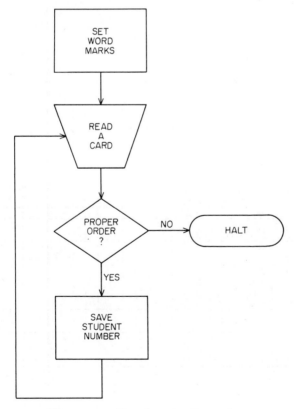

Figure 8–1. Flowchart for Example 8–7

IBM 1401 SYMBOLIC PROGRAMMING SYSTEM
CODING SHEET

Program: EXAMPLE 8-7 Page No. 01 of 1
Programmed by: ____ Date: 11/2 Identification: CHECK (76–80)

LINE (3–5)	COUNT (6–7)	LABEL (8–13)	OPERATION (14–16)	(A) OPERAND ADDRESS (17)	± (23)	CHAR. ADJ.	IND. (27)	(B) OPERAND ADDRESS (28)	± (34)	CHAR. ADJ.	IND. (38)	d (39)	COMMENTS (40–55)
010		BEGIN	SW	0002									DEFINE
020			SW	0102									FIELDS
030		MOVE	MCW	0006				0106					SAVE PREV NUMBER
040		READ	R										READ A CARD
050			C	0006				0106					COMPARE NUMBERS
060			B	MOVE								T	RETUR IF OKAY
070			H										
080			B	READ									START AGAIN
090			END	BEGIN									
100													
110													
120													
130													
140													
150													
160													
170													
180													
190													
200													

AREA-DEFINITION CHARACTER COUNT ⟶ 1 5 10 15 20 25 30 32

Figure 8–2. Sequence Checking

read in, and so on. On the other hand, if the B field is greater than the A field, the HIGH indicator will be turned on; if they are equal, the EQUAL indicator will be turned on. Both of these will represent an incorrect sequencing. Since the LOW indicator will not be on, the BRANCH will not be executed and the next instruction in the sequence (HALT) will be executed. Following the HALT instruction is an unconditional BRANCH. The purpose of these two instructions is to allow the programmer or computer operator to check the cards if an error in sequencing has been detected and restart the computer, which would involve taking the next instruction in sequence. Since that instruction is a BRANCH TO READ, processing of cards would be resumed.

Storage Contents

The cards in Figure 8–3 are the last two cards processed, and Figure 8–4 shows the storage contents after the computer has been halted following execution of the READ instruction. In addition to the contents of the last card in positions 001–080 the file number from the preceding card is stored in positions 102–106. As we would expect, the program is stored beginning in location 333. Here we can observe

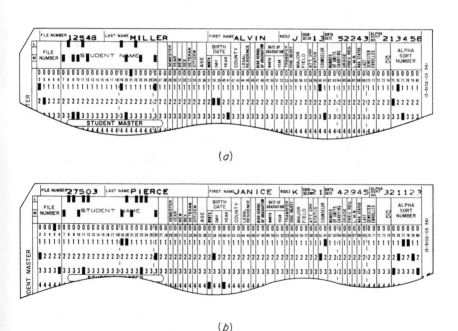

Figure 8–3. Final Cards in the Deck of Example 8–7

that the absolute address 341 is substituted for the symbolic address MOVE in the first BRANCH instruction, and 348 has been substituted for READ in the second BRANCH instruction. Of greater interest in this program is the appearance of these two instructions. The second one, stored beginning at 362, is an unconditional BRANCH, and consists of a three-character I address in addition to the single-character operation code, a total of four characters. The instruction beginning at 356 is the conditional BRANCH, which consists of the same operation code and a three-digit I address. It has in addition to these a T for a d character, which indicates that this is a conditional BRANCH and that the indicator to be tested is the LOW indicator.

The preceding example represents an elementary application of the conditional BRANCH instruction. Even at that, the student can probably

```
I-REG  OP-REG
 349      1
```

000 – 049	2750 1	3PIE	RCE		JANICE	K		429	45	
050 – 099		21			32112 3					
100 – 149	1254 8 1									
150 – 199										
200 – 249										
250 – 299										
300 – 349								,002, 1	102M 1	006 1 0610 11
350 – 399	00610 1	6B341 11	T.B34	8						
400 – 449										
450 – 499										
500 – 549										
550 – 599										
600 – 649										
650 – 699										
700 – 749										
750 – 799										
800 – 849										
850 – 899										
900 – 949										
950 – 999										

Figure 8–4. Storage Dump for Example 8–7

see several methods of rewriting the program to accomplish the required task.

Controlled Loops

Another common application for the conditional BRANCH is to allow the computer to break out of a loop after a designated number of passes have been made. This involves a counting procedure and results in a *controlled* loop. As an example, consider the following problem:

EXAMPLE 8-8

A deck of cards has information punched in columns 1–75. Write a program that will read the first 15 cards and reproduce them. In addition, the cards must be numbered 001–015 in columns 78–80 in the order that they are read.

Program Planning

In this problem it will be necessary to set up a counting device to serve a control function, in order to break out of the loop after 15 cards have been processed. In addition, the counter will provide the numbers for punching into the cards. The general flow of logic is illustrated in the flowchart of Figure 8–5.

The Program

Figure 8–6 is an SPS program that will process a deck of cards as required. Two program constants are defined. The first, LIMIT, consists of the three-digit number 015, which is the number of data cards to be processed when the program is ultimately executed. The second, ONE, consists of the single digit 1. ONE is used to increment the counter each time through the loop (the fifth instruction), and LIMIT is used in the COMPARE instruction to set the proper indicator for the following conditional BRANCH instruction. The first time through the loop, the following will take place:

1. A card will be read.
2. The card field will be moved.
3. One will be added to a field of blanks at 180, resulting in 001 located at 178–180.
4. A duplicate of the card read, with the addition of 001 in columns 78–80, will be punched.
5. 001 will be compared to 015, resulting in an UNEQUAL COMPARE.
6. The UNEQUAL indicator will be tested for the conditional BRANCH. Since it will be on, the computer will BRANCH TO INPUT for the next instruction.

Thus, after one card has been processed, the counter is set on 001. During the fifteenth pass through the program, the sequence of events will be as follows:

1. The fifteenth data card will be read.
2. The card field will be moved.
3. At location 180, one will be added to the field 014, which will become 015.
4. A duplicate of the fifteenth card read, with the addition of 015 in columns 78–80, will be punched.

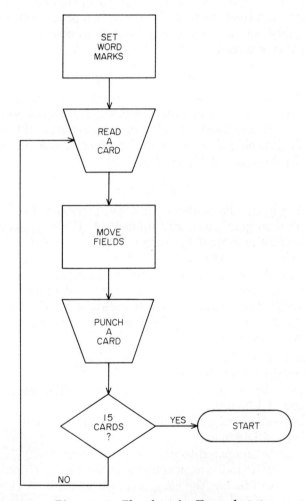

Figure 8–5. Flowchart for Example 8–8

IBM 1401 SYMBOLIC PROGRAMMING SYSTEM
CODING SHEET

Program EXAMPLE 8-8 — Programmed by ______ — Date 11/2 — Page No. 01 of 1 — Identification NUM 1

LINE 3–5	COUNT 6–7	LABEL 8–13	OPERATION 14–16	(A) OPERAND ADDRESS 17	± 23	CHAR. ADJ.	IND. 27	(B) OPERAND ADDRESS 28	± 34	CHAR. ADJ.	IND. 38	d 39	COMMENTS 40–55
010		SET	SW	0001									DEFINE
020			SW	0178									FIELDS
030		INPUT	R										
040			MCW	0075				0175					
050			A	ONE				0180					ADD ONE TO COUNT
060			P										
070			C	0180				LIMIT					CHECK FOR LIMIT
080			B	INPUT								/	IF FINISHED
090			H										THEN HALT
100	03	LIMIT	DCW	*		015							
110	01	ONE	DCW	*		1							
120			END	SET									
130													
140													
150													
160													
170													
180													
190													
200													

AREA-DEFINITION CHARACTER COUNT → 1 5 10 15 20 25 30 32

Figure 8–6. Card Numbering

5. The field 015 located at 180 will be compared to LIMIT (015), resulting in an EQUAL COMPARE.
6. The UNEQUAL indicator will be tested for the conditional BRANCH. Since the previous instruction turned it off, no branch will occur.
7. The computer will halt.

After a program has been written, it is always good practice to step through it in the above fashion prior to attempting a run. Always perform each instruction as coded, not as you, the programmer, want the program to function. The two will frequently differ. This is especially valuable to determine whether or not the computer breaks out of the loop after the desired number of passes.

Processing a Variable Number of Cards

Now we will consider the changes necessary in the program in order to process 150 cards instead of 15. A careful inspection of the program indicates that this could easily be accomplished by replacing the first DCW with a new card using 150 as the constant instead of 015. However, it would be necessary to reassemble and reload a new object deck, which is troublesome and time consuming. This would be especially inefficient if several data decks of different sizes were to be processed.

A means of making programs such as this one more versatile and efficient is to feed in as part of the data a header card containing a field to specify the number of cards that follow. The use of a header is illustrated by Example 8–9.

EXAMPLE 8-9

Rewrite the problem of Example 8–8 to use a header card in the data deck to specify the number of data cards to be processed.

Program Planning

The program logic will be essentially the same as that of Example 8–8; the flowchart would be different only because of the additional READ requirement. For the program, we shall arbitrarily use columns 1–3 of the header card to indicate the value of LIMIT for that given run.

The Program

Figure 8–7 is the SPS program written in the required fashion. The SPS program, combined with the flowchart, is practically self-explanatory. As indicated in the flowchart, the header card is read and the field moved to LIMIT prior to the execution of the loop. Once the computer enters the loop, it functions exactly as in Example 8–8.

IBM 1401 SYMBOLIC PROGRAMMING SYSTEM
CODING SHEET

Program EXAMPLE 8-9 Page No. 01 of 1

Programmed by ______ Date 11/2 Identification NUM 2

LINE (3–5)	COUNT (6–7)	LABEL (8–13)	OPERATION (14–16)	(A) OPERAND ADDRESS (17)	± (23)	CHAR. ADJ.	IND. (27)	(B) OPERAND ADDRESS (28)	± (34)	CHAR. ADJ.	IND. (38)	d (39)	COMMENTS (40–55)
010		SET	SW	0001									DEFINE
020			SW	0178									FIELDS
030			R										READ HEADER AND
040			MCW	0003				LIMIT					MOVE TO LIMIT
050		INPUT	R										
060			MCW	0075				0175					
070			A	ONE				0180					ADD TO COUNTER
080			P										
090			C	0180				LIMIT					CHECK FOR LIMIT
100			B	INPUT								/	AND IF FINISHED
110			H										THEN HALT
120	03	LIMIT	DCW	*									
130	01	ONE	DCW	*		1							
140			END	SET									
150													
160													
170													
180													
190													
200													

AREA-DEFINITION CHARACTER COUNT → 1 5 10 15 20 25 30 32

Figure 8–7. Variable Numbering

The Need for Documentation

The COMPARE and BRANCH IF INDICATOR ON instructions increase the scope and versatility of our programming capabilities many times. The three examples that we have considered only scratch the surface of the potential strength of the tools we have at our disposal. However, we are now at the point where programming can become a confusing chore if some type of over-all sketch of the program logic is not presented. Perhaps the student has already recognized difficulties that might occur when several conditional branches are involved. For this reason we will devote the next chapter to program documentation and flowcharting techniques.

■ CHAPTER SUMMARY

The COMPARE instruction is used to check the relative sizes of two fields and turn on appropriate indicators, depending upon whether the fields are equal or unequal and, if unequal, whether the A field is larger than the B field, or vice versa.

The BRANCH IF INDICATOR ON instruction is a conditional BRANCH instruction that will test the indicators set by the COMPARE instruction. If the designated indicator is on, a branch will be executed; otherwise the computer will continue to the next instruction.

■ EXERCISES

8.1 What would be the setting of each indicator if the following fields were compared?

(a) A field: 56228	B field: 6228
(b) A field: 15331	B field: 6228
(c) A field: bbbb12	B field: bb12
(d) A field: 6983	B field: bb123
(e) A field: JONESbb	B field: JOHNSON
(f) A field: 01532	B field: Z1532
(g) A field: /1234	B field: B1567

(Note that the lower-case b indicates a blank.)

8.2 If a conditional BRANCH instruction follows the COMPARE in Exercise 8.1, after which cases will the computer execute a branch if the d character is (a) /? (b) S? (c) T? (d) U?

8.3 Write a program that will update a customer's charge account after a new purchase has been recorded. A new balance card is to be punched and a listing of each customer's name, new balance, and limit is to be printed. If the new balance exceeds the customer's limit, the words OVER LIMIT are also to be printed on his entry. The card columns and print positions are as follows:

FIELD	*INPUT CARD*	*OUTPUT CARD*	*LISTING*
Name	1–20	1–20	11–30
Balance	25–30	25–30	40–45
Charge	35–40	——	——
Limit	75–80	75–80	54–59
OVER LIMIT	——	——	63–72

8.4 Write a program that will number a deck of SPS cards in columns 1–5. Columns 1 and 2 should contain the page number, and columns 3–5 the line number. Assume 20 lines per page. For example, card 7 on page 1 would be numbered 01070, and card 13 on page 2 would be 02130.

8.5 A deck of cards contains statistical data. Each card has an identification number in columns 1–3 and a data field in columns 11–15. The last card has 999 for an identification number but contains no data. Write a program that will read a deck, and upon detecting the last card, type out the smallest field and its card number.

8.6 Each card of a deck of cards contains eight 10-digit fields in columns 1–10, 11–20, and so on. Write a program that will type out the largest field from each card.

Chapter Nine

PROGRAM
DOCUMENTATION

At this point in our study of programming we can begin to see the value of carefully recording not only the program of instructions for a given problem but also notes and directions on how the program functions and how it is to be used. This type of documentation can be valuable to the programmer in debugging the program after it has been written, and is usually necessary if the program is to be used by others. In fact, many times a programmer will barely recognize his own program after several months of time have elapsed.

COMMENT CARDS

The organization of the SPS language reflects the above problems. The card itself provides columns 76–80 for program identification, and columns 40–55 may be used for making descriptive comments, as we have done in each of the example programs. One other provision to make an SPS program nearly independent of additional documentation is the *comment card*, which may be included in the source deck. By placing an asterisk in column 8, comments may be punched in columns 9–55 of that card. When the source deck is assembled, the object deck will also contain the comment, so that a listing will include the comment for use by the programmer. However, when the program is loaded into storage, the comment card will be ignored and none of its contents will be entered into storage. Use of a comment card is shown in Figure 9–1.

IBM 1401 SYMBOLIC PROGRAMMING SYSTEM
CODING SHEET

Program ______________ Page No. 0 1 of 1

Programmed by ______________ Date 11/3 Identification R E P O (76–80)

LINE (3–5)	COUNT (6–7)	LABEL (8–13)	OPERATION (14–16)	(A) OPERAND ADDRESS (17)	(A) ± (23)	(A) CHAR. ADJ.	(A) IND. (27)	(B) OPERAND ADDRESS (28)	(B) ± (34)	(B) CHAR. ADJ.	(B) IND. (38)	d (39)	COMMENTS (40–55)
010		* TH	IS	PROGRA	M	WI	L	L REPR	O	DUC	E		A DECK OF CARDS
020		START	SW	0001									
030		READ	R										
040			MCW	0080				0180					
050			P										
060			B	READ									
070			END	START									
080													
090													
100													
110													
120													
130													
140													
150													
160													
170													
180													
190													
200													

AREA-DEFINITION CHARACTER COUNT ⟶ 1 5 10 15 20 25 30 32

Figure 9–1. Program Use of the Comment Card

PROGRAM REPORTS

Although it would be possible to include sufficient comment cards to completely document a program and its use, this is not normally done. More often, the program will be included as part of a report that describes, not only the program itself, but also the problem from which the program arose. Although each computer installation in business or industry has its own rules and format, most will include such items as those that follow:

1. *Problem definition*—a complete description of the problem for which the program is written.
2. *Methods*—means and methods used in the program.
3. *Program*—a listing of the source program.
4. *Flowchart*—mainline and detailed flowcharts for the program (flowcharting will be discussed in detail later in this chapter).
5. *Program usage*—a detailed description of how to use the program, including switch settings if any, input format, output format, and special limitations.
6. *Sample run*—a sample run showing expected output from the sample input.

All too frequently a programmer will complete a problem, and, in his anxiety to proceed to another, will write an incomplete report, if any at all. In documenting work that has been completed, the programmer should continually consider his report from the point of view of a person who needs to use the program but knows nothing about it.

FLOWCHARTING

A flowchart can be useful to not only a future user of the program but also to the programmer himself when he is attempting to organize his thoughts and spell out the basic program logic. In fact, a visual representation is so valuable that flowcharting is widely used in the whole field of information processing. However, in many situations confusion has resulted from a lack of uniformity in terminology and in the meaning and use of specific symbols. In order to reduce these misunderstandings, standard symbols and terminology have been developed for use in the data processing field by the X3.6 Committee on Problem Definition and Analysis of the American Standards Association. The material in this text reflects these recommendations.

Flowchart Categories

A flowchart is a means for presenting graphically a set of steps necessary to perform a given function. There are two general categories into which flowcharts may be classified. First is the *program* flowchart, which we have used in writing several of our programs. As the name implies, a program flowchart describes what takes place in a stored program. It displays specific operations and decisions, and indicates their sequence within the program. One of the most important uses of a program flowchart is to provide the programmer with a means of visualizing, during the development of a program, the sequence in which operations occur. Further, it serves to display the relationship of one portion of a program to another. The program flowchart is frequently called a *block diagram*.

The second category is the *system* flowchart, which describes the flow of data through all parts of an over-all system. For example, a system flowchart might represent the processing and handling of student grades by the teacher, the necessary computation of grade-point averages, the printing of them on grade reports, and the distribution of grade reports to the students. In a system flowchart, an entire program flowchart is normally represented as a single phase of the over-all operation. The problems that we will consider in this text do not involve system flowcharting; however, we will use program flowcharts extensively.

Basic Flowchart Symbols

Common to program and system flowcharts are three basic symbols, indicating *flow directions*, *processing*, and *input/output*. These three are illustrated in Figure 9–2.

Flow Direction. The flow-direction symbol represents the direction of processing flow, which is generally from top to bottom and left to right. However, most programs involve decisions that result in multiple courses of action. Frequently, the net effect is a complicated flowchart. In order to avoid ambiguity, flow lines are usually drawn with an arrowhead at the point of entry to a symbol. Good practice also dictates that flow lines should not cross each other and that "jogs" be avoided whenever possible.

Processing. The processing symbol is used to represent general processing functions not represented by other symbols. These functions are generally those that contain the actual information processing operations of the program, such as arithmetic and data-movement instructions.

Input/Output. The input/output symbol is used to denote any function of an input/output device in the program. In the 141 system, the card reader is the input device; for output, both the printer and card punch are available. In addition, making information available for processing is generally considered an input function and recording processed information an output function.

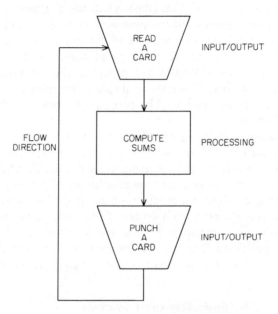

Figure 9–2. Three Basic Flowchart Symbols

Special Flowchart Symbols

In addition to the three basic symbols, there are six special processing symbols that aid immeasurably in clarifying over-all problems. Figure 9–3, the flowchart of Example 8–7, shows two of these.

Decision. The decision symbol is used to indicate a point in the program at which a branch to one of two or more alternate points is possible. Decisions in the 141 system are based on testing an indicator which has been set with a COMPARE instruction. The criterion for making the choice should be indicated clearly, as shown in Figure 9–3. Also, the condition upon which each of the possible exit paths will be executed should be identified and all possible conditions should be accounted for. In a given program, one decision symbol may be used to represent one or more conditional BRANCH instructions. Three additional examples of the decision symbol are shown in Figure 9–4.

Termination. The termination symbol represents any point at which a program originates or terminates. With normal program operations, such points will be at the start and completion of the program, and frequently at a terminal point under error conditions, as is shown in Figure 9–3. It is also in some types of subroutines.

The problems up to this point have been relatively easy and have not required the remaining symbols. In the following chapters, programs will become longer and more complex and will require all of the symbols. For future reference, all nine symbols are summarized in Figure 9–5, with a brief description of each.

Program Modification. Perhaps the student has surmised that it should be possible to treat instructions as data and actually operate on them with other instructions. This is another important aspect of the computer, and is discussed in detail in Chapter 12. To represent this graphically, the program modification symbol is used, to indicate that an instruction or group of instructions changes the program itself.

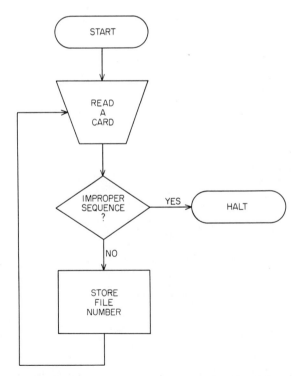

Figure 9–3. Two Special Processing Symbols

The purpose of the modification performed should be clearly indicated on the symbol.

Connector. When a program becomes sufficiently complex that the number and direction of flow lines is confusing, it is frequently convenient to use the connector symbol. This symbol represents an entry from, or an exit to, another part of the program flowchart. A pair of identically labeled connector symbols is frequently used to indicate a continued flow when the use of a line is confusing.

Offpage Connector. The offpage connector symbol is similar to the connector symbol except that it is used to designate exit from or entry to a page when the flowchart consists of more than one page. The symbol should be oriented so that its point indicates the direction of flow. Identification for both of the connector symbols should be placed within the symbol.

Predefined Process. The predefined process symbol represents a group of operations not detailed on the particular flowchart being used. It is commonly used to indicate subroutines, a subject discussed in Chapter 11.

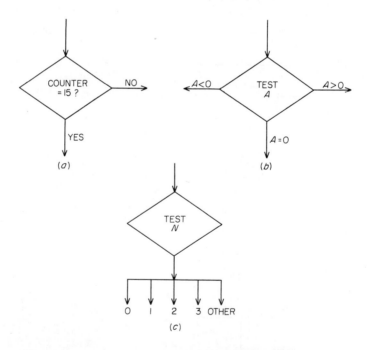

Figure 9-4. (a) *A Single* CONDITIONAL BRANCH *Instruction* (b) *and* (c) *Two or More* BRANCH *Instructions*

Flowcharting Template

In order to promote standardization in the use of flowchart symbols, various types of flowcharting templates are available, such as the one shown in Figure 9–6. Note that grid lines are provided as an aid to centering the symbols. In addition to the nine program symbols, standard system symbols are included.

Other Devices

One of the primary uses of a flowchart is to aid the programmer in determining the basic flow of logic in his problem. By flowcharting, the sequence and relationships among the various parts of the program can be seen. The flowchart provides a means of experimenting with various approaches to laying out program logic. It is much easier to move and to rearrange logic by moving blocks of a flowchart than by rewriting segments of a program. Many programmers draw their charts on a chalkboard to facilitate continuous changing.

Once the over-all picture or over-all mainline logic has been developed, detailed flowcharts of large segments may be charted. To indicate the existence of a more detailed flowchart for a given block in a main flowchart, the symbol is indicated with a heading line, as shown in Figure 9–7. Normally, the detailed flowchart is identified in the space provided above the line and a description of its function is indicated below it. Once the mainline and detailed flowcharts are completed, they should serve as a guide for writing the program. Here it is important to remember that the flowchart is a working device. As the problem is coded, it is frequently necessary to make changes in program logic because of such things as machine logic, incorrect flowcharting, and so on. However, when changes in logic become apparent, the flowchart should be changed accordingly. Otherwise its value as a programming aid is lost.

Once the problem is coded, the flowchart can frequently serve a valuable function in debugging the program. Consistent with this is the practice of cross referencing, which relates the source-language program to the flowchart. One way to cross reference is to locate an instruction either by its label or page and line number from the coding sheet. When used, the identification should be placed above the upper left-hand corner of the symbol and should indicate the first instruction of the given set. Figure 9–7 shows an example of cross referencing, in which the processing instruction is located on page 2 line 040 of the coding sheets and the decision is referenced by its label OUT.

PROGRAM FLOWCHART SYMBOLS

SYMBOL	REPRESENTS
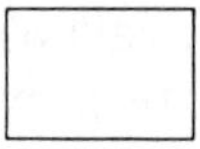	**PROCESSING** A group of program instructions which perform a processing function of the program.
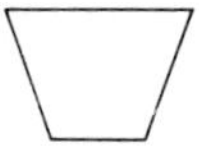	**INPUT/OUTPUT** Any function of an input/output device (making information available for processing, recording processing information, tape positioning, etc.).
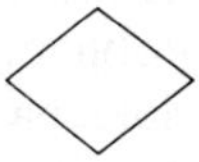	**DECISION** The decision function used to document points in the program where a branch to alternate paths is possible based upon variable conditions.
	**PROGRAM MODIFICATION** An instruction or group of instructions which changes the program.
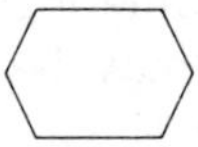	**PREDEFINED PROCESS** A group of operations not detailed in the particular set of flowcharts.
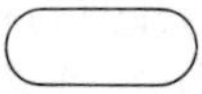	**TERMINAL** The beginning, end, or a point of interruption in a program.
	CONNECTOR An entry from, or an exit to, another part of the program flowchart.
	OFFPAGE CONNECTOR A connector used instead of the connector symbol to designate entry to or exit from a page.
◁ ▷ ▽ △	**FLOW DIRECTION** The direction of processing or data flow.

SUPPLEMENTARY SYMBOL FOR SYSTEM AND PROGRAM FLOWCHARTS

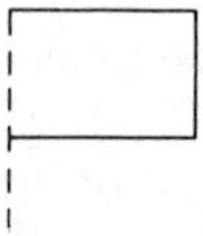	**ANNOTATION** The addition of descriptive comments or explanatory notes as clarification.

Figure 9–5. Flowchart Symbols and Descriptions (IBM)

SYSTEM FLOWCHART SYMBOLS

PROCESSING	**INPUT/ OUTPUT**
A major processing function.	Any type of medium or data.
PUNCHED CARD	**PERFORATED TAPE**
All varieties of punched cards including stubs.	Paper or plastic, chad or chadless.
DOCUMENT	**TRANSMITTAL TAPE**
Paper documents and reports of all varieties.	A proof or adding machine tape or similar batch-control information.
MAGNETIC TAPE	**DISK, DRUM, RANDOM ACCESS**
OFFLINE STORAGE	**DISPLAY**
Offline storage of either paper, cards, magnetic or perforated tape.	Information displayed by plotters or video devices.
ONLINE KEYBOARD	**SORTING, COLLATING**
Information supplied to or by a computer utilizing an online device.	An operation on sorting or collating equipment.
CLERICAL OPERATION	**AUXILIARY OPERATION**
A manual offline operation not requiring mechanical aid.	A machine operation supplementing the main processing function.
KEYING OPERATION	**COMMUNICATION LINK**
An operation utilizing a key-driven device.	The automatic transmission of information from one location to another via communication lines.
FLOW ◁ ▷ ▽ △	The direction of processing or data flow.

Figure 9–5. Continued

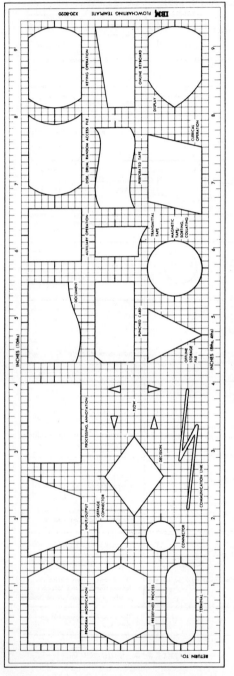

Figure 9–6. Flowcharting Template (IBM)

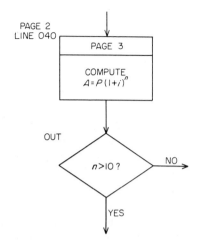

Figure 9–7. Flowchart Use of Heading Line

Using the Flowchart

In drawing flowcharts, the programmer should keep in mind that the primary functions of the flowchart are to provide him with a better insight into his problem while preparing the program, and to document and explain the program to others who might want to use it. The following pointers may frequently be of help in producing useful results:

1. First chart the main line of logic, then incorporate detail.
2. Do not chart every detail or the chart will only be a graphic representation, step by step, of the program. If the reader is interested, he can refer to the source program.
3. Use descriptive titles written in English rather than a machine-oriented language.
4. Use the flowchart as a genuine reference while coding, not as something to be discarded once coding is begun; do not be afraid to change it when required during the program coding.
5. Put yourself in the position of a reader and try to anticipate his problems in understanding your chart.

The importance of flowcharting cannot be overemphasized. Usually, the most complex part of programming a problem is to determine the basic logic required. Recognizing this, some large business firms employ trained individuals to reduce problems for computer solution to a series of flowcharts. From there, the somewhat less difficult task of coding is performed by someone with a lesser degree of training.

DEBUGGING

Prior to coding, the programmer should exercise care in defining his problem (on paper) and in preparing a flowchart. Further, while coding, he should fill in the comment portion of the cards, use comment cards liberally, and keep marginal notes. Once the program is completed, the programmer should proceed through it step by step (as we did in studying earlier examples). He should follow every path when multiple paths occur as a result of a conditional branch, and he should investigate each condition. Prior to assembling the program, he should list the source deck and check for key-punching errors. If these practices are followed, many programming errors will be eliminated before they can cause any difficulty.

However, when the program doesn't run, the programmer has problems. Finding the "bugs" is frequently a painstaking, exasperating chore and there is no set formula for doing it. In general, errors can be classed in two broad categories. First are errors in program logic. This is a serious type of error and one that usually results from insufficient preplanning in defining the problem and making the flowchart. The second type is the careless or "bonehead" error, such as writing an address as 0401 instead of 0104. The advice here is to take a deep breath, for these will always be with us.

Perhaps the best general rule in debugging is to run a set of simplified data, and when the program functions improperly take a storage dump, list the object deck, and study the two. Frequently the operation and instruction register contents from the dump can be of help. Otherwise it may be necessary to go through the program, instruction by instruction. There are many techniques that may be used, but usually each is peculiar to a given situation and the learning of these techniques comes from many hours of experience.

ADDITIONAL EXAMPLES

In Chapter 8, only a few simple examples of programs using the conditional branch were described. Now that we have established documentation techniques and flowcharting procedures to clarify complex problems, we shall consider further examples.

EXAMPLE 9-1

Write a program that will add the fields in columns 1–8 from twelve cards, print out the total in print positions 10–17, process 12 more, and so on, until the read hopper is empty. Do not be concerned with overflows.

Program Planning

In this problem, it will be necessary to set up a counting device in order to break out of the READ-ADD loop. We might note that it also will be necessary to initialize the working area after processing each group of twelve cards. A flowchart showing the program logic is shown in Figure 9–8.

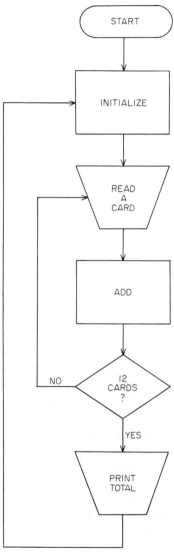

Figure 9–8. Program Flowchart for Example 9–1

The Program

Figure 9–9 is the source listing of a program that will perform the required function. In this listing, note that the page and line numbers have been printed and separated. Likewise, there is a space between the line number and count, the count and the label, and so on. The format is for convenience and ease of reading. We can see by studying the flowchart or the program that we have not one but two loops. More significantly, one of these loops is within the other. Twelve passes through the inner loop are required to complete one pass through the outer loop. Necessarily the inner loop must contain a conditional BRANCH.

```
01 005     *              SOURCE PROGRAM     EXAMPLE 9-1
01 006     *
01 010     START  SW   0210                 DEFINE FIELD
01 020     INITAL MCW  ZEROES    0217        INITIALIZE
01 030            MCW  ZROCNT    CNT         ZERO CNT
01 040     CARDIN R                          READ A CARD
01 050            A    0008      0217        ADD FIELDS
01 060            A    ONE       CNT         ADD ONE TO COUNT
01 070            C    CNT       DOZEN       COMPARE CNT
01 080            B    CARDIN                /BRANCH
01 084     *
01 085     *  IF  12  CARDS PROCESSED THEN PRINT THE TOTAL
01 086     *
01 090            W                          PRINT TOTAL
01 100            B    INITAL                NEW SET OF 12 CD
01 110 09  ZEROES DCW  *         000000000
01 120 02  ZROCNT DCW  *         00
01 130 02  CNT    DCW  *
01 140 02  DOZEN  DCW  *         12
01 150 01  ONE    DCW  *         1
01 160            END  START
```

Figure 9–9. Source Program for Example 9–1

First let us consider the inner loop, which begins with the READ instruction. The first ADD instruction causes the number in the specified field of the card just read to be added to the total in the WRITE area. The other ADD instruction serves no purpose other than to count the number of times through the loop and retain the number in CNT for use by the following COMPARE. Each time through the loop, the COMPARE checks the number against 12 and sets the indicators for use by the following conditional BRANCH. The BRANCH contains / in the d character, which tells the machine to BRANCH on an UNEQUAL COMPARE. If CNT is not 12, the UNEQUAL indicator is turned on and the computer will return to CARDIN and read another card.

After 12 cards have been processed the UNEQUAL indicator will be turned off and the machine will take the next instruction in sequence,

WRITE, and print out the total. Thus it will have broken out of the inner loop and will proceed to the unconditional BRANCH that marks the outer loop. The first MOVE instruction to which it will branch initializes the area in which totals are computed; then it moves to the next instruction, which initializes the number CNT. That is, in both cases the numbers are set equal to zero in order to "start with a new slate" for the next group of 12 cards. The computer will then continue on to the next instruction, which again represents the beginning of the inner loop.

Multiple Branches

Example 9–1 used a single criterion for the BRANCH condition. In actual practice, we will frequently encounter situations where several conditions must be evaluated before the proper branch can be made. Since the conditional BRANCH will test only one indicator and will either branch to a designated instruction or continue on to the next one, it is often necessary to employ more than one conditional BRANCH. To illustrate this, let us consider Example 9–2.

EXAMPLE 9-2

Write a program that will print a senior honor-roll list from a deck of student cards. The qualifications are that each student be a senior, be carrying 15 units of course work, and have a grade-point average of 3.2 or better. The student cards contain the following information:

CARD COLUMN	FIELD
1–6	not used*
7–18	Last name
19–25	First name
26	Middle initial
27–61	not used
62–64	Number of units
65–67	Grade point average
68–72	not used
73–74	Grade level
75–80	not used

* Those columns which are indicated "not used" *may* have information punched in them but that information is not used in this problem. It is not possible to assume they are blank.

The numerical fields use the following format:

xx∧x	number of units
x∧xx	grade-point average

12 indicates senior
11 indicates junior } grade level
10 indicates sophomore
09 indicates freshman

The printed list should have the title SENIOR HONOR ROLL beginning in print position 30, and the list should follow in the printing positions indicated below after first skipping a line:

PRINT POSITION	FIELD
20–26	First name
28	Middle initial
30–41	Last name
55–58	Grade-point average

The output format for the grade point average must be x.xx; that is, the decimal which is understood on the punched card must be printed on the list.

Program Planning

Prior to execution of the loop, it will be necessary to provide for the title and proper spacing. Within the loop, the machine will have to determine eligibility for the honor roll by testing the grade level, the grade-point average, and the number of units. If a student meets all of the requirements, he is placed on the honor roll. If he fails to satisfy any one of them, he does not qualify and another student card should be processed.

Flowchart

Figures 9–10 and 9–11 are flowcharts that illustrate the principles involved. The flowchart of Figure 9–10 represents the testing of all three requirements by a single decision symbol. On the other hand, the second flowchart is somewhat more detailed in that it indicates each qualification to be met by a decision symbol. In addition, these charts illustrate other principles of flowcharting discussed earlier in the chapter. Most significant is the use of the connector symbol from each of the decisions. Note that they are numbered the same as the connector that feeds into the input/output symbol.

The Program

The SPS source listing for this program is shown in Figure 9–12 and the output after processing a deck of cards is shown in Figure 9–13. This program is more sophisticated in several respects than any dis-

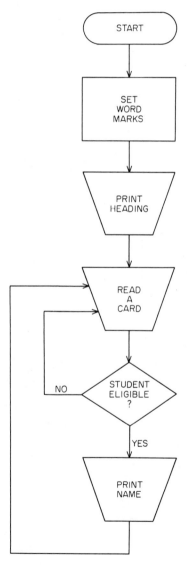

Figure 9–10. Program Flowchart for Example 9–2

cussed to date, so we shall examine it carefully. According to the flow-chart, the first function after setting word marks is to print the heading, which is accomplished by instructions 01 059 and 01 060. Instruction 01 090 places the decimal point in the proper position for future use in printing out the grade-point averages.

The READ instruction marks the beginning of the loop. Following this is the test to determine whether or not the student is a senior. The student grade level is compared to LEVEL, which has a value of 12. With this COMPARE, as with the other two, the A field is the one read from a card and has no word mark. The B field has a word mark by virtue of its definition. However, the B field word mark terminates the COMPARE, so a word mark is not required in the A field. If an UNEQUAL COMPARE results, instruction 01 120 causes the program to branch back

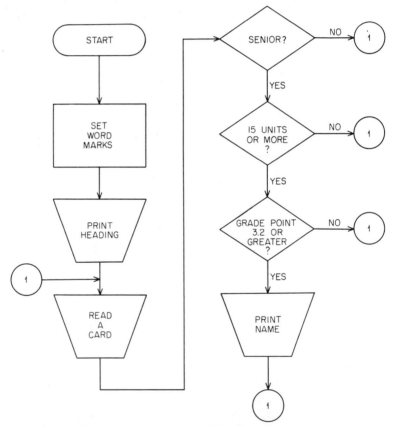

Figure 9–11. Alternate Program Flowchart for Example 9–2

to CARD and read another student card. If an UNEQUAL COMPARE does not result, the next instruction in sequence will be executed, and so on until the card is completely processed. If all the qualifications are met, the students' names and grade-point averages are printed. Instructions 01 170, 01 180 and 01 190 move the name to the printing area. Instructions 01 200 and 02 010 serve an editing function in moving the digits of the grade-point average so that they are properly positioned around the decimal point.

```
01 005    *                    SOURCE PROGRAM    EXAMPLE 9-2
01 006    *
01 010    START    SW   0007                     DEFINE FIELD
01 020             SW   0019
01 030             SW   0026
01 040             SW   0257
01 050             SW   0255
01 059             MCW  TITLE      0246           MOVE HEADING
01 060             W                              PRINT HEADING
01 070             CS   0246                      CLEAR PRINT AREA
01 080             W                              RETURN CARRIAGE
01 090             MCW  POINT      0256           PLACE DECIMAL
01 100    CARD     R                              READ A CARD
01 110             C    0074       LEVEL          COMPARE LEVEL
01 120             B    CARD                      /BRANCH IF NO GD
01 130             C    0064       UNITS          COMPARE UNITS
01 140             B    CARD                      UBRANCH IF NO GD
01 150             C    0067       AVRAGE         COMPARE GRDE AVE
01 160             B    CARD                      UBRANCH IF NO GD
01 170             MCW  0025       0226           MOVE FIRST NAME
01 180             MCW  0026       0228           MOVE MID INITIAL
01 190             MCW  0018       0241           MOVE LAST NAME
01 200             MCW  0067       0258           MOVE GRADE PT
01 201             MCW  0065       0255           MOVE GRADE PT
01 202             W                              PRINT NAME
01 203             B    CARD                      BRANCH TO READ
02 020 01 POINT    DCW  *          .
02 030 02 LEVEL    DCW  *          12
02 040 03 UNITS    DCW  *          150
02 050 03 AVRAGE   DCW  *          320
02 060 17 TITLE    DCW  *          SENIOR HONOR ROLL
02 070             END  START
```

Figure 9–12. Source Program for Example 9–2

```
                 SENIOR HONOR ROLL

        JAMES     F  ARNOLD              3.29
        RENEST       JOHNSON             3.21
        ALLEN     A  FINNEY              3.20
        JOANNE    D  FRANKLIN            3.29
        DEBRA        HERRERA             3.72
        ARLIN     L  JACKSON             3.70
        JOANNE    C  LEEDS               3.31
        DONALD    G  RAAB                3.24
        MANUEL       RAMIREZ             3.29
        MICHAEL      RAMIREZ             3.34
        JUNE      D  THOMAS              3.38
        RICHARD      VIXON               3.20
        DONALD    A  CHEW                3.25
        DEBBY     M  BROWN               3.97
```

Figure 9–13. Sample Output for Example 9–2

To illustrate more complex principles of flowcharting, consider the following example:

EXAMPLE 9-3

A deck of personnel cards is to be examined to find all persons who (1) have either been with the company 25 years or more or are 65 years of age or over, and (2) have 120 days or more of accumulated sick leave. Each card contains a department number, employee number (in sequence), job class, age (in years), service (in years), sick leave (in days), and monthly salary. When a card of a person meeting the above requirements is found, a card is to be punched containing the same information as the input card plus the value of his equivalent accumulated sick leave. The value of equivalent accumulated sick leave is calculated by a predefined process. The computer is to halt if an employee number is out of sequence.

Program Planning

In this problem, it will be necessary to examine the employee card to determine if he meets the age requirement *or* if he meets the length-of-employment requirement. In *either* case he may be eligible. Then, in addition, he must meet the days-of-sick-leave requirement. This is in contrast to Example 9–2, in which it was necessary that all three conditions be met.

The Flowchart

Figure 9–14 is a flowchart illustrating the logic involved in this problem. Note the use of connector symbols to avoid many confusing flow lines. An important part of the logic of this program is represented by the decision symbols. The decisions labeled number 1 and number 2 represent a parallel construction. If the employee qualifies by either 1 *or* 2, then he may be considered further. In addition he must qualify under condition number 3; that is, he must qualify according to 1 or 2 *and* 3.

Computation of accumulated sick leave is represented by the predefined process symbol. The page number shown in the upper portion of the symbol shows the page where the detailed flowchart of this predefined process can be found.

The examples of this chapter have served to introduce us to the proper use of flowcharts. In the following chapters, we will continue to emphasize use of the flowchart in planning and clarifying problems to be programmed.

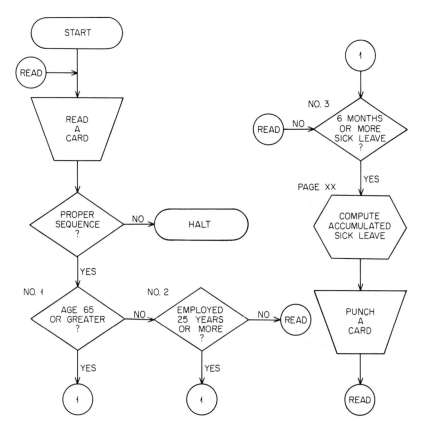

Figure 9–14. Flowchart for Example 9–3

■ CHAPTER SUMMARY

The system flowchart and the program flowchart are the two basic types of flowchart. We have emphasized only the program flowchart.

The nine standardized symbols for program flowcharting are summarized in Figure 9–4.

The flowchart serves two basic purposes. It is a valuable aid both in understanding the problem logic and in programming, and it serves as a valuable record of the program.

■ EXERCISES

9.1 *Commission Problem.* Each salesman's card contains an account number, commission rate, amount of sales, minimum commission, and maximum commission. The program is to check the sequence of the cards by account number and stop if any are out of sequence.

The salesman's commission is to be calculated by multiplying the rate times sales and rounding off. The commission paid will depend upon the maximum or minimum in the following way: (a) If the commission is less than the minimum, the minimum is paid. (b) If the commission is over the maximum, the maximum is paid. (c) If the commission is in between the maximum and minimum, the calculated commission is paid. The output card is to contain all the information from the input card, plus the appropriate commission. Draw the flowchart.

9.2 *Inventory Problem.* For each item in an inventory there is a master card and a transaction summary card. The master card contains a card code, part number, description, and old balance. The transaction summary card contains a card code, part number, total receipts, and total issues. The card code is a 1 for a master card and a 2 for a transaction card.

Draw a flowchart for a program that will compute the new balance and punch an updated master card. Check that the cards have the appropriate card code and that the cards are in sequence by part number. If the cards are out of sequence, print OUT OF SEQUENCE on the printer and stop the machine. The transaction card should follow the master card. If the cards are not in proper order or have invalid card codes, print WRONG CODE and stop.

Chapter Ten

ADDITIONAL INSTRUCTION FORMS

The instructions that we have studied thus far are the most fundamental forms in the 141 system. However, all of the problems that we shall discuss in this text (with the exception of the loading routine described in Chapter 14) could be programmed using this basic set. In fact, with only a few exceptions, all example programs are written without using the additional forms that we shall now discuss.

SET AND CLEAR WORD MARK

The two instructions, SET WORD MARK and CLEAR WORD MARK, consist of an operation code and three-position address specifying the location at which the word mark is to be set or from which it is to be cleared. In other words, these are four-position instructions consisting of an operation code and an A address. If two word marks are to be set, two instructions are used. Since setting and clearing word marks are common and frequent operations, the 141 system is designed to set (or clear) either one or two word marks with a single instruction. This is done merely by using both the A and B addresses. Thus, the two instructions to set word marks at 245 and 262, shown in Figure 10–1 on lines 010 and 020, could be replaced by the single instruction shown on line 040. In storage, the first two instructions would appear as

,245,262

and their equivalent as

,245262

LINE	COUNT	LABEL	OPERATION	(A) OPERAND				(B) OPERAND				d	
3	6 7	8	13 14 16	ADDRESS 17	± 23	CHAR. ADJ.	IND. 27	ADDRESS 28	± 34	CHAR. ADJ.	IND. 38	39	40
0 1 0			S W	0 2 4 5									
0 2 0			S W	0 2 6 2									
0 3 0													
0 4 0			S W	0 2 4 5				0 2 6 2					

Figure 10-1

For obvious reasons, the latter is frequently called a *seven-position* SET WORD MARK instruction. When the computer encounters a SET WORD MARK instruction in storage, it will set either one or two word marks, depending upon whether the instruction has only an A address or both an A and a B address. For instance, if the previous two instructions were followed by a MOVE instruction, they would appear in storage as

$$,245,262M125221$$

The computer would determine the end of the first instruction by the word mark of the second and the end of the second by the word mark at the op code of the MOVE instruction. The seven-position SET WORD MARK instruction does not require the presence of the terminating word mark, although one almost always follows in the normal program. This added refinement will be useful in later work.

The seven-position CLEAR WORD MARK instruction functions in much the same manner as the SW; that is, word marks are cleared from both the A and B address positions. However, unlike the SW instruction, the CW always requires a word mark immediately following it.

BRANCHING FORMS

Four instructions, READ, WRITE, PUNCH, and HALT, consist of only one position, the operation code. Frequently, after performing input or output functions, we may wish the program to branch. Also, after computer operation has been stopped by a HALT instruction, we may wish to restart computation by branching to another instruction in the program. For instance, if we are processing a deck of cards and, in doing so, are checking the card-number sequencing, detection of a card out of order could cause the computer to branch to a HALT instruction and terminate processing. After checking the deck to find the error, we would normally continue processing.

In all of these situations, this is accomplished by using two instructions, the second one being an unconditional BRANCH. Four examples are shown in Figure 10–2. For the first instruction, program execution will be halted, and after depression of the start key, the computer will branch to READ. In the second, a card will be read and then a branch to 472 executed. Similar functions will be performed by the other two pairs.

LINE	COUNT	LABEL	OPERATION	(A) OPERAND				(B) OPERAND				d
				ADDRESS	±	CHAR. ADJ.	IND.	ADDRESS	±	CHAR. ADJ.	IND.	
3	5	6 7	8	13 14	16 17	23		27 28		34		38	39 40
0 1 0			H									
0 2 0			B	R E A D								
0 3 0												
0 4 0			R									
0 5 0			B	0 4 7 2								
0 6 0												
0 7 0			W									
0 8 0			B	G O								
0 9 0												
1 0 0			P									
1 1 0			B	I N P U T								

Figure 10–2

Each of these pairs of instructions can be combined into a single equivalent instruction, as shown in Figure 10–3. The first instruction is HALT AND BRANCH, the second is READ AND BRANCH, the third is WRITE AND BRANCH, and the last is PUNCH AND BRANCH. The formal definition for each of these four instructions is as follows:

READ AND BRANCH (R)

Op code	I address
1	iii

LINE	COUNT	LABEL	OPERATION	(A) OPERAND				(B) OPERAND				d
				ADDRESS	±	CHAR. ADJ.	IND.	ADDRESS	±	CHAR. ADJ.	IND.	
3	5	6 7	8	13 14	16 17	23		27 28		34		38	39 40
0 1 0			H	R E A D								
0 2 0												
0 3 0			R	0 4 7 2								
0 4 0												
0 5 0			W	G O								
0 6 0												
0 7 0			P	I N P U T								

Figure 10–3

Description. The READ AND BRANCH instruction causes the computer to read one Hollerith-coded card (in the same manner as the READ A CARD instruction), then branch to the instruction specified by the I address.

WRITE AND BRANCH *(W)*

Op code	I address
2	iii

Description. The WRITE AND BRANCH instruction causes the computer to print the contents of the PRINT area (in the same manner as the WRITE A LINE instruction), then branch to the instruction specified by the I address.

PUNCH AND BRANCH *(P)*

Op code	I address
4	iii

Description. The PUNCH AND BRANCH instruction causes the computer to punch the contents of the PUNCH area (in the same manner as the PUNCH A CARD instruction), then branch to the instruction specified by the I address.

HALT AND BRANCH *(H)*

Op code	I address
:	iii

Description. The HALT AND BRANCH instruction causes the computer to stop. Depressing the start key will cause the computer to proceed to the instruction designated by the I address.

Note that the operation codes for these four instructions are identical to the READ, WRITE, PUNCH, and HALT instructions, respectively.

CLEAR STORAGE

Another instruction with which BRANCH may be combined is CLEAR STORAGE. However, the CS instruction consists of an operation code and an A address, that is, the location at which clearing is to commence. Thus, in order to extend the CLEAR STORAGE instruction to CLEAR STORAGE AND BRANCH, it is necessary to use the B address as well. On the other hand, whenever an instruction uses an I address (the location of another instruction), the I address is used in place of an A address.

The situation is similar with the CLEAR STORAGE AND BRANCH instruction; the computer will branch to the location specified by the I address. Thus the single instruction shown on line 040 in Figure 10–4 is equivalent to the two instructions on lines 010 and 020. The complete definition of this instruction is as follows:

CLEAR STORAGE AND BRANCH (CS)

Op code	I address	B address
/	iii	bbb

LINE	COUNT	LABEL	OPERATION	(A) OPERAND				(B) OPERAND				d
				ADDRESS	±	CHAR. ADJ.	IND.	ADDRESS	±	CHAR. ADJ.	IND.	
3	5 6	7 8	13 14 16	17	23		27	28	34		38	39 40
0 1 0			C S	0 2 2 5								
0 2 0			B	C O M P								
0 3 0												
0 4 0			C S	C O M P				0 2 2 5				

Figure 10–4

Description. The CLEAR STORAGE AND BRANCH instruction causes the storage to be cleared (including word marks) to blanks, beginning at the location specified by the B address and continuing downward through the nearest hundreds positions, in the same manner as the CLEAR STORAGE instruction. Upon completion of the clearing operation, the program branches to the instruction specified by the I address.

Two additional factors concerning this instruction are that it does not require a terminating word mark in order to be executed (similar to the seven-position SW in that respect), and it can clear itself and still execute a branch. This instruction is most commonly used in the object program as assembled by the computer. In Chapter 6 we discussed the END card and referred to it as the *transition* card. Furthermore we stated that, after the program is loaded and execution begun, no trace of the END statement remains in storage. However, after assembly, an instruction is punched in the END card (beginning in column 56). For example, the student is referred back to Figure 6–3, where the END card contains the instruction

/333080

Execution of this instruction will cause the entire READ area (000–080) to be cleared; the computer will then branch to 333, the location of the first instruction. Since the instruction is located in the READ area at this time, it will clear itself prior to branching. Further details of this process are described in Chapter 14.

ARITHMETIC

In each of the preceding forms an instruction has been made longer by adding an I address. In each case, however, the resulting instruction has saved space by combining two operations. The ADD and SUBTRACT instructions can also be abbreviated, but in this case to serve a special purpose. If we wish to add a field to itself or to subtract one from itself, as is frequently the case when zeroing, the A address and B address are normally identical, as shown in lines 010 and 030 of Figure 10–5.

LINE	COUNT	LABEL	OPERATION	(A) OPERAND ADDRESS	±	CHAR. ADJ.	IND.	(B) OPERAND ADDRESS	±	CHAR. ADJ.	IND.	d
3 5	6 7	8 13	14 16	17 23	27	28 34	38	39	40			
0 1 0			A	0 1 2 2				0 1 2 2				
0 2 0												
0 3 0			S	S U M				S U M				
0 4 0												
0 5 0												
0 6 0			A	0 1 2 2								
0 7 0												
0 8 0			S	S U M								

Figure 10–5

Equivalent operations will result if the instructions use the forms shown in lines 060 and 080. That is, if an ADD (or SUBTRACT) instruction consists only of an operation code and an A address, the A field will be added to (or subtracted from) itself. The formal definitions of these instructions are as follows:

ADD (A)

Op code	A address
A	aaa

Description. The four-position ADD instruction causes the A field to be added to itself, with the sum replacing the original A field.

Word Marks. The word mark is not affected.

SUBTRACT (S)

Op code	A address
S	aaa

Description. The four-position SUBTRACT instruction causes the A field to be subtracted from itself, with zeroes replacing the original A field.

Word Marks. The word mark is not affected.

BRANCH IF CHARACTER EQUAL

The unconditional BRANCH instruction consists of an op code and an I address; that is, it is four positions in length. In order to make it a conditional BRANCH, a *d* character is added, making it five positions. Of course, prior to its use, it is necessary to use a COMPARE instruction to set the indicators. For instance, let us assume that we wish to compare the character in the single location 032 to 7, and branch if they are equal. If the storage contents are

$$\underline{\quad |1|2|5|3|7| \quad}$$
$$0\,3\,2$$

we would require the two instructions and one declarative in Figure 10–6 to perform this function. In the 141 system, this operation can be performed by execution of a single instruction called BRANCH IF CHARACTER EQUAL, which is shown on line 080 of Figure 10–6.

LINE	COUNT	LABEL	OPERATION	(A) OPERAND ADDRESS	±	CHAR. ADJ.	IND.	(B) OPERAND ADDRESS	±	CHAR. ADJ.	IND.	d
0 1 0			C	0,0,3,2				S,E,V,E,N				
0 2 0			B	G,O								S
0 3 0												
0 4 0												
0 5 0	0,1	S,E,V,E,N	D,C,W	*		7						
0 6 0												
0 7 0												
0 8 0			B	G,O				0,0,3,2				7

Figure 10–6

Unlike any instruction previously studied, this one consists of eight characters, an op code, an I address, a B address and a *d* character. In machine language, it will appear as (assuming GO equivalent to 492)

$$\underline{B}4920327$$

Its execution will cause the computer to compare the *d* character, 7, to the single character at the B address (in this case 7) and branch to 492 if they are equal. In this illustration, a branch would be executed. Thus, the purpose of the DCW is achieved by placing 7 in the d character of the instruction, and the COMPARE is incorporated automatically by using a B address.

■ REMARKS

If the student reviews the example programs and those of his own, undoubtedly he will see instances where one or several of the additional instruction forms could have been used. The exercises that follow will, in general, not use these additional forms. It is hoped that the student will study each example and exercise with the idea of improving the program by the use of these forms, or by any other means that are available. It is further anticipated that the student will consider all of these instructions in their various forms as part of his programming vocabulary and will use them when appropriate.

■ EXERCISES

10.1 In the program of Example 8–7, reduce the number of instructions by two, using the techniques described in this chapter.

10.2 The program of Figure 7–9 will require 72 storage locations. Reduce the storage requirements as much as possible.

10.3 A deck of grade cards has the following format:

FIELD	CARD COLUMN
Name	6–26
Course description	29–40
Grade	44

Write a program that will process the deck and print out the name and course description for all F grades.

Chapter Eleven

SUBROUTINES AND PROGRAM SWITCHES

ADDRESS ADJUSTING

Whenever there has been a need to address an instruction or a program constant in writing SPS programs, we have provided it with a label, that is, a symbolic address. During program assembly these symbols were changed to absolute addresses in the object program. If a symbol were used to address an instruction, the high-order position, the operation code, was specified. If the label referred to a program constant defined by a DCW, the address of the low-order position was used. For each program constant, a separate DCW was written to define the constant no matter how similar any two of them may have been. In Example 9–1 two zero constants were defined, although by the nature of the problem, only the first was actually necessary. The first of them contained 9 zeros and the second 2 zeros. We will now study methods that will allow us, among other things, to define only one constant and use it in both cases first as a nine-position constant and then as a two-position constant.

The SPS instructions from Figure 9–9 of Example 9–1 are shown in Figure 11–1. After the program is assembled and placed in storage, these two instructions and the program constants appear as shown in Figure 11–2. With this knowledge of the machine-language program and actual addresses, we can see that the two-position zero is not necessary, since the other zero could be used by appropriate addressing. By changing the second MOVE instruction of the machine-language program to

M384395

LINE	COUNT	LABEL	OPERATION	(A) OPERAND ADDRESS	±	CHAR. ADJ.	IND.	(B) OPERAND ADDRESS	±	CHAR. ADJ.	IND.	d	
0 1 0		INITAL	MCW	ZERO				0217					
0 2 0			MCW	ZROCNT				CNT					

LINE	COUNT	LABEL	OPERATION	(A) OPERAND ADDRESS	±	CHAR. ADJ.	IND.	(B) OPERAND ADDRESS	±	CHAR. ADJ.	IND.	d	
1 0 0													
1 1 0	09	ZERO	DCW	*				0,0,0 0 0,0,0,0,0,0					
1 2 0	02	ZROCNT	DCW	*				0,0					

Figure 11-1

300 - 349								M39	1217M 39339
								1	1
350 - 399	5							0000000	000000
								1	1 1

Figure 11-2

the second zero constant would not be required. However, we must bear in mind that, when writing SPS programs, we do not normally know these addresses. Even at that, we can represent the constant in storage as shown below:

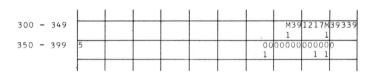

$$\underline{0}\ 0\ 0\ 0\ 0\ 0\ 0\ 0\ 0$$

Reference to the constant as a nine-character field could be made by addressing ZERO, and reference to it as a two-character field could be made by addressing ZERO − 7. In other words, we adjust the symbolic address in order to designate another position. This then extends the scope of the SPS language and provides means by which locations other than those with a label can be specified. We will call this practice *character adjustment*, although it is frequently referred to as *address adjustment* and *address arithmetic*.

Figure 11-3 shows the SPS program rewritten to use this technique with only the nine-position zero constant ZERO defined. In the third instruction, which previously used ZROCNT, the A operand is adjusted appropriately. The operation, subtraction, is indicated in column 23, and the number by which the address is adjusted is in columns 24–26,

IBM 1401 SYMBOLIC PROGRAMMING SYSTEM
CODING SHEET

Program ______________ Page No. 01 of 1

Programmed by ______________ Date 11/4 Identification SUM

LINE (3–5)	COUNT (6–7)	LABEL (8–13)	OPERATION (14–16)	(A) OPERAND ADDRESS (17)	(A) ± (23)	(A) CHAR. ADJ.	(A) IND. (27)	(B) OPERAND ADDRESS (28)	(B) ± (34)	(B) CHAR. ADJ.	(B) IND. (38)	d (39)	COMMENTS (40–55)
010		START	SW	0210									
020		INITAL	MCW	ZERO				0217					
030			MCW	ZERO	-	7		CNT					
040		CARDIN	R										
050			A	0008				0217					
060			A	DOZEN	-	1		CNT					
070			C	CNT				DOZEN					
080			B	CARDIN								/	
090			W										
100			B	INITAL									
110	09	ZERO	DCW	*		000	0	00000					
120	02	CNT	DCW	*									
130	02	DOZEN	DCW	*		12							
140			END	START									
150													
160													
170													
180													
190													
200													

AREA-DEFINITION CHARACTER COUNT → 1 5 10 15 20 25 30 32

Figure 11–3. Address Adjusting

and is right-justified. It should also be noted that the constant ONE was eliminated by adjusting DOZEN, thus using only the high-order digit 1.

In both of these cases, adjustment was used in the A operand, although it can be used with either the A or B operand when necessary. Although the above example only illustrates the principle with regard to addressing constants, it is also useful in addressing instructions and even particular characters of instructions. To illustrate this, we will consider the card reproducer program shown as the first program in Figure 11–4. Note that the label BEGIN is used to indicate the location of the first instruction as specified on the END card, and START is used to designate the location of the first instruction of the loop. From our knowledge of the machine language, we know that the first instruction will be located at 333 (through 336) and the second at 337. From a symbolic point of view, the first instruction will be located at BEGIN and the second instruction at BEGIN + 4. Using character adjustment, the label START may be eliminated, as shown in the second program of Figure 11–4. The final program shown has been rewritten, only this time the label BEGIN has been omitted and the END statement uses START − 4. These examples are obviously very simple uses of the concept of character adjusting. The principle provides us with a powerful tool, which will find many applications in the remainder of this chapter and in those following.

```
01 010    BEGIN  SW   0001
01 020    START  R
01 030           MCW  0080        0180
01 040           P
01 050           B    START
01 060           END  BEGIN
```

```
01 010    BEGIN  SW   0001
01 020           R
01 030           MCW  0080        0180
01 040           P
01 050           B    BEGIN +  4
01 060           END  BEGIN
```

```
01 010           SW   0001
01 020    START  R
01 030           MCW  0080        0180
01 040           P
01 050           B    START
01 060           END  START -  4
```

Figure 11–4. Card Reproducer Program

SUBROUTINES

All arithmetic operations up to this point have involved either addition or subtraction, since no multiplication instruction is available in the 141 system. However, since multiplication is nothing more than a series of successive additions, it is possible to write a short program that will multiply by performing the required additions. Whenever two numbers are to be multiplied together, this subprogram, commonly called a *subroutine*, can be used.

There are two means by which the subroutine may be properly included in the program. The obvious method is to insert the subroutine directly into the main program whenever and wherever it is needed. A subroutine used in this fashion is called an *open* subroutine. However, if a program requires multiplication in several different places, the use of an open subroutine is not practical, because of storage limitations. In any event, it would appear to be a waste of time and storage space to repeat the same set of instructions many times.

In the *closed* subroutine, the routine is included in the program only once, but referred to whenever the desired function is required by the main program. Figure 11-5 is a diagram representation of both types of subroutines. Note in both cases that shaded blocks represent the list of instructions making up the subroutine, and the unshaded blocks represent the instructions of the main program.

This visual representation readily shows the efficiency of the closed subroutine if the routine is of any length. However, using the closed subroutine presents the problem of returning to the main program at the proper place, which leads us to the subject of subroutine linkage.

SUBROUTINE LINKAGE

In general, linkage provides the means to enter and return from a subroutine and to designate the field or fields on which the subroutine is to operate. The three items of information needed in a linkage may be summarized as follows:

1. The location of the required subroutine.
2. The return address in the program after completion of the subroutine operation.
3. The location(s) of the field(s) to be operated upon by the subroutine.

Item 1 above is accomplished by simply using a BRANCH instruction, with the I address specifying the location of the subroutine. Item 2 is a little more subtle; once control of the machine is within the subroutine, the computer has no way of knowing from which part of the main program it came unless such information is transmitted before branching. This is done by moving a BRANCH instruction into the subroutine to designate the next main program instruction. Finally, item 3 is furnished by placing the fields to be operated upon, usually called *arguments*, in a predetermined location specified by the subroutine. In the case of a MULTIPLY subroutine, it would be necessary to specify the locations of both the multiplicand and multiplier.

We will now discuss the use of two different subroutines, one to suppress leading zeros in a field prior to printing, and the other to perform the MULTIPLY operation. A detailed explanation of these routines will be given in the next chapter, since principles are involved which we have not yet discussed. A standard description format will be used to

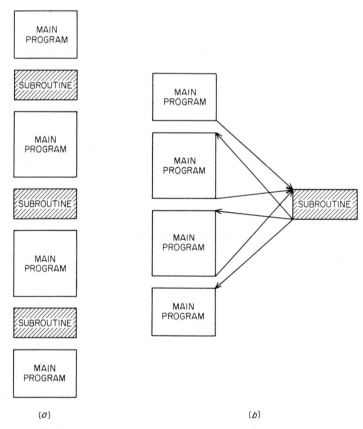

(*a*) (*b*)

Figure 11–5. (a) *Open Subroutine* (b) *Closed Subroutine* explain how to incorporate into a program each subroutine discussed in the text.

THE "SUPPRESS ZERO" SUBROUTINE

Title: Suppress Zero

Mnemonic: SUPZR

Purpose: Given a numeric field of 9 digits or less, suppress leading zeros (that is, change high-order zeros to blanks).

Storage Requirements:

Work area	091–099, addressed as SZARG.
Program	82 additional locations as assigned by the assembler.

Linkage: Move the numeric field of *m* digits to SZARG. The field will then occupy storage positions (100 − m) through 099. For example, a three-digit field would occupy positions 097–099. Move the RETURN BRANCH instruction to SUPZRX + 3. Branch to SUPZR. The linkage is illustrated in Figure 11–6.

	MCW	(argument)	SZARG
	MCW	RETURN-001	SUPZRX+003
	B	SUPZR	
	B	RETURN	
RETURN		(next instruction in program)	

Figure 11–6

After completion of the operation, the field with leading zeros suppressed will remain in its original location. If the entire field is zero, then one zero will remain.

Word Marks: A word mark is set at location 091 during processing by the assembler. If cleared during execution of the main program, it should be reset.

Clearing: Initially the work area will be zero. Further clearing is left to the programmer. Zeroing will always be necessary if the new field contains fewer digits than the previous quantity that used this area.

Use of the Subroutine

The first four instructions in the above SPS linkage instructions are the linkage, and they are inserted in the program where required. The next instruction in the main program following execution of the subroutine is on the fifth line, labeled RETURN. Remember that the operation code of this instruction will be addressed by the label RETURN. The first linkage instruction moves the argument (the field whose zeros are to be suppressed) to the subroutine work area. The second MOVE instruction specifies the field at RETURN − 1, which begins with the character just preceding the next main program instruction. But this is the low-order position of the instruction assembled from the SPS instruction

B   RETURN

so it is this instruction that will be moved, as a field, to SUPZRX + 3, the exit instruction in the subroutine. Thus, only after the return BRANCH instruction has been moved to the subroutine will the BRANCH instruction that designates the subroutine address, SUPZR, be executed.

It is important to recognize the significance of the second BRANCH instruction. It is never executed in the main program, but is placed there so that it can be moved to the subroutine exit prior to branching and thus provide the means of return.

The SPS version of the subroutine is shown in Figure 11–8, where it is used in the following example.

EXAMPLE 11-1

A deck of cards has columns 1–8 and 21–29 reserved for number fields. We wish to punch a new deck with leading zeros suppressed in these fields, and all other data on the cards should be undisturbed. If a field contains only zeros, punch a zero in the units position of the fields; if the card contains only one field, columns 21–29 will be blank and should remain blank.

Program Planning

Because we wish to reproduce the entire card, its contents will be moved to the PUNCH area before leading zeros are suppressed. If the second field is blank, there is no need to operate on it. Since the second field is longer than the first, it will be necessary to initialize the work area before operating on the first field. The self-explanatory program flowchart for this problem is shown in Figure 11–7; note that predefined process symbols are used to represent the subroutine.

The Program

In the main program of Figure 11–8, the two instances in which the subroutine is used are apparent by the linkages. Instructions 01 060 and 01 130 are the BRANCH instructions that direct the program to the subroutine. The address of the desired subroutine is specified by the I address in each BRANCH. However, before branching, the argument is moved to the work area and the return BRANCH is moved to the subroutine for the eventual return. Thus, after execution of the subroutine instructions, the computer will return to the required MOVE instruction.

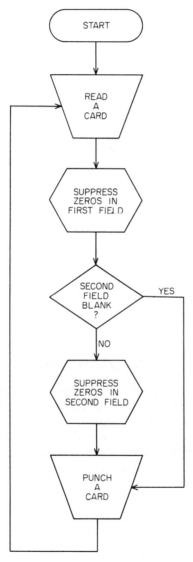

Figure 11-7. Program Flowchart for Example 11-1

```
01 004    *                    EXAMPLE 11-1
01 060    *
01 010    START   SW   0101
01 020    INPUT   R
01 030            MCW  0080        0180
01 035            S    SZARG       SZARG        INITIALIZE
01 040            MCW  0108        SZARG        MOVE ARG TO WORK
01 050            MCW  RETRN1-  1  SUPZRX+   3  AREA THEN RETRN
01 060            B    SUPZR                     ADDRESS THEN
01 070            B    RETRN1                    BRANCH TO SUBR
01 080    RETRN1  MCW  SZARG       0108         REMOVE ARG
01 090            C    BLANKS      0029         CHECK SECOND FLD
01 100            B    OUTPUT                   S FOR BLANK
01 110            MCW  0029        SZARG        MOVE ARG TO WORK
01 120            MCW  RETRN2-  1  SUPZRX+   3  AREA THEN RETRN
01 130            B    SUPZR                     ADDRESS THEN
01 140            B    RETRN2                    BRANCH TO SUBR
01 150    RETRN2  MCW  SZARG       0129         REMOVE ARG
01 160    OUTPUT  P                             PUNCH A CARD
01 170            B    INPUT
01 180 10 BLANKS  DCW  *
01 190    *                    SUPPRESS ZERO SUBROUTINE FOLLOWS ON
02 000    *                    CARDS 02010 THROUGH 02160
02 010    SUPZR   MCW  SZ15        SZ3   +   3
02 020            MCW  SZ15        SZ5   +   6
02 030    SZ3     C    SZARG -  8  SZ13  -   1
02 040            B    SUPZRX                    T
02 050    SZ5     MCW  SZ14        SZARG -   8
02 060            SW   SZ3   +  1  SZ5   +   4
02 070            A    SZ13        SZ3   +   3
02 080            A    SZ13        SZ5   +   6
02 090            CW   SZ3   +  1  SZ5   +   4
02 100            C    SZ3   +  3  SZ15  -   1
02 110            B    SZ3                       /
02 120    SUPZRX  B    0000
02 130 02 SZ13    DCW  *           01
02 140 01 SZ14    DCW  *
02 150 02 SZ15    DCW  *           91
02 160 09 SZARG   DCW  0099        000000000
02 170            END  START
```

Figure 11–8. Source Program for Example 11–1

SUBROUTINE PLACEMENT

It is important to note that the subroutine immediately follows the main program. The normal practice that we shall follow will be to place the subroutine deck(s) immediately following the main program, as illustrated by Figure 11-9, and then allow the assembler to position it (them) in storage. Thus, both the main program and the subroutine are included in the source program.

It is important to note that the END card, which signals completion of processing to the assembler, is the last one in the entire source deck and specifies the first instruction of the main program as the first one which should be eventually executed. Note also that we have not violated the rules and placed a DCW in the middle of a program. The DCW in Figure 11–8 represents the last card of the main program and it is followed by the first instruction of the subroutine. The computer will never attempt to execute the constant as an instruction because the program will always branch around it. The order in which the program and subroutines are loaded has no bearing on the order in which they are executed.

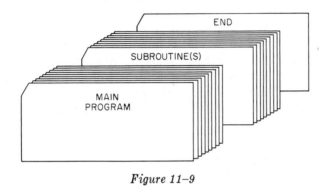

Figure 11–9

THE "MULTIPLY" SUBROUTINE

Title: Multiply

Mnemonic: MULT

Purpose: To provide the capability of multiplying a number containing up to 8 digits by a second number containing up to 8 digits to form a product up to 16 digits in length.

Storage Requirements:

Multiplicand	081–089
Multiplier	091–099
Product	181–196
Additional work areas	197–200
Program	100 additional locations as assigned by assembler

Linkage: Move the multiplicand of m digits to MULTD. This field will then occupy storage positions $(090 - m)$ through 089. Move the multiplier of n digits to MULTR. This field will then occupy storage positions $(100 - n)$ through 099. Move the return BRANCH instruction to MULTX $+ 3$. Branch to MULT. The linkage is illustrated in Figure 11–10. After completion of the operation, the product of $m + n$ digits will be in PROD. Both the multiplicand and multiplier remain in their respective areas.

Word Marks: Word marks are placed in locations 081, 091, and 181 with DCW's during assembly, and care must be exercised to insure that they are not cleared during execution of the main program.

Clearing: Initially all three work areas will be zero. Further clearing is left to the programmer. Blanking or zeroing of the multiplicand and multiplier areas will only be necessary if the new values contain fewer digits than the previous quantities that used these areas. Zeroing of the product accumulator will always be necessary unless we wish to sum products. If the accumulator is not zeroed after prior use, the product will be summed with the quantity originally in this area.

Scaling: Decimal alignment is the responsibility of the programmer. The number of decimal places in the product is equal to the sum of the number of decimal places in the multiplicand and the multiplier.

0			M,C,W	(multiplicand)		M,U,L,T,D
0			M,C,W	(multiplier)		M,U,L,T,R
0			M,C,W	R,E,T,U,R,N - 0,0,1		M,U,L,T,X + 0,0,3
0			B,	M,U,L,T		
0			B,	R,E,T,U,R,N		
0		R,E,T,U,R,N		(next instruction in program)		

Figure 11–10

Use of the Subroutine

Note that the linkage is virtually the same as that of the SUPPRESS ZERO subroutine except here it is necessary to move two arguments (multiplier and multiplicand) to their respective work areas. Use of this subroutine is illustrated by the following example:

EXAMPLE 11-2

Each card of a deck contains four numeric fields, A, B, C, and D. Write a program that will compute $E = A \times B + C \times D$ and punch a new card with all five quantities. Card format is as follows:

FIELD	CARD COLUMNS	CARD
A	1–3	Input and output
B	4–9	Input and output
C	21–25	Input and output
D	26–30	Input and output
E	71–80	Output only

Program Planning

Since we wish to add $A \times B$ and $C \times D$, the first product may be left in the product area when forming the second. Because of the nature of the MULTIPLY subroutine, they will be automatically summed. The program flowchart for this problem is shown in Figure 11–11.

In this case, the flowchart is relatively simple, so both multiplications are represented by a single predefined process symbol. The inclusion of more detail would add little to the basic understanding of program logic.

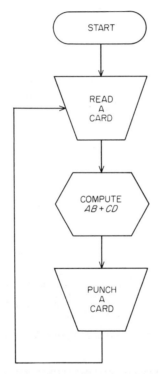

Figure 11–11. Flowchart for Example 11–2

The Program

Figure 11–12 is the program written to perform the required function. The MULTIPLY subroutine is shown immediately following the main program. The logic involved is reasonably straightforward, so study of the program will be left to the student. Note that in each instance when the subroutine is used a return BRANCH is defined.

```
01 010    *                           EXAMPLE 11-2
01 020    *
01 030    START   SW   0101          0104
01 040            SW   0121          0126
01 050            SW   0171
01 060    READ    R
01 070            MCW  0003          0103
01 080            MCW  0009          0109
01 090            MCW  0025          0125
01 100            MCW  0030          0130
01 110            MCW  0103          MULTD
01 120            MCW  0109          MULTR
01 130            MCW  RETRN1-  1 MULTX  +  3
01 140            B    MULT
01 150            B    RETRN1
01 160    RETRN1  MCW  ZEROES-  4 MULTD
01 170            MCW  0125          MULTD
01 180            MCW  0130          MULTR
01 190            MCW  RETRN2-  1 MULTX  +  3
01 200            B    MULT
02 010            B    RETRN2
02 020    RETRN2  MCW  PROD          0180
02 030            P
02 040            MCW  ZEROES-  5 MULTD
02 050            MCW  ZEROES        PROD
02 060            B    READ
02 070 10 ZEROES  DCW  *         0000000000
02 080    *                MULTIPLY SUBROUTINE FOLLOWS ON
02 090    *                CARDS 02100 THROUGH 03110
02 100    MULT    MCW  M16           M3   +  3
02 110            MCW  M17           M6   +  6
02 120    M3      MCW  MULTR -  7 M19   -  1
02 130    M4      C    M19   -  1 M18   -  1
02 140            B    M9                       U
02 150    M6      A    MULTD         PROD  -  7
02 160            S    M18           M19
02 170            B    M4
02 180    M9      SW   M3    +  1 M6    +  4
02 190            A    M18   -  1 M3    +  3
02 200            A    M18   -  1 M6    +  6
03 010            CW   M3    +  1 M6    +  4
03 020            C    M3    +  3 M16   -  2
03 030            B    M3                       /
03 040    MULTX   B    0000
03 050 03 M16     DCW  *         092
03 060 02 M17     DCW  *         89
03 070 02 M18     DCW  0198      10
03 080 02 M19     DCW  0200      00
03 090 09 MULTD   DCW  0089      000000000
03 100 09 MULTR   DCW  0099      000000000
03 110 16 PROD    DCW  0196      0000000000000000
03 120            END  START
```

Figure 11-12. Source Program for Example 11-2

ANOTHER SUBROUTINE LINKAGE

In devising subroutine linkages, it is necessary to save the return address so that it can be placed at the end of the subroutine to allow return to the main program. In the example programs, we have specified each return location by a symbolic address (for example, RETURN). The absolute address that the machine assigned to this symbolic location was stored as the I address of a dummy BRANCH instruction as part of the linkage.

A common practice is to store only the return address and not the entire instruction. However, we cannot define the address as a constant using the DCW since we know the address only by its symbolic equivalent and not by its absolute value. What is needed then is some means to require the computer to store, as an *address constant*, the machine-language equivalent of the symbol (for example, the equivalent of RETURN). For this purpose, an additional declarative, the DEFINE SYMBOLIC ADDRESS (DSA), is provided for use with the assembler. The complete definition of this pseudo instruction is as follows:

DEFINE SYMBOLIC ADDRESS (DSA)

The DSA statement causes a three-character machine-language address (which the assembler has assigned to a label) to be stored as a constant when the program is loaded. The number of characters need not be specified in the COUNT area of the coding sheet, since it is automatically assigned three storage positions by the processor. If we wish to refer to the address of the address field, a symbol may be written in the LABEL portion of the coding sheet. Column 17 may contain an asterisk, thus allowing the assembler to assign the storage positions, or columns 17–20 may contain the desired storage locations of the low-order position for the address field. The symbol whose equivalent address is to be the address field is written beginning in column 28 of the B operand. The MULTIPLY subroutine linkages shown in Figure 11–13 have been modified to use this instruction.

LINE	COUNT	LABEL	OPERATION	(A) OPERAND ADDRESS	±	CHAR. ADJ.	IND.	(B) OPERAND ADDRESS	±	CHAR. ADJ.	IND.	d
0 1 0			M C W	(multiplicand)				M U L T D				
0 2 0			M C W	(multiplier)				M U L T R				
0 3 0			M C W	L I N K				M U L T X	+	0 0 3		
0 4 0			B	M U L T								
0 5 0		L I N K	D S A	*				R E T U R N				
0 6 0		R E T U R N		(next instruction in program)								
0 7 0												
0 8 0		or										
0 9 0												
1 0 0			M C W	(multiplicand)				M U L T D				
1 1 0			M C W	(multiplier)				M U L T R				
1 2 0			M C W	R E T U R N	−	0 0 1		M U L T X	+	0 0 3		
1 3 0			B	M U L T								
1 4 0			D S A	*				R E T U R N				
1 5 0		R E T U R N		(next instruction in program)								

Figure 11–13

Note that the label whose absolute address we want in storage is placed beginning in column 28, and the programmer can refer to this address field (or address constant) by the label beginning in column 8. When the computer assembles this card, the actual address will be punched in columns 24–26 of the object deck card and loaded as any other constant. Further use of the DSA in subroutine linkages is left to the student.

THE PROGRAM SWITCH

The next example that we shall consider also uses the MULTIPLY subroutine and illustrates another principle. Several of the programs studied have required that a number field from a card be stored so that it could be compared to a corresponding number field on a new card. For this, an area in storage was defined for storing the number of the previous card. In a sense, this area could be considered to represent a switch, which would, for instance, be considered *on* if the new number and the stored number were the same, and *off* otherwise; the *on* state might effect a branch and the *off* state not.

Perhaps more along the lines of an actual switch would be a single character indicator with 1 to indicate *on* and 0 to indicate *off*, which is in keeping with the binary system used in computers. In a broad sense of the term, this is called a *program switch*, the use of which is illustrated by the following example.

EXAMPLE 11-3

A deck of cards consists of a customer record card followed by a card for each purchase that he has made, another customer record and purchase cards, and so on. Card format is specified below:

CARD	CARD COLUMNS	FIELD	FORMAT
Record Card	2–5	Customer number	
	6–19	Customer	
	74	Indicator	
Purchase Card	6–10	Item cost	$xxx_\wedge xx$
	20–22	Mark-up rate	$x_\wedge xx$

If the indicator in column 74 of the record card is punched with a 1, the customer qualifies for a 15 percent discount. If it contains a zero, he must pay the full price. Columns 2–5 and 74 on the purchase card will be blank. Write a program that will compute the total purchases for each customer and print a report with the following output:

FIELD	PRINT POSITIONS	FORMAT
Customer number	30–33	
Customer	37–50	
Total charge	61–67	xxxxx$_\wedge$xx

Program Planning

For the first card, multiply the item cost by the mark-up rate to obtain the item selling price, then process the next card. If it is another purchase card, handle it the same way. If it is a customer record card and the customer qualifies, multiply the gross amount by 0.85; leave it unchanged if he does not. Thus, it will be necessary to store the indicator; that is, set a switch for later use whenever a record card is read. We will assume that no overflows occur.

The program flowchart is shown in Figure 11–14; Figure 11–15 is the main program for this problem. In the flowchart, special provisions have been made to accommodate the first card. If this were not done, the program would write a blank line initially. Although in this problem the blank line would create no difficulty, situations frequently arise in which such extra operations are undesirable, so special means are required for starting the program.

After the first card has been read in, the computer will process purchase cards until another record card is encountered. At that time, processing of the complete figures for the previous customer will be done. The 1 or 0 setting of SWITCH, which may have been set many cards previous to its use, will determine whether or not the discount is applied. Then the various work areas will be initialized and the new card contents recorded, including a new setting of SWITCH.

To illustrate the use of two subroutines in one program, this problem has been expanded to include suppression of leading zeros using the SUPZR subroutine from Example 11–1. The main program is shown in Figure 11–16. The subroutines MULT and SUPZR follow in that order, although they have not been listed.

USING THE NOP

In the program of Figure 11–15, it was necessary to use two COMPARE instructions, one for each decision. We will now consider another means for accomplishing the same thing using only one COMPARE. If SWITCH contains 1, the discount will be applied; if it contains 0, the discount computation will be omitted. The BRANCH instruction for this determination is represented in SPS as instruction 02 040 of Figure 11–15.

Another means to accomplish this is to make the BRANCH instruction

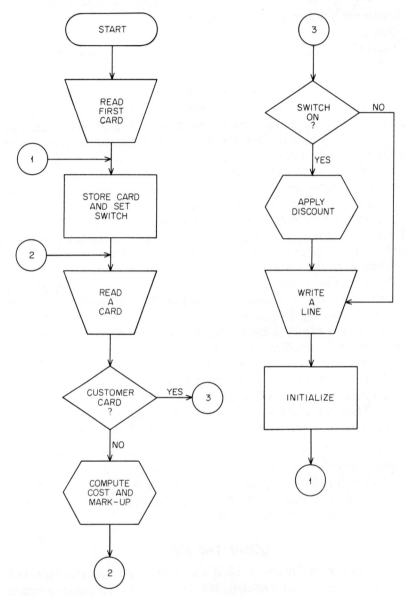

Figure 11–14. Program Flowchart for Example 11–3

```
01 010    *                         EXAMPLE 11-3
01 020    *
01 030    START   SW   0002          0261        SET UP
01 040            SW   0006          0020                 FIELDS
01 050            MCW  HEAD          0260        PRINT
01 060            W                              HEADINGS
01 070            CS   0260
01 080            W
01 090            W
01 100            R                              READ FIRST
01 110    MOVE    MCW  0005          0233            RECORD CARD
01 120            MCW  0074          SWITCH          AND STORE
01 130            MCW  0019          0250        READ A CARD
01 140    INPUT   R
01 150            C    BLANKS        0005        IF ANOTHER PURCH
01 160            B    COMPSW                    / MULT COST BY
01 170            MCW  0010          MULTD - 1   .MARK UP RATE
01 180            MCW  0022          MULTR - 1       AND SUM IN
01 190            MCW  RETRN1-  1 MULTX + 3   PRODUCT AREA
01 200            B    MULT
02 010            B    RETRN1
02 020    RETRN1  B    INPUT                     READ ANOTHER CRD
02 030    COMPSW  C    ONE           SWITCH      IF ALL CUSTOMER
02 040            B    RETRN2                    / CARDS THEN
02 050            MCW  PROD   -  3 MULTD           CHECK FOR DISC
02 060            S    MULTR         MULTR
02 070            S    PROD          PROD        IF DISCOUNT,
02 080            MCW  RATE          MULTR          MULT TO OBTAIN
02 090            MCW  RETRN2-  1 MULTX + 3   TOTAL CHARGES
02 100            B    MULT
02 110            B    RETRN2
02 120    RETRN2  A    POINT5        PROD   - 3
02 130            MCW  PROD   -  4 026/
02 140            W                              PRINT CHARGES
02 150            S    PROD          PROD
02 160            S    MULTD         MULTD
02 170            B    MOVE
02 180 01 POINT5  DCW  *         5
02 190 01 ONE     DCW  *         1
02 200 01 SWITCH  DCW  *
03 010 05 BLANKS  DCW  *
03 020 03 RATE    DCW  *          850
03 030 22 HEAD    DCW  *    DISCOUNT SALES SUMMARY
03 040    *            MULTIPLY SUBROUTINE FOLLOWS ON
03 050    *                 CARDS 03060 THROUGH 04070
03 060    MULT    MCW  M16           M3   + 3
03 070            MCW  M17           M6   + 6
03 080    M3      MCW  MULTR -  7 M19   - 1
03 090    M4      C    M19   -  1 M18   - 1
03 100            B    M9                             U
03 110    M6      A    MULTD         PROD   - 7
03 120            S    M18           M19
03 130            B    M4
03 140    M9      SW   M3    +  1 M6    + 4
03 150            A    M18   -  1 M3    + 3
03 160            A    M18   -  1 M6    + 6
03 170            CW   M3    +  1 M6    + 4
03 180            C    M3    +  3 M16   - 2
03 190            B    M3                             /
03 200    MULTX   B    0000
04 010 03 M16     DCW  *          092
04 020 02 M17     DCW  *          89
04 030 02 M18     DCW  0198       10
04 040 02 M19     DCW  0200       00
04 050 09 MULTD   DCW  0089       000000000
04 060 09 MULTR   DCW  0099       000000000
04 070 16 PROD    DCW  0196       0000000000000000
04 080            END  START
```

Figure 11-15. Source Program for Example 11-3

unconditional and use the NO OPERATION instruction. Remember that, when a different customer card is read in, SWITCH is set so that the conditional BRANCH will cause omission of the discount computation later. If the customer qualifies, SWITCH is set accordingly and the discount is computed.

If, instead of setting SWITCH, a NO OPERATION (N) were moved in to replace the B of instruction 02 040 (in the machine language, of course) when the customer qualified for a discount, and a B when he did not, the function would be performed properly. Thus if the instruction were

```
01 010      *                EXAMPLE 11-3  (WITH SUPPRESS ZERO)
01 020      *
01 030  START   SW   0002      0261         SET UP
01 040          SW   0006      0020              FIELDS
01 050          MCW  HEAD      0260         PRINT
01 060          W                                HEADING
01 070          CS   0260
01 080          W
01 090          W
01 100          R                           READ FIRST
01 110  MOVE    MCW  0005      0233            RECORD CARD
01 120          MCW  0074      SWITCH          AND STORE
01 130          MCW  0019      0250
01 140  INPUT   R                           READ A CARD
01 150          C    BLANKS    0005
01 160          B    COMPSW                  /IF ANOTHER PURCH
01 170          MCW  0010      MULTD -   1   MULT COST BY
01 180          MCW  0022      MULTR -   1   MARK UP RATE
01 190          MCW  RETRN1-  1 MULTX +  3   AND SUM
01 200          B    MULT                       IN PROD
02 010          B    RETRN1
02 020  RETRN1  B    INPUT                   READ ANOTHER CRD
02 030  COMPSW  C    ONE       SWITCH       IF ALL CUSTOMER
02 040          B    RETRN2                 / CARDS THEN
02 050          MCW  PROD  -   3 MULTD       CHECK FOR DISC
02 060          S    MULTR     MULTR
02 070          S    PROD      PROD         IF DISCOUNT,
02 080          MCW  RATE      MULTR          MULT TO OBTAIN
02 090          MCW  RETRN2-  1 MULTX +  3   TOTAL CHARGES
02 100          B    MULT
02 110          B    RETRN2
02 120  RETRN2  A    POINT5    PROD  -   3
02 130          MCW  PROD  -   4 SZARG       SUPPRESS
02 140          MCW  RETRN3-  1 SUPZRX+  3   ZEROES
02 150          B    SUPZR                   FOR
02 160          B    RETRN3                     OUTPUT
02 170  RETRN3  MCW  SZARG     0267
02 180          W                           PRINT
02 190          S    MULTD     MULTD
02 200          S    PROD      PROD
03 010          B    MOVE
03 020  01 POINT5 DCW  *       5
03 030  01 ONE    DCW  *       1
03 040  01 SWITCH DCW  *
03 050  05 BLANKS DCW  *
03 060  03 RATE   DCW  *       850
03 070  22 HEAD   DCW  *     DISCOUNT SALES SUMMARY
03 080      *              MULTIPLY SUBROUTINE FOLLOWS ON
03 090      *                 CARDS 03100 THROUGH 04110
04 120      *              SUPPRESS ZERO SUBROUTINE FOLLOWS ON
04 130      *                 CARDS 04140 THROUGH 05090
05 100          END  START
```

Figure 11–16. Example 11–3 with SUPPRESS ZERO

a NO OPERATION, the next instruction in the sequence would be executed, which begins the discount computation. If it were a BRANCH, the computation would not be performed.

For this problem this method represents no particular advantage over the previous program, but in many instances the technique is very useful. In order to show a variety of programming techniques, the program of Example 11-3 has been entirely rewritten. The program in Figure 11-17 uses not one but two program switches (as before, the MULTIPLY subroutine is not repeated here in the listing). The first, named SWICH1, is on, causing a branch with the first card only, thus

```
01 010    *                      EXAMPLE 11-3 (USING NOP)
01 020    *
01 030    START   SW   0002        0261
01 040            SW   0006        0020
01 050            MCW  HEAD        0260
01 060            W
01 070            CS   0260
01 080            W
01 090            W
01 100    RETRN2  R
01 110            C    0074        POINT5-  1
01 120    *                 ON FIRST CARD,BRANCH TO SW1OFF
01 130    *                   IF CC 74 BLANK,BRANCH TO MPY
01 140    *                    IF NEW CUST THEN OUTPUT PREV TOTALS
01 150            B    MPY                          U
01 160    *                 IF CUST QUALIFIES FOR DISCOUNT,OP CODE
01 170    *                     OF LINE 01180 WILL BE N
01 180    SWICH1  B    SW1OFF
01 190    SWICH2  B    RETRN1
01 200            MCW  PROD   -  3 MULTD       APPLY
02 010            S    PROD        PROD          DISCOUNT
02 020            S    MULTR       MULTR
02 030            MCW  RATE        MULTR
02 040            MCW  RETRN1-  1 MULTX +   3
02 050            B    MULT
02 060            B    RETRN1
02 070    RETRN1  A    POINT5      PROD   -   3
02 080            MCW  PROD   -  4 0267
02 090            W
02 100            S    PROD        PROD
02 110            S    MULTD       MULTD
02 120    SW1OFF  MCW  OFF         SWICH1
02 130            MCW  ON          SWICH2
02 140            B    STORE                  S
02 150            MCW  OFF         SWICH2
02 160    STORE   MCW  0005        0233       STORE CUST
02 170            MCW  0019        0250          CARD
02 180            B    RETRN2
02 190    MPY     MCW  0010        MULTR -   1 COMPUTE
02 200            MCW  0022        MULTD -   1  SUB TOTALS
03 010            MCW  LINK   +  3 MULTX +   3
03 020            B    MULT
03 030    LINK    B    RETRN2
03 040 02 POINT5  DCW  *       05
03 050 03 RATE    DCW  *       850
03 060 01 OFF     DCW  *       N
03 070 01 ON      DCW  *       B
03 080 22 HEAD    DCW  *    DISCOUNT SALES SUMMARY
03 090    *             MULTIPLY SUBROUTINE FOLLOWS ON
03 100    *                   CARDS 03110 THROUGH 04120
04 130            END  START
```

Figure 11-17. Example 11-3 using the NOP *Instruction*

omitting the undesired WRITE. This is a common method of providing for special handling of the first card or initial computations to be performed. Execution of instruction 02 120 (SW1OFF) will turn SWICH1 off, that is, place an N in the operation code, and the branch will not be executed again. On the other hand, SWICH2 is set each time a customer card is processed. Either instruction 02 130 or 02 150 will be the last executed to set SWICH2, depending upon the results of the COMPARE, instruction 01 110.

Again it is suggested that the student study all examples with a critical eye. Without a doubt, many of these example programs can be shortened or made more efficient. However, too much sophistication in attempting to make the shortest and "best" program can often lead to confusion and a long, involved debugging task.

■ CHAPTER SUMMARY

A subroutine is a set of predefined instructions programmed to perform a given function.

Two types of subroutines are commonly used in programming. The open subroutine is placed within the program wherever and whenever it is required. The closed subroutine is included in the program only once but is referred to whenever the programmed function is required.

The closed subroutine requires the following three items of information: (1) the location of the required subroutine, (2) the return address, (3) the location(s) of the argument(s).

Two subroutines, one to suppress leading zeros and the other to multiply, were introduced in this chapter.

A program switch is a form of dynamic program alteration. The most common method is to change the operation code of a BRANCH instruction from B to N, or vice versa. This results in a temporary change in the sequence of instruction execution.

■ EXERCISES

11.1 In the program of Figure 8–6, how could the constant LIMIT be used in place of ONE by address adjusting?

11.2 By address adjusting, eliminate the label INPUT in the program of Figure 8–6.

11.3 What three items of information are furnished by the subroutine linkage? How is each supplied in the SUPPRESS ZERO subroutine?

11.4 What is the distinction between a closed subroutine and an open subroutine?

11.5 Why must the END card follow the last subroutine in the source program and not the last card of the main program?

11.6 In Example 11–1, would the program function properly if the subroutine were placed at the beginning of the main program? Explain.

11.7 Rewrite the program of Figure 7–9 to include suppression of leading zeros for M, N and P on the output.

11.8 Write a program for Exercise 7.9 using the MULTIPLY subroutine (do *not* use the method of differences). Compare the running times.

11.9 Write a program that will compute current and cumulative grade-point averages for each card in a deck of student record cards. Card format is as follows:

CARD COLUMN	FIELD	FORMAT
Input Card		
1–20	Not used in this program	
21–23	Current units	xx∧x
24–26	Current points	xx∧x
27–32	Not used in this program	
33–36	Cumulative units	xxx∧x
37–40	Cumulative points	xxx∧x
41–80	Not used in this program	
Output Card		
1–74	Same as input	
75–77	Current GPA	x∧xx
78–80	Cumulative GPA	x∧xx

The use of a DIVIDE subroutine is described in Appendix III.

Chapter Twelve

ADDRESS MODIFICATION

DATA AND INSTRUCTIONS

In the 141 system, we find that data and instructions are stored side-by-side in storage but addressed differently. That is, an instruction is addressed by its high-order character and a data field by its low-order character. Because of this, the beginner often assumes that they are completely different entities in storage. However, during our study of subroutines, we moved instructions and parts of instructions just as we would data. By now it should be apparent that the main distinction between the two in storage is the manner in which they are used. For instance, the field

$$\underline{|\underline{B}|5|0|2|}_{\overset{3}{\underset{4}{7}}}$$

is a four-character field stored in locations 371–374. It does have the appearance of a BRANCH instruction, but it could be, for instance, a file number that has been read in from a card and stored at 374. The important point here is that if it is to be used as an instruction it will be referred to by the address 371; if it is to be used as data, it will be addressed by 374. Further, if it is to be used as an instruction it can still be operated upon as data at any time during execution of the program. In fact, this is what is done in providing subroutine linkages, since a BRANCH instruction containing the return address is moved to replace the return BRANCH in the subroutine. After execution of the subroutine instructions, this branch is then treated as an instruction and executed.

188

The program switch that uses an NOP also represents a situation in which an instruction is treated as a data field. Both of these techniques, which result in modifying the program, use only the MOVE instruction to replace part or all of an instruction with a previously defined field. Perhaps the student has already guessed that, in addition to program modification by the movement of fields, it is possible to perform arithmetic on the operands of instructions. Herein lies one of the most powerful tools of the stored-program computer. Perhaps now the student will begin to appreciate this concept and the historical significance of the EDVAC type of computer described in Chapter 1.

A SIMPLE PROGRAM

Suppose that 13 four-digit fields are punched in columns 2-5, 7-10, 12-15, ···, 62-65 of a card (other columns blank). We wish to write a program that will read the card, sum these 13 fields, and punch a new card with the sum in columns 76-80 (assume no overflows). A simple and straightforward set of instructions for performing this function is shown in Figure 12-1. The only difference between each of the 13 ADD instructions is that each A address increases by 5 over the previous one. To simplify programming, we could use only one ADD instruction and increase the A address by 5 after each addition, looping back again as shown in Figure 12-2.

The first nine instructions are identical to those of Figure 12-1, but there the similarity ends. The next five instructions serve the purposes of modifying the ADD instruction and controlling the loop. In order to perform the address modification, it is necessary to set a word mark at the high-order position of the A operand. During the first time through the loop, the ADD instruction would appear in storage as follows:

Before execution of instruction 110 (SW):

$$\underline{\quad |\underline{A}|0|0|5|1|8|0|\quad}$$

After execution of instruction 110 (SW):

$$\underline{\quad |\underline{A}|\underline{0}|0|5|1|8|0|\quad}$$

IBM 1401 SYMBOLIC PROGRAMMING SYSTEM

CODING SHEET

Program **Summation of Fields**

Programmed by

Date 11/4

LINE	COUNT	LABEL	OPERATION	(A) OPERAND ADDRESS	±	CHAR. ADJ.	(B) OPERAND ADDRESS	±	CHAR. ADJ.	d	COMMENTS
0 1 0		START	SW	0 1 1 7 6			0 0 0 0 2				
0 2 0			SW	0 0 0 0 7			0 0 0 1 2				
0 3 0			SW	0 0 0 1 7			0 0 0 2 2				
0 4 0			SW	0 0 0 2 7			0 0 0 3 2				
0 5 0			SW	0 0 0 3 7			0 0 0 4 2				
0 6 0			SW	0 0 0 4 7			0 0 0 5 2				
0 7 0			SW	0 0 0 5 7			0 0 0 6 2				
0 8 0		READ	R								
0 9 0			A	0 0 0 0 5			0 1 1 8 0				
1 0 0			A	0 0 0 1 0			0 1 1 8 0				
1 1 0			A	0 0 0 1 5			0 1 1 8 0				
1 2 0			A	0 0 0 2 0			0 1 1 8 0				
1 3 0			A	0 0 0 2 5			0 1 1 8 0				
1 4 0			A	0 0 0 3 0			0 1 1 8 0				
1 5 0			A	0 0 0 3 5			0 1 1 8 0				
1 6 0			A	0 0 0 4 0			0 1 1 8 0				
1 7 0			A	0 0 0 4 5			0 1 1 8 0				
1 8 0			A	0 0 0 5 0			0 1 1 8 0				
1 9 0			A	0 0 0 5 5			0 1 1 8 0				
2 0 0			A	0 0 0 6 0			0 1 1 8 0				
			A	0 0 0 6 5			0 1 1 8 0				
			P	0 1 1 8 0							
			S	R E A D							
			B	S T A R T							
			END								

AREA-DEFINITION CHARACTER COUNT → 1

Figure 12–1. Summing Twelve Fields

IBM 1401 SYMBOLIC PROGRAMMING SYSTEM
CODING SHEET

Program: Summation of Fields
Programmed by: ___
Date: 11/4
Page No. 01 of 1
Identification: MOD

LINE	COUNT	LABEL	OPERATION	(A) ADDRESS	±	CHAR. ADJ	ONI	(B) ADDRESS	±	CHAR. ADJ	d	COMMENTS
010		START	SW	0176				0002				SET WORD
020			SW	0007				0012				MARKS
030			SW	0017				0022				FOR
040			SW	0027				0032				INPUT
050			SW	0037				0042				FIELDS
060			SW	0047				0052				
070			SW	0057				0062				
080			R									
090		ADD	A	0005				0180				ADD FIELD TO SUM
100			C	ADD	+	3		FINISH				THEN, CHECK FOR
110			SW	ADD	+	1						LAST FIELD
120			A	FIVE				ADD	+	3		INCREMENT FOR
130			CW	ADD	+	1						NEXT FIELD AND
140			B								/	RETURN IF NOT
150			P									FINISHED
160			S	0180				0180				OTHERWISE PUNCH
170			MCW	FIVE				ADD	+	3		AND INITIALIZE
180			B	ADD	-	1						
190	03	FINISH	DCW	*		065						
200	03	FIVE	DCW	*		005						
210			END	START								

AREA-DEFINITION CHARACTER COUNT → 1

Figure 12-2. Address Modification

After execution of instruction 120 (ADD):

$$\underline{\underset{\underset{D}{D}A}{A} \mid 0 \mid 1 \mid 0 \mid 1 \mid 8 \mid 0 \mid}$$

After execution of instruction 130 (CW):

$$\underline{\underline{A} \ 0 \ 1 \ 0 \ 1 \ 8 \ 0}$$

If the word mark were not set at ADD + 1, the operation code "$\underline{A}$" would be included in the addition and would result in an incorrect instruction. When the A operand reaches a value of 065, the conditional branch will cause the program to proceed to the PUNCH instruction. After punching the sum on a new card, the output area is initialized and the original address of 005 is moved to the A operand of the ADD instruction in preparation for processing a new card.

Although this method saves only four cards over the previous program, the former requires 149 positions in storage and the latter uses only 109. In most programming it is best to economize on storage space rather than on the number of instructions, so this represents a significant saving.

THE "SUPPRESS ZERO" SUBROUTINE

Initial Considerations

With the background given above, we can now discuss in detail the two subroutines presented in the previous chapter. The first, which is used to suppress the leading zeros of a numeric field, is a relatively simple and direct application of address modification. In writing such a routine, the programmer must ask himself, (1) "Should the field length (number of characters in the field) be fixed or variable? (2) If fixed, how long should it be? If variable, how can the length be specified in the subroutine linkage? (3) How should special cases be handled?"

As we have seen, the 141 system uses variable word-length instructions and data. However, elements of a fixed word-length machine have been incorporated into our studies by the subroutines. In both of these routines a predetermined field of fixed length has been set aside as a working area. The subroutine operates on the complete area, whether or not the number field that we move into the work area completely fills the area. Thus computing time is sacrificed to obtain simple straightforward routines.

With the decision made to use fixed word-length subroutines, it is necessary to decide upon optimum length. To a degree this is arbitrary; the important thing is to plan each of the subroutines in order to assure reasonable compatibility. With the SUPPRESS ZERO subroutine, 9 digits are chosen to be consistent with the MULTIPLY and DIVIDE routines.

The needs of a given situation usually determine the means provided for handling special cases. For instance, in the SUPPRESS ZERO subroutine, if a field consists of zeros, the last zero will be saved (this is the reason for right-justifying the work area); if the field is blank, it remains blank. In a similar fashion, most subroutines have both practical and/or programmer-imposed requirements that dictate, to an extent, how the program is to be written.

The Program

Before proceeding further, we will now relate the program flowchart shown in Figure 12–3 to the SUPPRESS ZERO program of Figure 12–4. Each flowchart symbol has the equivalent instruction or instructions listed above and to the left of it. Beginning with instruction 3, the leading digit is compared to zero; if the digit is greater than zero, the next instruction causes a return to the main program. If the next digit is zero or anything lower in the collating sequence, a blank replaces it. Instructions 6, 7, 8, and 9 increase the addresses of the two operands designating the leading digit of the subject field.

After incrementing the addresses, a check is made to determine whether or not the loop has been completed 8 times and, if not, the next digit is processed. If 8 passes have been made, the A address of sz3 will be 099 and the computer will return to the main program. Thus the last digit (if all the digits preceding it are zero or blank) would be left unchanged. Instruction sz13 is a DCW that performs double duty, inasmuch as it is used as 01, and then by address adjusting as 0.

THE "MULTIPLY" SUBROUTINE

Initial Considerations

The other subroutine used in the preceding chapter performs the operation of multiplication. In writing this subroutine, it is again necessary to ask such questions as, "How long should the factors be?" and "Where should the work areas be located?"

In the interest of conserving storage, positions 081–100 and 181–200 are chosen as work areas for the four subroutines included in this text. This automatically places a restriction on the lengths of the fields. In order to insure that the routines work on both the 1620 with the simulator and the 1401, and that they be compatible with one another when used in the same program, fields of 8 characters are chosen for both the multiplicand and multiplier, with a resulting 16-character product. It should be emphasized that these choices are completely arbitrary and

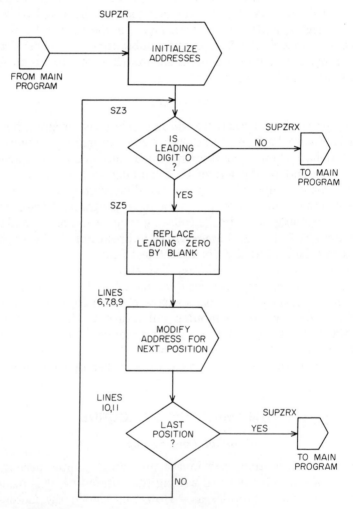

Figure 12-3. Flowchart for SUPPRESS ZERO *Subroutine*

IBM 1401 SYMBOLIC PROGRAMMING SYSTEM
CODING SHEET

Program **Suppress Zero Subroutine**

Programmed by _____   Date 11/4

LINE	COUNT	LABEL	OPERATION	(A) ADDRESS	±	CHAR. ADJ	ONI	(B) ADDRESS	±	CHAR. ADJ	ONI	d	COMMENTS
0 1 0		SUPZR	MCW	SZ15				SZ3	+	3			INITIALIZE,
0 2 0			MCW	SZ15				SZ5	+	6			ADDRESSES
0 3 0		SZ3	C	SZARG	−			SZ13	−	1			IF LEADING DIGIT
0 4 0			B	SUPZRX		8							NOT ZERO, RETURN
0 5 0		SZ5	MCW	SZ14				SZARG	−	8			TO MAIN PROGRAM
0 6 0			SW	SZ3	+			SZ5	+	4			IF ZERO REPLACE,
0 7 0			A	SZ13				SZ3	+	3			WITH BLANK AND,
0 8 0			A	SZ13				SZ5	+	6			INCREMENT FOR
0 9 0			CW	SZ3				SZ15	+	4			NEXT POSITION
1 0 0			C	SZ3	+	3		SZ15	−	1		/	IF LAST POSITION
1 1 0		SUPZRX	B	0000									RET TO MAIN PRG
1 2 0	0 2	SZ13	DCW	*		01							
1 3 0	0 1	SZ14	DCW	*									
1 4 0	0 2	SZ15	DCW	*		91							
1 6 0	0 9	SZARG	DCW	0099		00		0000000					
1 7 0													
1 8 0													
1 9 0													
2 0 0													

AREA-DEFINITION CHARACTER COUNT ——→ 1

Figure 12–4. SUPPRESS ZERO *Subroutine*

do not characterize the 141 system. Another programmer could readily write his own routines using entirely different methods and working areas.

An Arithmetic Algorithm

The standard method used to determine the product of two numbers, say 1384 and 253, is as follows:

$$
\begin{array}{r}
1384 \\
253 \\
\hline
4152 \\
6920 \\
2768 \\
\hline
350152 \\
\end{array}
$$

This process involves multiplying each digit by each of the other digits using a simple multiplication table learned in grade school. Since the 141 system has no such table, we must devise other means to do this by using only addition, in the following manner:

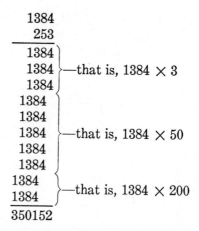

Obviously this is not the only format that can be used in performing multiplication; any convenient means for keeping check on place value can be employed. In multiplying two algebraic quantities, we normally consider terms from left to right in the following way:

$$
\begin{array}{r}
1384 \\
253 \\
\hline
1384 \\
1384 \\
1384 \\
1384 \\
1384 \\
1384 \\
1384 \\
1384 \\
1384 \\
1384 \\
\hline
350152
\end{array}
$$

Obviously, all of these methods produce the same answer. For convenience, the latter method is used in the 141 MULTIPLY subroutine.

The Program

The program flowchart for the MULTIPLY routine is shown as Figure 12-5, and the program itself follows as Figure 12-6. The first two instructions serve, as with the SUPPRESS ZERO subroutine, to initialize the addresses to be modified. Instruction M3 moves the high-order digit of the multiplier (located at 092) to the tens position of a two-position work area. If the digit is not 0, the multiplicand is added to the leftmost position of the product area, 1 is subtracted from the multiplier digit in the work area, and the computer branches back to M4. Again the COMPARE is executed until the multiplier has been decremented to 0, and the computer breaks out of the loop and proceeds to M9.

Both the M18 and M19 fields use two positions to keep the test digit separate from its sign. This assures compatibility with the 1401 system (see Chapter 15, on Sign Control). In the example multiplication, the computer would now have completed the function of adding 1384 to the high-order positions of the product area twice.

The four instructions beginning with M9 cause the A operand in M3 to be increased by 1 to 093, which is the address of the next multiplier digit. The B operand of M6 would also be incremented to 193, which would result in a shift in the subsequent addition of the multiplicand corresponding to the lower significance of the new multiplier digit. Then the computer would return to M3 (assuming that the multiplication had not been completed as determined by instruction 013) and proceed with the required operations. This time the next digit of the multiplier would be moved to the work area and would control the inner loop. After the outer loop had been completed 8 times, the operation would be terminated and the computer would branch back to the main program.

Although MULTD and MULTR are defined as nine-digit fields with resulting word marks in 081 and 091, only eight-digit fields can be multiplied. Again, this is to insure compatibility with the DIVIDE subroutine. A more detailed step-by-step study of the program is left to the student.

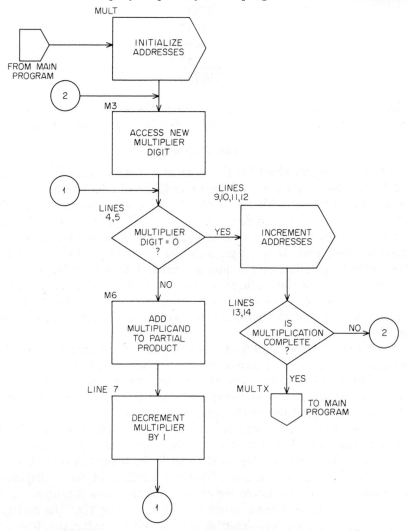

Figure 12-5. Flowchart for MULTIPLY *Subroutine*

Program: MULTIPLY SUBROUTINE
Programmed by: _____
Date: 11/4

LINE	COUNT	LABEL	OPERATION	(A) ADDRESS	(A) ±	(A) CHAR. ADJ.	(A) d/zONI	(B) ADDRESS	(B) ±	(B) CHAR. ADJ.	(B) d/zONI	(B) d	COMMENTS
010		MULT	MCW	M16				M3		3			INITIALIZE
020			MCW	M17				M6		6			ADDRESSES
030		M3	MCW	MULTR		7		M19	−	1			MOVE FIRST DIGIT
040		M4	C	M19	−			M18	−	1			OF MULTR TO WRK
050			B	M9								U	IF 0, NEXT POSIT
060		M6	A	MULTD				PROD	−	7			OTHERWISE ADD
070			S	M18				M19					MULTD UNTIL
080			B	M4									MULTR DIGIT ZERO
090		M9	S	M3	+			M6	+	4			THEN MODIFY
100			A	M18	−			M3	+	3			ADDRESS TO
110			A	M18	−			M6	+	6			OBTAIN NEXT
120			C	M3	+			M6	+	4			MULTR DIGIT
130			C	M3		3		M16	−	2			IF MULTIPLICATION
140			B	M3									COMPLETE RETURN
150		MULTX	B	0000									TO MAIN PROGRAM
160	03	M16	DCW	*		092							
170	02	M17	DCW	*		99							
180	02	M18	DCW	0198		10							
190	02	M19	DCW	0200		00							
200	09	MULTD	DCW	0089		00		000000000			0	0	
210	09	MULTR	DCW	0099		00		0000000000			0	0	
220	16	MULT	DCW	0196		00		00000000					

AREA-DEFINITION CHARACTER COUNT →

Figure 12–6. MULTIPLY Subroutine

TABLE LOOK-UP

Let us assume that we have a problem in which it is necessary to use the number of days in any given month. Thanks to the ancient Romans, there is no neat formula that will give these, so we remember them either by verse or by counting on our knuckles. Unfortunately (or perhaps fortunately) the computer does not use such means, so it is necessary to provide this information to the computer in tabulated form, such as that shown in Table 12–1.

Table 12–1
DAYS PER MONTH

MONTH	MONTH NUMBER	NUMBER OF DAYS
January	1	31
February	2	28 (usually)
March	3	31
April	4	30
May	5	31
June	6	30
July	7	31
August	8	31
September	9	30
October	10	31
November	11	30
December	12	31

If we were working on a problem and came to a place where the number of days in July were required, we would search the left-hand column to find July, and read across to obtain 31 from the right-hand column. If we stored this information in the computer, we could instruct the machine to do the same thing. However, in storage, this information would not appear as a table, but rather as a series of fields as shown below (which have been arbitrarily placed, beginning in location 701):

0131022803310430053106300731083109301031113012 31

$$7_0 \quad 7_0 \quad \quad \quad 7_2$$
$$1 \quad \quad 4 \quad \quad \quad 8$$

Consider the first field (701–704). The first two digits, 01, (usually called the *argument*) represent the month, and the second two digits, 31, (usually called the *function*) represent the number of days in that month. Thus, for any given argument, we can refer to the table and determine the function. In this case the pairs are separated from each other in storage by use of a word mark, although this need not be so.

In finding the number of days for July from Table 12–1, the reader probably fixed his glance at the middle portion of the table, since July is approximately in the middle of the year. Had the table been randomly ordered, it would have been necessary to search the table month by month to find the proper entry. These approaches are suggestive of methods used with the computer. In practice, many techniques are used, but the two (and their variations) that we shall discuss are commonly employed and therefore representative.

Sequential Searching

This technique might be termed a "brute-force" approach; it basically involves running through the list until finding the desired argument. For instance, let us use this method to find the number of days in July (month 07). First we compare 07 to the field at 702 and, obtaining negative results, increment the address by four and compare 07 to the field at 706, and so on until reaching 726, at which time we get an equal comparison. We then move the function from 728 and continue with the main program. Each time the program requires the number of days in a given month, this routine is executed.

Whenever the number of days in January is desired, the answer will be found immediately. However, if the number of days in December is to be obtained, considerable searching is required. A method frequently employed to save time is to enter the table in the middle; that is, compare 07 to the field at 722 for the first check. This comparison indicates whether the desired field is equal to, above, or below the initial point. It is necessary to check, at most, half of the table. However, if the elements of the table were ordered in a completely random fashion, this refinement could not be used; a complete search from the beginning would be necessary.

Another commonly used variation on this method is to enter the table in the vicinity of the most frequently used points, if they are clearly defined. For instance, if the program were used primarily for computations prior to the Christmas season, the table might be entered at the end (that is, December) and searched in reverse.

Direct Look-up

Perhaps the student has recognized an even faster and more efficient method that could be used in this particular problem. Since the values for the argument are conveniently ordered and vary in increments of one, a direct table look-up procedure may be employed. The first argument and its function are stored at 704 and, since each field consists of four digits, the second is at 708; that is, the second is stored at $704 + 4 = 708$. Using this, we can find the information for the seventh month by subtracting 1 from 7, multiplying by 4, and adding to 704 to obtain

$$704 + 4\,(7 - 1) = 728$$

which is the address of the desired field. Obviously, this is the most efficient method for a table of this type.

If we give some thought to this particular table, we can see that storage of each argument is not necessary since the location implies the value of the argument. For instance, the data field below shows the same table in storage; this time only values of the function are included:

$$\underline{31\underline{28}31\underline{30}31\underline{30}31\underline{31}30\underline{31}30\underline{31}}$$

$$\overset{7}{\underset{\underset{1}{0}}{}} \qquad \overset{7}{\underset{\underset{4}{1}}{}}$$

In this case each month occupies only two positions, so applying the previous arithmetic rule to find the number of days in July gives

$$702 + 2\,(7 - 1) = 714$$

which is the address of 31, the required function.

The Assembler

Whenever we assemble an SPS program, we use the process of table look-up in two places. Recall that the assembly process is completed in two passes. During the first pass, actual addresses are computed for all symbolic addresses and a label table is set up in storage. During the second pass, whenever the assembly program encounters a symbolic address in the SPS program, it refers to the label table and places the equivalent machine-language address in the object program. In this case the symbolic address is the argument and the actual address is the function.

The other instance in which the table look-up procedure is employed during assembly is to change symbolic operation codes to equivalent machine-language codes during assembly. The table used to perform this function is included in the assembler and contains all of the symbolic operation codes as the arguments and the corresponding machine-language codes as the functions. The assembler itself is an interesting data processing program.

TABLE LOOK-UP APPLICATIONS

To further illustrate table look-up methods, we will consider two modifications of Example 11–3.

EXAMPLE 12-1

Direct Look-up. A deck of cards consists of one customer record followed by a card for each purchase, another customer record card and purchase cards, and so on. The card format is as follows:

FIELD	CARD COLUMN	FORMAT
Record Card		
Customer number	2–5	
Customer	6–19	
Purchase Card		
Blank	1–5	
Item	6–15	
Item cost	21–24	xx$_\wedge$xx
Department code number	30	

For each purchase, the customer receives a discount (shown in Table 12–2) that depends upon the department from which the purchase was

Table 12–2
DEPARTMENT DISCOUNTS

DEPARTMENT	DISCOUNT	COST FACTOR
1	5%	0.95
2	7%	0.93
3	15%	0.85
4	8%	0.92
5	22%	0.78
6	23%	0.77
7	9%	0.91
8	22%	0.78
9	20%	0.80

made. Compute the total bill for each customer by applying the appropriate discounts, that is, by multiplying the item cost by the cost factor and summing the charges for each. The output should consist of a listing with the following information:

FIELD	PRINT POSITIONS	FORMAT
Customer	37–50	
Total charge	63–69	$xxx.xx

Program Planning

Since the department number (the argument) varies by increments of one, we may use the method of direct table look-up. By loading the table into storage as part of the data, it will be possible to make quick changes if the discount rates change. In this situation it will be necessary to store only the function, since position in storage is indicative of the argument. For convenience, as we will see later, the table will be punched into columns 30–47 of the card, and the table will be moved to storage from the READ area. An arbitrary choice for storing the table is 999, as shown below:

$$959385927877917880$$

9
8
3
9
9
3
9
9
9

The cost factor for department 1 is in location 983, department 2 in 985, and so on, and they may be addressed accordingly. The over-all flow of program logic is shown in the flowchart of Figure 12–7. Each purchase card is processed by applying the appropriate cost factor from the table; if a new card is a customer record card, the previous result is edited and printed.

The Program

A program that will accomplish the above is shown in Figure 12–8. Word marks for three input fields (the customer name, the item cost, and the department number) are set at the beginning of the program. These fields are given mnemonic symbols during assembly by using DS instructions at the end of the program. The third SW also provides the defining word mark when the table is moved to 999 in instruction 01 060 of Figure 12–8.

Whenever a purchase card is read, twice the department number is added to the A operand of instruction 01 170. For instance, if a purchase card from department 6 is read, 6 + 6 will be added to 981, giving 993. Following this, the field at 993 is moved to FACTOR, a two-position field, which will then contain 77, the cost factor for department 6. The product is obtained by using the MULTIPLY subroutine, and totals are automatically accumulated in the product area.

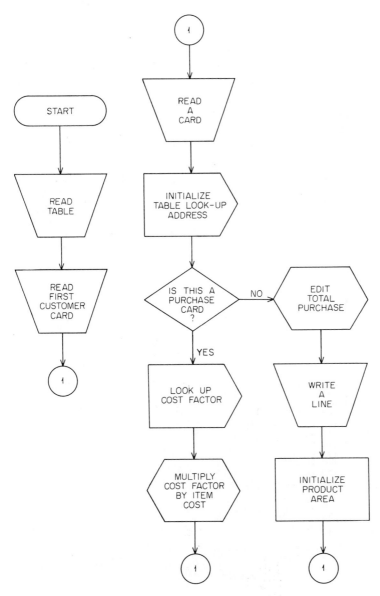

Figure 12–7. Flowchart for Example 12–1

```
01 010      *                    TABLE LOOK-UP (DIRECT)
01 020      *
01 030  START   SW   0006            0021
01 040          SW   0030
01 050          R                                    READ TABLE
01 060          MCW  0047            0999             STORE AT 999
01 070          R                                    READ FIRST CUST
01 080  MOVE1   MCW  CUST            0250             CARD AND STORE
01 090  READ    R                                    READ A NEW CARD,
01 100          C    CUSTNO          BLANKS           IF CUST THEN
01 110          B    TOTALS                         / BRANCH TO TOTAL
01 120          MCW  INITAL          MOVE2 +   3      IF NOT,INITIALIZ
01 130          SW   MOVE2 +  1                       TABLE ADDRESS
01 140          A    CODE            MOVE2 +   3      THEN CALCULATE
01 150          A    CODE            MOVE2 +   3      CORRECT TABLE
01 160          CW   MOVE2 +  1                       ENTRY ADDRESS
01 170  MOVE2   MCW  0981            FACTOR
01 180      *
01 190      *                    MULTIPLY ROUTINE (OPEN ROUTINE)
01 200          MCW  COST            MULTD            TAKE PRODUCT
02 010          MCW  FACTOR          MULTR            OF COST
02 020          MCW  M16             M3    +   3      FACTOR
02 030          MCW  M17             M6    +   6      AND ITEM
02 040  M3      MCW  MULTR -   7 M19       -   1      COST
02 050  M4      C    M19   -   1 M18       -   1      USING THE
02 060          B    M9                           U  MULTIPLY
02 070  M6      A    MULTD           PROD  -   7      SUBROUTINE
02 080          S    M18             M19              AS AN OPEN
02 090          B    M4                               SUBROUTINE
02 100  M9      SW   M3    +   1 M6        +   4      TO SHOW
02 110          A    M18   -   1 M3        +   3      THAT IT CAN
02 120          A    M18   -   1 M6        +   6      BE DONE.
02 130          CW   M3    +   1 M6        +   4  TOTALS ARE
02 140          C    M3    +   3 M16       -   2      SUMMED IN
02 150          B    M3                            /  PRODUCT AREA
02 160          B    READ
02 170      *
02 180      *                    PROCESS TOTALS
02 190  TOTALS  A    FIVE            PROD  -   1  ALL CARDS
02 200          MCW  PROD  -   2 EDIN              PROCESSED FOR
03 010          MCW  RETRN2-   1 EDITX +   3       THIS CUSTOMER
03 020          B    EDIT                          SO HALF ADJ,
03 030          B    RETRN2                        EDIT RESULTS,
03 040  RETRN2  MCW  EDOUT           0269          INITIALIZE
03 050          W                                  AND BRANCH
03 060          S    EDIN            EDIN          BACK TO READ
03 070          S    PROD            PROD          ANOTHER CARD
03 080          B    MOVE1
03 090 02 FACTOR DCW  *
03 100 03 INITAL DCW  *              981
03 110 01 FIVE   DCW  *              5
03 120 04 BLANKS DCW  *
03 130 04 CUSTNO DS   0005
03 140 00 CUST   DS   0019
03 150 00 COST   DS   0024
03 160 00 CODE   DS   0030
03 170 03 M16    DCW  *              092
03 180 02 M17    DCW  *              89
03 190 02 M18    DCW  0198           10
03 200 02 M19    DCW  0200           00
04 010 09 MULTD  DCW  0089           000000000
04 020 09 MULTR  DCW  0099           000000000
04 030 16 PROD   DCW  0196           0000000000000000
04 040     *                    EDIT SUBROUTINE FOLLOWS ON
04 050     *                      CARDS 04 060 THROUGH 05 080
05 090             END START
```

Figure 12-8. Source Program for Example 12-1

Whenever another customer card is encountered, the program branches to instruction 02 190 and the total charges are edited by using the EDIT subroutine (described in Appendix III). In this program the MULTIPLY subroutine is used as an open routine, which is always possible, especially if the subroutine is only used once in the program. However, it is considered best practice to use these subroutines as packages, hence as closed routines. The multiplication is done with an open subroutine only as an illustration.

Figure 12–9 is the storage dump after the table card has been placed in storage. Note the table in positions 982–999.

```
I-REG   OP-REG
 353      1
```

000 - 049		1			1		95938	59278	77917	880
							1			
050 - 099							00000	00000	00000	00000
							1		1	
100 - 149										
150 - 199							00000	00000	00000	00100
							1			1 1
200 - 249	0									
250 - 299										
300 - 349							,00602	1	,0301	M0479
								1	1 1	
350 - 399	991M0	19250	1C005	582B5	18/M5	77405	,403A	03040	5A030	405)4
	11		11	1	1		1 1	1	1	1
400 - 449	03M98	1574M	02408	9M574	099M5	85440	M5874	62M09	2199C	19919
	1	1	1	1	1		1 1	1	1	
450 - 499	7B474	UA089	189S1	98200	B444,	43846	0A197	440A1	97462	)4384
	1	1	1	1	1		1 1	1	1	1
500 - 549	60C44	0583B	437/B	360A5	78195	M1940	89M54	6706B	588B5	47M19
	1	1	1	1	1		1	1	1	1
550 - 599	12692	S0890	89S19	6196B	353	9815	09289	M7106	47M7106	
	11		1	1	1	1 11	1 1	1		
600 - 649	62M08	9191M	71418	9M087	188M7	13185	M0841	84M71	2181C	18270
	1	1	1	1	1 1	1	1	1	1	
650 - 699	7B703	TM712	182,6	45660	A7086	47A70	8662)	64566	0C647	709B6
	1	1	1	1	1	1	1	1	1	
700 - 749	44/B0	00018	2 $,.							
	1	1 1	1							
750 - 799										
800 - 849										
850 - 899										
900 - 949										
950 - 999							95938	59278	77917	880

Figure 12–9. Storage Dump for Example 12–1

EXAMPLE 12-2

Random Table Look-up. An input deck consists of the same customer record and purchase cards used in Example 12–1.

FIELD	CARD COLUMN	FORMAT
Record Card		
Customer number	2–5	
Customer	6–19	
Purchase Card		
Blank	1–5	
Item	6–15	
Item cost	21–24	xx∧xx

In this case, the customer receives a discount dependent upon the total purchase amount, according to Table 12–3.

Table 12–3
TOTAL-PURCHASE DISCOUNTS

TOTAL COST	COST FACTOR
0.00–$49.99	1.00
$50.00–$99.99	0.95
100.00–499.99	0.92
500.00–599.99	0.90
600.00–799.99	0.88
800.00 and up	0.85

We wish to process the cards and compute the total charges for each customer by applying the appropriate discount according to Table 12–3. The output should consist of a listing with the following information:

FIELD	PRINT POSITIONS	FORMAT
Customer	37–50	
Total charge	63–69	$xxx.xx

Program Planning

In this problem, it will be necessary to total all purchases for a given customer and determine the appropriate discount rate. Other than that, the program logic illustrated by Figure 12–10 is very similar to that of the previous example. For the convenience of the particular program, the table will be entered in the following form:

COST FACTOR	COST
100	04999
095	09999
092	49999
090	59999
088	79999
085	99999

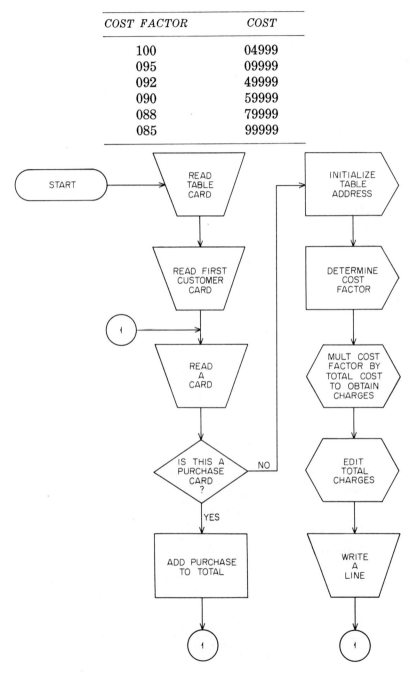

Figure 12–10. Flowchart for Example 12–2

However, unlike Example 12–1, the storage positions allocated for the table are determined by the computer using the 32-character DCW in conjunction with a 16-character DC pseudo instruction, which is labeled TABLE (Figure 12–11). Since the table address is not known prior to assembly, it is necessary to use the DSA pseudo instruction (labeled INITAL) to store the address of the first table value for later use in initializing. In the machine-language version of the program, shown in Figure 12–12, the table has been assigned storage positions 528–575,

```
01 010     *                 TABLE LOOK-UP (SEARCH)
01 020     *
01 030     START   SW   0006          0021
01 040             R                            READ AND
01 050             MCW  0068          TABLE       STORE TABLE
01 060             R                            READ AND STORE
01 070     MOVENO  MCW  CUST          0250      FIRST CARD
01 080     READ    R                            READ AND IF
01 090             C    CUSTNO        BLANKS    PURCHASE CARD
01 100             B    MOVE                  / ADD TO TOTALS
01 110             A    COST          MULTD     THEN READ NEW
01 120             B    READ                     CARD
01 130     MOVE    MCW  INITAL        LOOK  + 3
01 140     LOOK    MCW  TABLE - 40    WORK      IF FINISHED
01 150             SW   MULTD -  4              ACCESS FIRST
01 160             C    WORK          MULTD     ARG AND FUNCTON
01 170             B    MODIFY                 UIF INCORRECT
01 180             B    CLEAR                   VALUE FROM TABL
01 190     MODIFY  SW   LOOK  +  1             INCREMENT  TO
01 200             A    EIGHT         LOOK  + 3 THE NEXT TABLE
02 010             CW   LOOK  +  1             VALUE THEN
02 020             B    LOOK                   BRANCH TO MOVE
02 030     *
02 040     *                 MULTIPLY TOTAL BY CUST FACTOR
02 050     CLEAR   CW   MULTD -  4             IF CORRECT VALUE
02 060             MCW  WORK   -  5 MULTR      FROM TABLE THEN
02 070             MCW  RETRN1-  1 MULTX + 3     MULTIPLY
02 080             B    MULT                   TOTAL COST BY
02 090             B    RETRN1                 CUST FACTUR AND
02 100     RETRN1  A    FIVE          PROD  - 1 HALF ADJ TOTAL
02 110             MCW  PROD   -  2 EDIN        CHARGES
02 120             MCW  RETRN2-  1 EDITX + 3 EDIT
02 130             B    EDIT                    RESULTS
02 140             B    RETRN2                 THEN PRINT
02 150     RETRN2  MCW  EDOUT         0269      THEM
02 160             W                            OUT
02 170             S    MULTD         MULTD
02 180             S    PROD          PROD
02 190             B    MOVENO
02 200  08 WORK    DCW  *
03 010  04 BLANKS  DCW  *
03 020  01 EIGHT   DCW  *             8
03 030  01 FIVE    DCW  *             5
03 040  32         DCW  *
03 050  16 TABLE   DC   *
03 060  03 INITAL  DSA  *             TABLE - 40
03 070  00 COST    DS   0024
03 080  00 CUST    DS   0019
03 090  00 CUSTNO  DS   0005
03 100     *           EDIT SUBROUTINE FOLLOWS ON
03 110     *              CARDS 03 120 THROUGH 04 140
04 150     *           MULTIPLY SUBROUTINE FOLLOWS ON
04 160     *              CARDS 04 170 THROUGH 05 180
05 190             END  START
```

Figure 12–11. Source Program for Example 12–2

and the address of the first function and argument, 535, immediately follows it.

For a more complete description of the program the student is referred to the comments in Figure 12–11.

```
I-REG   OP-REG
 349      1

000 - 049                               1000 4999 095099 990924 999909059
               1              1
050 - 099  999088 799990859 9999             000000000 000000000
                                                   1         1
100 - 149

150 - 199                                    000000000 000000000100
                                                   1              1 1
200 - 249  0

250 - 299

300 - 349                                    ,006021 1M068 5751M
                                                  1      11     11
350 - 399  01925 01C00 5525B 380/A 02408 9B356 M5783 90M53 5521, 085C5
            11      1     1         1     1     1     1       1     1
400 - 449  21089 8414U B433, 388A5 26390 )388B 387)0 85M51 6099M 45880
            1      1    1     1           1    1     1     1
450 - 499  0B706 B459A 52719 5M194 089M4 8769 7B579 B488M1 91269 2S089
            1      1    1     1     1     1    1      1            11
500 - 549  089S1 96196 B349              8510 0049 99 9095 0 9999 0 92499
            1      1    1          1      111
550 - 599  99090 5 9999 0887 9 99908 59999 9535M 70163 8M701 653M0 89191
                  1                        1 1       1      1
600 - 649  M7051 89M08 7188M 70418 5M084 184M7 03181 C1826 98B69 4TM70
            1 1    1     1     1     1     1     1     1     1
650 - 699  3182, 63665 1A699 638A6 99653 )636 65 1C638 7 00B 635/B 00001
            1      1     1     1     1     1       1      1     1     1
700 - 749  82 $, .M803 723M8 05745 M0921 99C1 99197B 757UA 08918 9S198
            1 1   1     1     1     1     1     1      1     1
750 - 799  200B7 27,72 1743A 19772 3A197 745) 721743 C7238 01B72 0/B00
            1      1     1     1     1     1          1     1     1
800 - 849  009289
            1 1
850 - 899

900 - 949

950 - 999
```

Figure 12–12. Storage Dump for Example 12–2

INDEX REGISTERS

In all of the programs examined in this chapter, many of the instructions serve only to modify addresses. It is notable that none of these instructions are directly involved in processing data. In order to facilitate variable addressing, many machines, including the IBM 1401, use methods for indexing addresses.

In the 1401 system, whenever an instruction is to be executed, the A and B addresses are moved respectively to the A and B address registers.

These registers are in the control section of the computer, and it is from them that the instructions are executed. Thus, whenever we wish to increment an address, it is done in the registers, leaving the program in storage unchanged. This is accomplished by using index registers, which can be set at the value by which addresses are to be incremented. As the program progresses it is necessary to modify only the contents of a single index register, which may be used by several instructions, and thus avoid operating on each individual instruction.

Such features do not provide additional capabilities which are beyond those of the 141 system; the primary advantage is convenience.

■ CHAPTER SUMMARY

Within storage a *field* is a group of characters with a defining word mark at the high-order position. If that field is to be operated upon as an instruction, it is referred to by the address of its high-order position; if it is to be used as data, it is referred to by the address of its low-order position. There is no distinction between data and instructions other than the manner in which they are used.

If arithmetic is to be performed on the A or B address of an instruction, a word mark must be set to avoid including the operation code in the process. Otherwise the code will be affected and may become an invalid operation code.

The method of direct table look-up is normally used when values for the argument of the table change at a constant rate.

Sequential searching methods of table look-up are used when no simple relationships among values of the argument exist.

■ EXERCISES

12.1 Suppress leading zeros on the two numbers 000623456 and 000000000, following the step-by-step procedure of the SUPPRESS ZERO subroutine. Make a table to keep check on all counters and addresses as you proceed.

12.2 Multiply the two numbers 231 and 42, following the step-by-step procedure of the MULTIPLY subroutine.

12.3 The BRANCH IF CHARACTER EQUAL instruction can often be used to replace a COMPARE and a CONDITIONAL BRANCH. Can one be readily used in either of the subroutines for simplification? What changes would be necessary?

12.4 A deck of cards contains experimental data for statistical studies, with the following card format:

FIELD	CARD COLUMNS
Card number	1–3
Data	11–15

The last card contains no data, only 999 in columns 1–3, and is used to indicate the end of the deck. Write a program that will read these cards in groups of 16 and punch an output card with the following format:

FIELD	CARD COLUMNS
Data	1–5
Data	6–10
.	.
.	.
.	.
Data	76–80

Since the number of cards in the deck may *not* be a multiple of 16, special provisions must be made for the last card punched.

12.5 In Figure 12–11, why is the symbolic address defined by the DSA specified as TABLE–40?

12.6 A deck of cards contains, in addition to other information, the month of the year (for instance, MARCH) beginning in column 1. Write a program that will punch a new deck with the same information as the old one except that columns 10 and 11 will contain the number of days in the month.

12.7 A deck of student master cards contains a code in columns 47–48 indicating high school of graduation. In order to reflect a change in the coding system, we wish to punch a new deck with the new high school code but with all other information unchanged. The new and old codes are

OLD CODE	01 02 03 04 05 06 09 11 12 13 14 15 16 17 18 21 25 26 27 28 00
NEW CODE	02 04 06 08 10 12 14 16 18 20 22 24 26 28 30 32 34 36 38 40 42

In the process, check file numbers (columns 2–6) for ascending sequence. Use the direct table look-up method.

12.8 Write a program for Exercise 12.7 treating the table as a random one and use searching techniques. Which method will be faster?

Chapter Thirteen

PROBLEMS AND SOLUTIONS

Preceding chapters have been devoted to introducing basic elements of the 141 system, and simple programs were used to illustrate each of the concepts. We will now direct our endeavor to the study of eight typical problems, which include mathematics, science, and business applications.

1. *Grade-point Average.* Student records are updated by processing current semester records and combining them with cumulative records. Cumulative and current grade-point averages are calculated.

2. *Gross to Net.* This is a typical payroll calculation in which withholding tax and FICA are deducted from gross pay to obtain net pay. Withholding and FICA are updated to obtain yearly totals. Being a typical business problem, it is also used in Chapter 16 to demonstrate the Cobol language.

3. *Money and Interest.* The amortization of a loan is programmed. The lengthy output consists of the month, payment, principal, interest, and unpaid balance. Special means are used to determine the final payment.

4. *Sorting.* The problem of sorting 8 ten-digit fields on a card is programmed by three different methods, each more sophisticated than the previous one.

5. *Statistical Computations.* The analysis of information by statistical means is common to all disciplines. This problem concerns

calculation of mean and variance from a set of data. This problem is also programmed in Chapter 16 to illustrate Fortran techniques.

6. *Prime Numbers.* A classical subject in mathematics is the prime number. A program is written to find prime numbers.

7. *Square Root.* Although no subroutine for computing square root is included in the text, the interesting technique for obtaining square root by Newton's method of successive approximations is programmed.

8. *Perfect Gas Law.* Almost all students in engineering and science study the perfect gas law. This program allows the computation of volumes for up to 10 temperatures and 10 pressures. Later in Chapter 16, the perfect gas law is used to illustrate Fortran.

The first four problems are business-oriented, and are in approximate order of difficulty. The fifth problem represents a transition; that is, it is commonly used in both business and science applications. Problems six and seven are mathematical in nature, and are also in order of difficulty. The eighth is a science problem.

Except in a few instances, all of the programs use only the elementary instructions, and, undoubtedly, many improvements could be made in them. In fact, no attempt was made to write the most sophisticated program in any case. It is hoped that the student will make improvements where possible. In all programs, wide use is made of mnemonics.

GRADE-POINT AVERAGES

The Problem

Of considerable interest to most students are grades and grade-point averages. A common method of grading uses grades *A* through *F*, with numerical equivalents as shown in Table 13–1.

Table 13–1
LETTER-GRADE NUMERICAL EQUIVALENTS

GRADE	POINTS	DESCRIPTION
A	4	Excellent
B	3	Good
C	2	Average
D	1	Poor
F	0	Failing
W		Withdrawal

Total points earned by a student are normally computed by summing the points earned for each course, as done in the following example. Assume that a student receives the following grades.

COURSE	CREDIT	GRADE
History	3 units	C
English	3 units	B
Data processing	4 units	A
Math	4 units	C
Typing	2 units	W

Using for each course the formula

$$\text{Total Points} = (\text{Units}) \times (\text{Points})$$

shows that the student would have earned a total of 39 points from 14 units of course work. His grade-point average would be 39 divided by 14, or 2.79, for that semester. Neither the total units nor total points are affected by the typing course because the student withdrew.

Generally, computations such as these are part of the periodic updating of student records undertaken at the completion of each school term. Processing of these records not only consists of determining both current and cumulative grade averages but also of compiling scholarship and deficiency lists, assembling grade reports, updating permanent records, and other functions which the institution may require. As a programming example we shall consider that portion of the over-all operation in which grade-point averages are computed and a master card is updated.

Each student has a master card and several scholarship cards, one for each course in which he is enrolled. The complete deck consists of all the cards, merged so that the master for a given student is followed by his scholarship cards. Table 13–2 summarizes the card format.

Program Planning

Whenever a card is read, it is necessary to check the file number against that of the previous card. If it is the same as the previous file number, it is a scholarship card; if not, it is a master card for a new student.

In processing each scholarship card, the number of units is added to the total units for the term, and the points are totaled by multiplying the units by 4 if the grade is A, 3 if B, and so on. If a grade of W

Table 13–2
CARD FORMAT

FIELD	*CARD* *COLUMN*	*FORMAT*
INPUT		
Master Card		
File number	1–5	
Name	6–26	
Not used in this problem	27–60	
Not used for input	61–69	
Cumulative units	70–73	xxx∧x
Cumulative grade points	74–77	xxx∧x
Cumulative grade-point average	78–80	x∧xx
Scholarship Card		
File number	1–5	
Name	6–26	
Units	27–28	x∧x
Not used in this program	29–43	
Grade	44	
Not used in this program	45–80	
OUTPUT		
Same as input master card	1–60	
Current units	61–63	xx∧x
Current grade points	64–66	xx∧x
Current grade-point average	67–69	x∧xx
Cumulative units	70–73	xxx∧x
Cumulative grade point	74–77	xxx∧x
Cumulative grade-point average	78–80	x∧xx

is found, the card is ignored. When all the scholarship cards have been processed for a given student, the cumulative computations are completed. A program flowchart is shown in Figure 13–1.

The updating is done by computing total units, total points, and grade-point average (GPA) for the current term from the information on the scholarship cards, and determining cumulative units, cumulative points, and grade-point average by using the master. All of this information is punched in a new updated master card, which is used as an input card at the completion of the next term.

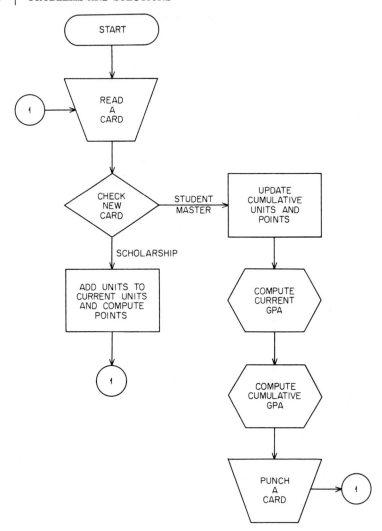

Figure 13–1. Program Flowchart for Grade-point Averaging

The Program

In the program shown in Figure 13–2, extensive use has been made of mnemonics. Table 13–3 describes the meaning of each symbol used in addressing the various fields.

Since the program is reasonably well described by the flowchart and by the comments in the listing, we need not proceed with a step-by-step discussion. On the other hand, we should note the use of the eight-

position BRANCH instruction (that is, BRANCH IF CHARACTER EQUAL).
Although the practice in this text is to use only the most fundamental
instructions, here is an ideal application for this instruction. Instruction
01 140 will cause a branch to AGRADE if the student receives an *A* in

```
01 010     *              GRADE POINT AVERAGES
01 020     *
01 030     START  SW   0001
01 040            R                        READ FIRST
01 050     MOVE   MCW  0060      0160       MASTER CARD AND
01 060            MCW  ZERO      CURUN      MOVE TO OUTPUT
01 070            MCW  ZERO      CURPTS     THEN INITIALIZE
01 080            MCW  0073      CUMUN
01 090            MCW  0077      CUMPTS
01 100     READ   R                        READ A CARD AND
01 110            SW   UNITS -  1
01 120            C    0105      0005       CHECK FOR NEW
01 130            B    AVRAGE               / FILE NO. IF NEW
01 140            B    AGRADE    GRADE      A BRANCH TO OUTP
01 150            B    BGRADE    GRADE      BOTHERWISE CHECK
01 160            B    CGRADE    GRADE      C GRADE FOR A,B,
01 170            B    DGRADE    GRADE      D C,D,F OR W
01 180            B    TOTAL     GRADE      F
01 190            B    READ      GRADE      WIF W THEN READ
01 200            H    READ                 ERROR HALT
02 010     AGRADE A    UNITS     CURPTS     COMPUTE
02 020     BGRADE A    UNITS     CURPTS     PROPER NUMBER
02 030     CGRADE A    UNITS     CURPTS     OF GRADE POINTS
02 040     DGRADE A    UNITS     CURPTS
02 050     TOTAL  A    UNITS     CURUN      TOTAL THE UNITS
02 060            CW   UNITS -  1
02 070            B    READ                 PROCESS NEW CARD
02 080     *
02 090     *              COMPUTE AVERAGES FOR EACH STUDENT
02 100     AVRAGE MCW  ZERO      DIVD
02 110            MCW  ZERO      DIVR       INITIALIZE WORK
02 120            MCW  ZERO      QUOT       AREAS THEN
02 130            MCW  CURPTS    DIVD  - 2  DIVIDE TOTAL
02 140            MCW  CURUN     DIVR       POINTS BY TOTAL
02 150            MCW  RETRN1-  1 DIVX  + 3 UNITS FOR
02 160            B    DIV                  CURRENT GPA
02 170            B    RETRN1
02 180     RETRN1 MCW  QUOT      CURGPA     MOVE CUR GPA TO
02 190            A    CURUN     CUMUN      OUTP.ADD CUR
02 200            A    CURPTS    CUMPTS     UNITS AND PTS
03 010            MCW  ZERO      QUOT       TO CUM UNITS
03 020            MCW  ZERO      DIVD       AND PTS THEN
03 030            MCW  CUMPTS    DIVD  - 2  DIVIDE PTS BY
03 040            MCW  CUMUN     DIVR       UNITS FOR
03 050            MCW  RETRN2-  1 DIVX  + 3 CUMULATIVE
03 060            B    DIV                  GPA
03 070            B    RETRN2
03 080     RETRN2 MCW  QUOT      CUMGPA     MOVE CUM GPA TO
03 090            P                         OUTP THEN RETRN
03 100            B    MOVE                 FOR MASTER CARD
03 110  04 ZERO   DCW  *         0000
03 120  03 CURUN  DCW  0163
03 130  03 CURPTS DCW  0166
03 140  03 CURGPA DCW  0169
03 150  04 CUMUN  DCW  0173
03 160  04 CUMPTS DCW  0177
03 170  03 CUMGPA DCW  0180
03 180  00 GRADE  DS   0044
03 190  00 UNITS  DS   0028
03 200     *              DIVIDE SUBROUTINE FOLLOWS ON
04 010     *                  CARDS 04 020 THROUGH 05 100
05 110            END START
```

Figure 13–2. Source Program for Grade-point Averaging

Table 13–3

MNEMONIC ADDRESS SYMBOLS

SYMBOL	MEANING
CUMGPA	Cumulative grade-point average
CUMPTS	Cumulative grade points
CUMUN	Cumulative units
CURGPA	Current grade-point average
CURPTS	Current grade points
CURUN	Current units
GRADE	Course grade from scholarship cards
UNITS	Course units from scholarship cards

his course, and the units will be added to CURPTS four times to give the points earned for that course. If the grade is a B, the branch is to BGRADE, thus performing the addition only three times, and so on. If the grade is F, no points, only units, are added in, and if a W is detected, another card is read. If none of these is punched in the card, the computer stops at an error HALT.

GROSS TO NET

Most of us have received a payroll check for services performed and have noted, perhaps with considerable distress, the difference between gross pay and net pay. This difference is usually due to withholding tax, social security tax (FICA), and other deductions such as insurance, charity contributions, and so on.

From a computational point of view the withholding tax and FICA are the most interesting, since they include variable factors; other deductions are usually constant values, explicitly stated. As a result, we will consider a gross-to-net program in which the only deductions are for withholding tax and FICA.

The Problem

As part of a biweekly payroll operation, the following information is furnished as input for a computation:

Employee number
Employee name
Number of exemptions
Year-to-date gross pay
Year-to-date FICA deductions
Year-to-date withholding tax deductions
Gross pay for pay period

It is required that withholding tax, FICA, and net pay be computed and that year-to-date gross, FICA, and withholding tax be updated. The output must consist of all of the input items (except gross pay) plus net pay, FICA, and withholding tax.

In preparing a program that is part of a larger operation, considerable attention is given to input/output card format, since it is always desirable to organize the most efficient over-all system. With this in mind, the format specified in Table 13–4 will be used.

Table 13–4
CARD FORMAT

FIELD	CARD COLUMN	FORMAT
INPUT		
Employee number	1–6	
Name	7–35	
Exemptions	36	
YTD gross pay	37–43	xxxxx∧xx
YTD FICA	44–48	xxx∧xx
YTD withholding tax	49–55	xxxxx∧xx
Not used	56–74	
Gross pay	75–80	xxxx∧xx
OUTPUT		
Employee number	1–6	
Name	7–35	
Exemptions	36	
YTD gross pay (updated)	37–43	xxxxx∧xx
YTD FICA (updated)	44–48	xxx∧xx
YTD withholding tax (updated)	49–55	xxxxx∧xx
Net pay	56–61	xxxx∧xx
FICA	62–65	xx∧xx
Withholding tax	66–71	xxxx∧xx
Not used	72–74	
Blank	75–80	

The information punched in columns 56–71 of the output card can be used to prepare the employees check and stub. At the end of the next pay period, the output card can be used as the input card by punching the new gross pay in columns 75–80. This is convenient because columns 1–36 contain identifying information, columns 37–55 contain necessary year-to-date totals to be used in further updating, and columns 56–71, which contain information from the previous pay period, are not used in the input card.

Computations

The amount of withholding tax is determined from gross pay by the formula

Withholding Tax = 0.14 [Gross Pay − 13.00 × (Exemptions)]

For instance, a person with three exemptions and gross pay of 250 dollars would have the following amount deducted for withholding tax:

$$WT = 0.14 [250.00 − 13.00 × (3)]$$
$$WT = 0.14 [250.00 − 39.00]$$
$$WT = 29.54$$

The amount deducted for FICA is $3\frac{5}{8}$ percent of the gross pay until a yearly total of 174 dollars ($3\frac{5}{8}$ percent of 4800 dollars) has been reached, since this is the maximum yearly amount any one individual must pay. The resulting net pay will be determined by subtracting from gross pay, the withholding tax and the FICA, but only until the yearly FICA deduction is 174 dollars.

The Program

The program flowchart shown in Figure 13–3 reflects the relatively simple logic of the program. The first computations involve determining exempted income from the number of exemptions listed in card column 36 of the input card. If the exempted income exceeds the gross income, there is nothing to be taxed, so the program proceeds to the FICA computation. If the accumulated FICA amount is 174 dollars, no computation is made, and the program immediately branches to the net pay determination and subsequently to output.

This flowchart is deceptively simple in a sense because of the method used to compute FICA. For instance, if a card showed a year-to-date FICA amount of 172 dollars, a deduction would be made. But if $3\frac{5}{8}$

percent of the current gross were greater than 2 dollars, the 174 dollars would be exceeded. As a result, special provisions are made in the program for calculating this final amount (see lines 03 070–03 110 of Figure 13–4).

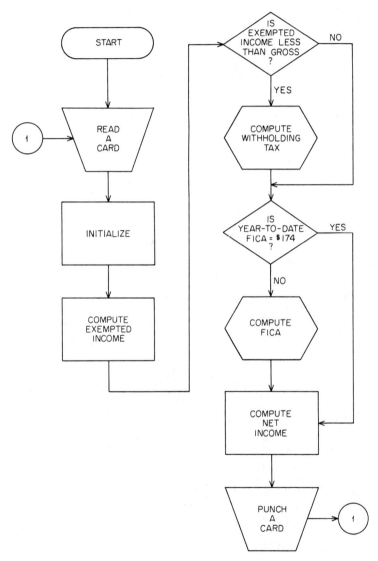

Figure 13–3. Program Flowchart for Payroll Deduction

```
01 010    *                GROSS TO NET
01 020    *
01 030    SET    SW  0001         0075
01 040    READ   R
01 050           MCW 0036         0136          SET UP OUTPUT
01 060           MCW 0043         YTDGRO        FIELDS
01 070           MCW 0048         YTDFIC        FOR FUTURE
01 080           MCW 0055         YTDWTX        CALCULATIONS
01 090           MCW GROSS        NETPAY
01 100           A   GROSS        YTDGRO
01 110           MCW ZEROES       COUNTR        INITIALIZE
01 120           MCW ZEROES       MULTR         WORK
01 130           MCW ZEROES       FICA          AREAS
01 140           MCW ZEROES       WITHTX        REQUIRING
01 150           S   PROD         PROD          INITIALIZATION
01 160           MCW GROSS        MULTD
01 170           C   0036         ONE           IF ANY EXEMPTION
01 180           B   COMPUT                     U THEN COMPUTE
01 190    ADD    A   THTEEN       EXEMP         EXEMPTED INCOME
01 200           A   ONE          COUNTR        BY MULTIPLYING
02 010           C   0036         COUNTR        TOTAL NUMBER OF
02 020           B   ADD                        / EXEMPTION BY 13
02 030           C   EXEMP        GROSS         IF GROSS INCOME
02 040           B   FICACM                     T GREATER THAN
02 050           S   EXEMP        MULTD         EXEMPTION INCOM
02 060    COMPUT MCW PNT14        MULTR         THEN COMPUTE
02 070           MCW RETRN1-  1   MULTX +   3   WITHOLDING TAX
02 080           B   MULT                       BY MULTIPLYING
02 090           B   RETRN1                     TAXABLE INCOME
02 100    RETRN1 A   POINT5       PROD   -  1   BY 0.14 THEN
02 110           MCW PROD   -  2  WITHTX        HALF ADJUST,
02 120           A   WITHTX       YTDWTX        UPDATE AND SUBT
02 130           S   WITHTX       NETPAY        FROM GROSS
02 140    FICACM C   YTDFIC       MAXFIC        IF FICA TOTAL IS
02 150           B   PUNCH                      S 174 , NO DEDUCT
02 160           S   PROD         PROD          CLEAR PROD AREA
02 170           MCW FCRATE       MULTR         THEN COMPUTE
02 180           MCW GROSS        MULTD         FICA BY
02 190           MCW RETRN2-  1   MULTX +   3   MULTIPLYING
02 200           B   MULT                       GROSS BY 3.625
03 010           B   RETRN2                     THEN
03 020    RETRN2 A   POINT5       PROD   -  2   HALF ADJUST AND
03 030           MCW PROD   -  3  FICA          MOVE TO FICA
03 040           A   FICA         YTDFIC        UPDATE TOTAL
03 050           C   YTDFIC       MAXFIC        IF NEW UPDATED
03 060           B   NET                        U FICA EXCEEDS174
03 070           S   FICA         YTDFIC        COMPUTE PREVIOS
03 080           S   YTDFIC       MAXFIC        TOTAL AND STORE
03 090           MCW MAXFIC       FICA          THEN UPDATE TOT
03 100           A   FICA         YTDFIC        TO 174 AND
03 110           MCW YTDFIC       MAXFIC        READJUST MAX TO
03 120    NET    S   FICA         NETPAY        174.COMPUTE NET
03 130    PUNCH  P                              PAY THEN PUNCH
03 140           B   READ                       NEW EMPLOYEE
03 150 01 COUNTR DCW *        0
03 160 01 POINT5 DCW *        5
03 170 01 ONE    DCW *        1
03 180 02 PNT14  DCW *        14
03 190 04 THTEEN DCW *        1300
03 200 04 FCRATE DCW *        3625
04 010 05 MAXFIC DCW *        17400
04 020 06 EXEMP  DCW *        000000
04 030 06 ZEROES DCW *        000000
04 040    GROSS  DS  0080
04 050 06 NETPAY DCW 0161
04 060 04 FICA   DCW 0165
04 070 07 YTDGRO DCW 0143
04 080 05 YTDFIC DCW 0148
04 090 06 YTDWTX DCW 0155
04 100 06 WITHTX DCW 0171
04 110    *                MULTIPLY SUBROUTINE FOLLOWS ON
04 120    *                    CARDS 04 130 THROUGH 05 140
05 150           END SET
```

Figure 13-4. Source Program for Payroll Deduction

MONEY AND INTEREST

The Problem

The "pigeon-hole" analogy in Chapter 2 consisted of computing compound interest, that is, determining the amount of money earned with savings. The problem of computing the cost of borrowed money makes an interesting computer program, and is especially appropriate with the present-day emphasis on credit spending.

Although several different methods can be used for computing interest, we will consider a situation in which the interest is computed as a certain percentage (rate) per month of the unpaid balance. For example, if a person borrowed 1000 dollars at a rate of 2 percent per month, the interest for the first month would be 20 dollars. A 50-dollar monthly payment would reduce the principal by only 30 dollars; the following amortization table illustrates this:

MONTH	PAYMENT	PRINCIPAL	INTEREST	BALANCE
1	$50.00	$30.00	$20.00	$970.00
2	$50.00	$20.60	$19.40	$939.40
.	.	.	.	.
.	.	.	.	.
.	.	.	.	.

Note that the interest and principal payments and the new balance are obtained by multiplying the balance for the previous month by the rate to obtain interest, subtracting from the payment to obtain principal, and then subtracting the principal from the previous balance.

Computations

Before setting forth general program requirements, we shall translate the problem definition into a set of algebraic equations around which the program will be written. Table 13–5 summarizes symbols used in the equations and also mnemonics used in the program.

Table 13–5
SYMBOLS AND MNEMONICS USED TO CALCULATE INTEREST

ITEM	EQUATION SYMBOL	MNEMONIC
Payment	M	PAYMT
Portion of payment applied to interest	I	INT
Portion of payment applied to principal	P	PRINC
Rate	r	RATE
Balance	B	BAL

The equations are

$$I_2 = B_1 \cdot r$$
$$P_2 = M - I_2$$
$$B_2 = B_1 - P_2$$

The subscripts denote the month; for example, I_2 is the interest for the second month and B_1 is the balance from the first month. A general way of expressing this is

$$I_{i+1} = B_i \cdot r$$
$$P_{i+1} = M - I_{i+1}$$
$$B_{i+1} = B_i - P_{i+1}$$

where the i stands for any desired month, say the third, in which case $i + 1$ represents the fourth. Such subscripting is discussed more extensively in Chapter 16, in the section on Fortran programming.

The above equations can be expressed in another form, which, although not as obviously correct, are more useful for programming:

$$I_{i+1} = B_i \cdot r$$
$$P_{i+1} = M - I_{i+1}$$
$$B_{i+1} = (B_i + I_{i+1}) - M$$

With a little algebra, these two methods can be shown to be identical. In computing a complete amortization table, the only deviation from this procedure would be for computation of the last payment which, in all probability, would be other than an even 50 dollars. Let us now consider a program to perform the complete function.

Program Planning

Input/output format is summarized in Table 13–6. The task of planning the format for this problem is significant, so we shall consider it in detail.

The exact input card and output printing format were determined with the aid of the layout form shown in Figure 13–5. The first input card contains the heading AMORTIZATION TABLE; it is used by reading it in, moving it to the WRITE area, and writing it out; similarly, the second card contains more such information. The third card contains the input data with the format shown in Figure 13–5 (all leading zeros must be punched). The fourth card contains each of the output headings, which is consistent with the output format. As we shall see, this program occupies nearly all of the storage, so it is necessary to read the headings from input cards.

The computational portion of this program is clearly defined by the preceding equations and the flowchart of Figure 13–6.

Table 13–6
INPUT/OUTPUT FORMAT

FIELD	FORMAT
INPUT	
Amount of loan	xxxx∧xx
Monthly payment	xxx∧xx
Monthly interest rate	x∧xxx
OUTPUT	
Month	xx
Payment	$xxx.xx
Payment to principle	$xxx.xx
Payment to interest	$xxx.xx
Unpaid balance	$xxxx.xx

The Program

The first 25 instructions of the program shown in Figure 13–7 are required to obtain proper headings and format. Only a minor part of the processing is done in the main program, since most of the operations are performed by the MULTIPLY and EDIT subroutines. Another point worth mentioning is that this program, as did the gross-to-net problem, requires special means for computation of the final payment and terminating execution. Whenever the balance drops below the payment, the program branches to FINAL and sets up each field for the last computation. Before branching to MULTIPLY, the program switch is set so that the following HALT instruction will terminate operation. Further details of the program are contained in the COMMENTS area of the listing.

Program Limitations

Although the input format suggests a maximum loan amount of 9999.99 dollars, restrictions other than card format dictate a maximum value somewhat less. Since interest is added to the unpaid balance in the computations, the loan amount plus interest for the first time period cannot exceed 9999.99 dollars.

A Sample Run

The amortization table that we began computing at the beginning of this section has been completed by the computer and is shown here as Figure 13–8. The output includes input data that was used.

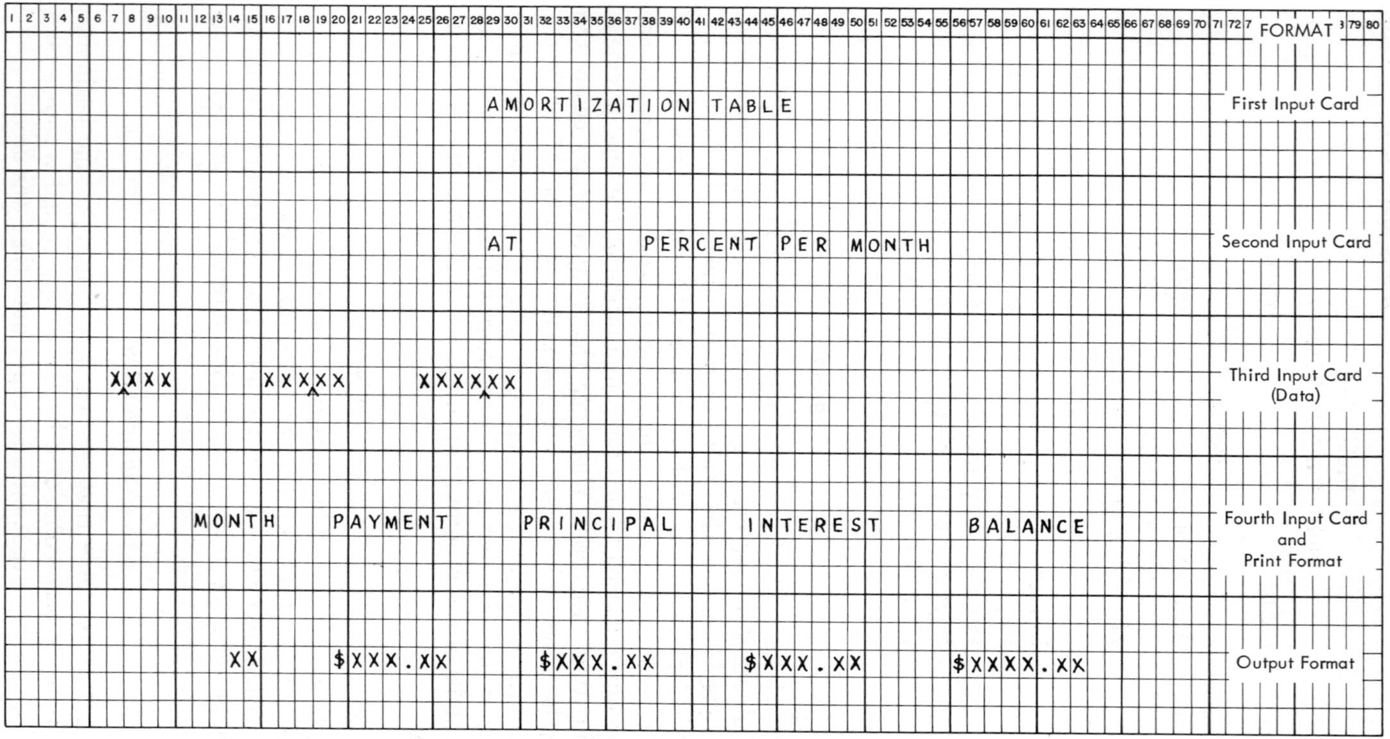

FORMAT

First Input Card

AMORTIZATION TABLE

Second Input Card

AT PERCENT PER MONTH

Third Input Card (Data)

XXXX XX XXXXXX XXXXX XXXXXX

Fourth Input Card and Print Format

MONTH PAYMENT PRINCIPAL INTEREST BALANCE

Output Format

XX $XXX.XX $XXXX.XX $XXX.XX $XXXX.XX

Figure 13–5. Layout Form for Loan Amortization

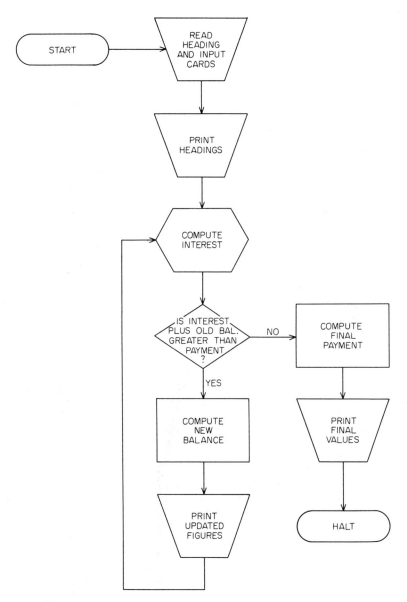

Figure 13-6. Program Flowchart for Loan Amortization

```
01 010    *                MONEY AND INTEREST (AMORTIZATION)
01 020    *
01 030    START   SW   0007
01 040            R                              READ   AND   WRITE
01 050            MCW  0080          0280         FIRST TITLE
01 060            W                               CARD
01 070            R                              READ SECOND
01 080            MCW  0080          0280          TITLE CARD
01 090            R                              READ DATA CARD
01 100            MCW  0030          BAL          STORE LOAN AMNT
01 110            MCW  0020          PAYMNT       STORE PAYMENT
01 120            MCW  RATE          MULTR        STORE RATE IN
01 130            MCW  RATE          0236         MULTR.MOVE AND
01 140            MCW  POINT         0233         EDIT RATE
01 150            MCW  0007          0232
01 160            MCW  BAL           EDIN         EDIT TOTAL LOAN
01 170            MCW  RETRN1-  1 EDITX +  3      AMOUNT WITH
01 180            B    EDIT                       SUBROUTINE
01 190            B    RETRN1                     THEN MOVE IT TO
01 200    RETRN1  MCW  EDOUT         0227         WRITE AND PRINT
02 010            W                               HEADING
02 020            CS   0280
02 030            W                               RETURN CARRIAGE
02 040            R                              READ AND WRITE
02 050            MCW  0080          0280         CARD GIVING
02 060            W                               FINAL HEADING
02 070            CS   0280
02 080            MCW  EDOUT         0263         PRINT AMOUNT OF
02 090            W                               LOAN AS FIRST
02 100            SW   0214                       BALANCE
02 110            MCW  PAYMNT        EDIN         EDITS PAYMENT
02 120            MCW  RETRN2-  1 EDITX +  3      FOR TABULATED
02 130            B    EDIT                       OUTPUT
02 140            B    RETRN2
02 150    RETRN2  MCW  EDOUT         0226
02 160    MOVE1   S    PROD          PROD         RATE IN MULTR SO
02 170            MCW  BAL           MULTD        MOVE BAL TO
02 180            MCW  RETRN3-  1 MULTX +  3      MULTD AND
02 190            B    MULT                       COMPUTE INT
02 200            B    RETRN3
03 010    RETRN3  MCW  PROD    -  5 INT           NEW BALANCE
03 020            A    INT           BAL          INCLUDES CURENT
03 030            C    BAL           PAYMNT       INT. IF PAYMENT
03 040            B    FINAL                      U GREATER, COMPUT
03 050            S    PAYMNT        BAL          FINAL PAYMENT.
03 060            MCW  PAYMNT        PRINC        OTHERWISE COMPUT
03 070            S    INT           PRINC        PRINC AND NEW
03 080    MOVE2   MCW  BAL           EDIN         BALANCE
03 090            MCW  RETRN4-  1 EDITX +  3
03 100            B    EDIT                       THEN
03 110            B    RETRN4
03 120    RETRN4  MCW  EDOUT         0263            EDIT
03 130            S    EDIN          EDIN
03 140            MCW  PRINC         EDIN            ALL THE
03 150            MCW  RETRN5-  1 EDITX +  3
03 160            B    EDIT                        QUANTITIES
03 170            B    RETRN5
03 180    RETRN5  MCW  EDOUT         0238            AND
03 190            MCW  INT           EDIN
03 200            MCW  RETRN6-  1 EDITX +  3         MOVE
04 010            B    EDIT
04 020            B    RETRN6                      TO OUTPUT
04 030    RETRN6  MCW  EDOUT         0250
04 040            A    ONE           0215         UPDATE MONTH
04 050            W                               AND WRITE
04 060    SWITCH  B    MOVE1                      SWICH IS CHANGED
04 070            H    START                      TO N LAST PAYMT
```

Figure 13–7. Source Program for Loan Amortization

```
04 080    *
04 090    *              COMPUTATION OF FINAL PAYMENT
04 100    FINAL  MCW BAL         EDIN        THE FINAL PAYMNT
04 110           MCW RETRN7-  1 EDITX +  3   WILL BE SAME
04 120           B   EDIT                    AS FINAL NON-
04 130           B   RETRN7                  ZERO BALANCE
04 140    RETRN7 MCW EDOUT        0226
04 150           S   INT          BAL
04 160           MCW BAL          PRINC
04 170           S   BAL          BAL
04 180           MCW OFF          SWITCH     RETURN TO MOVE2
04 190           B   MOVE2                   FOR FINAL OUTPT
04 200 06 BAL    DCW *       000000
05 010 05 INT    DCW *        00000
05 020 06 PAYMNT DCW *       000000
05 030 05 PRINC  DCW *        00000
05 040 01 ONE    DCW *            1
05 050 01 OFF    DCW *            N
05 060 01 POINT  DCW *            .
05 070    RATE   DS  0010
05 080    *               MULTIPLY SUBROUTINE FOLLOWS ON
05 090    *                 CARDS 05 100 THROUGH 06 110
06 120    *               EDIT SUBROUTINE FOLLOWS ON
06 130    *                 CARDS 06 140 THROUGH  07 160
07 170            END START
```

Figure 13–7. Continued

AMORTIZATION TABLE
$1,000.00 AT 2.000 PERCENT PER MONTH

MONTH	PAYMENT	PRINCIPAL	INTEREST	BALANCE
				$1,000.00
01	$50.00	$30.00	$20.00	$970.00
02	$50.00	$30.60	$19.40	$939.40
03	$50.00	$31.22	$18.78	$908.18
04	$50.00	$31.84	$18.16	$876.34
05	$50.00	$32.48	$17.52	$843.86
06	$50.00	$33.13	$16.87	$810.73
07	$50.00	$33.79	$16.21	$776.94
08	$50.00	$34.47	$15.53	$742.47
09	$50.00	$35.16	$14.84	$707.31
10	$50.00	$35.86	$14.14	$671.45
11	$50.00	$36.58	$13.42	$634.87
12	$50.00	$37.31	$12.69	$597.56
13	$50.00	$38.05	$11.95	$559.51
14	$50.00	$38.81	$11.19	$520.70
15	$50.00	$39.59	$10.41	$481.11
16	$50.00	$40.38	$9.62	$440.73
17	$50.00	$41.19	$8.81	$399.54
18	$50.00	$42.01	$7.99	$357.53
19	$50.00	$42.85	$7.15	$314.68
20	$50.00	$43.71	$6.29	$270.97
21	$50.00	$44.59	$5.41	$226.38
22	$50.00	$45.48	$4.52	$180.90
23	$50.00	$46.39	$3.61	$134.51
24	$50.00	$47.31	$2.69	$87.20
25	$50.00	$48.26	$1.74	$38.94
26	$39.71	$38.94	$0.77	$0.00

Figure 13–8. Sample Output for Loan Amortization

SORTING ROUTINES

The orderly arrangement of information is a common requirement in all fields of endeavor. For instance, the telephone directory consists of a list of names in ascending order (*A* through *Z*); in playing a game of cards we frequently order the cards according to suit and in ascending order within the suits. A common operation in data processing is to change a set of fields from a random ordering to some predetermined ordering, usually to an ascending sequence. This process is called *sorting*.

The Problem

For a demonstration of various sorting methods, we will consider a problem in which eight 10-digit data fields are stored on a card in columns 1–10, 11–20, and so on. The fields may consist of alphabetic, numeric, or mixed alphanumeric information. The problem is to process a deck of cards, rearrange the eight fields from each card into an ascending sequence, and punch a new card with this information.

Program Planning

Perhaps the most obvious method of sorting is to search the table to find the smallest field and place it in the first positions of the PUNCH area, then search the table for the second largest, and so on. Although this is a satisfactory method, it does not lend itself to some situations. A means somewhat more versatile consists of comparing and reordering adjacent pairs. For instance, let us arrange the following digits in ascending order using this method:

$$5 \ 4 \ 3 \ 2 \ 1$$

We first compare the 5 and the 4; since the former is larger we change the order, giving

$$4 \ 5 \ 3 \ 2 \ 1$$

Comparing the next pair, 5 and 3, we see that the 5 is once again larger, so we exchange these two, giving

$$4 \ 3 \ 5 \ 2 \ 1$$

Continuing in this manner, we would eventually obtain

$$4 \ 3 \ 2 \ 1 \ 5$$

Having completed this first pass, the largest of the digits would be last.

After four such passes have been completed the digits would be reordered as required:

5 4 3 2 1	original number
4 3 2 1 5	completion of first pass
3 2 1 4 5	completion of second pass
2 1 3 4 5	completion of third pass
1 2 3 4 5	completion of fourth pass

For the sake of simplicity, we compared each of the four pairs of digits during each of the passes. Note, however, that after the first pass we need not compare the last pair, 1 and 5, since 5 is already in its proper position. Similarly, after the third pass it is only necessary to compare the first two digits, not each of the four pairs. Although we would undoubtedly use this more efficient method if we were manually performing the sorting operation, special consideration of this factor is necessary in writing the computer program.

The above example required four passes to complete the sequencing. However, if the numbers are not completely out of sequence, the task is shorter. For instance, consider the following example:

        3 2 5 1 4   original number
        2 3 1 4 5   completion of first pass
        2 1 3 4 5   completion of second pass
        1 2 3 4 5   completion of third pass

In this case, it was not necessary to complete four passes since the desired sequencing was obtained in three. Once again this would probably be automatic if we were arranging the digits ourselves, but special provisions are required in the program in order to avoid the maximum number of passes when they are not necessary.

The flowchart of Figure 13–9 is sufficiently general so that it fits either of the three similar methods discussed, yet it consists of enough detail to adequately describe the program logic.

Three programs to perform this sorting function are given below. They are arranged in order, with the least efficient and sophisticated first and the most efficient and sophisticated last. In studying each of these examples, note that in all of them it is necessary to set aside a work area from which the fields may be compared, and saved during the process of interchanging adjacent fields.

EXAMPLE PROGRAM—SORT 1

The program shown in Figure 13–10 performs the function of sorting eight 10-digit fields into an ascending sequence. The method used is to move each pair to be compared to a 20-character working area (181–200). If they are already in the proper sequence they are left undisturbed. However, if they are out of sequence, they are interchanged. Appropriate addresses are then modified and the next pair is processed. This program will perform seven complete passes, and seven comparisons in each pass, regardless of the initial order of the fields. The sample output is shown in Figure 13–13; it is discussed after the descriptions of SORT 2 and SORT 3.

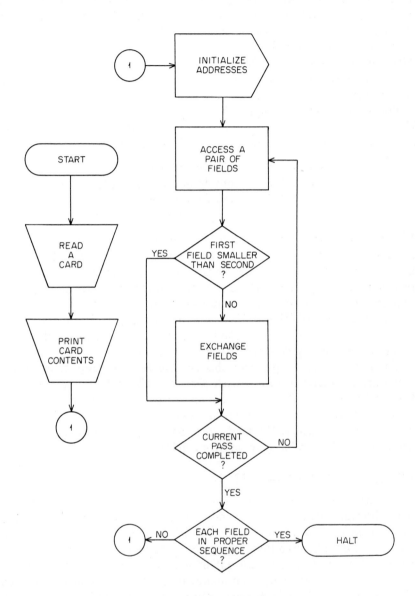

Figure 13–9. Program Flowchart for Sorting

EXAMPLE PROGRAM—SORT 2

The program for SORT 2, shown in Figure 13–11, is nearly identical to SORT 1 except that the address tested to break out of the inner loop is decremented after each pass. Thus succeeding passes require fewer compares, although seven passes will be required regardless of the initial ordering of the fields.

EXAMPLE PROGRAM—SORT 3

The most efficient method we will consider is programmed here as Figure 13–12. Again it is nearly identical to SORT 1 and SORT 2. However, at the beginning of each pass, a program switch is set to the OFF condition; that is, the instruction labeled SWITCH is given the operation code N. If, during the pass, at least one pair is out of sequence, the digits are interchanged and SWITCH is reset to the ON condition. If no sequencing errors are found, the instruction that resets SWITCH is not executed and the computer will halt, regardless of the preceding COMPARE instruction.

```
01 010      *             SORT 1
01 020      *
01 030   START  SW 0001       0181
01 040   READ   R
01 050          MCW 0080      0280
01 060          W
01 070          MCW ZERO      COUNT
01 080   LOOP1  MCW A220      LOOP2 +   3   INITALIZE ADRESS
01 090          MCW A220      REPLCE+006   FOR NEXT PASS
01 100   LOOP2  MCW 0220      0200         ACCESS A PAIR OF
01 110          C   0200      0190         FIELDS AND TEST
01 120          B   EXCHGE                 U
01 130          B   INSEQ                  IF THE FIRST OF
01 140   EXCHGE MCW 0200      HOLD         THE PAIR IS
01 150          MCW 0190      0200         LARGER,EXCHANGE
01 160          MCW HOLD      0190         THEM
01 170   REPLCE MCW 0200      0220
01 180   INSEQ  SW  LOOP2 +001 REPLCE+004  INCREMENT THE
01 190          C   LOOP2 +003 TEST        ADDRESSES FOR
01 200          A   TEN       LOOP2 +003   NEXT PAIR . IF
02 010          A   TEN       REPLCE+006   ALL PAIRS HAVE
02 020          CW  LOOP2 +001 REPLCE+004  NOT BEEN TESTED
02 030          B   LOOP2                  / THEN RETURN
02 040          W
02 050          A   ONE       COUNT        IF ALL TESTED,
02 060          C   COUNT     SEVEN        CHECK FOR 7
02 070          B   LOOP1                  / PASSES THROUGH
02 080          H                          OUTER LOOP
02 090          B   READ
02 100   03 TEST   DCW *      280 .
02 110   03 A220   DCW *      220
02 120   01 ZERO   DCW *      0
02 130   01 ONE    DCW *      1
02 140   01 SEVEN  DCW *      7
02 150   02 TEN    DCW *      10
02 160   10 HOLD   DCW *
02 170   01 COUNT  DCW *      0
02 180          END START
```

Figure 13–10. Source Program for Sort 1

Sample Outputs

Figure 13–13 shows the sample outputs from SORT 1 and SORT 2. The first line of each case contains the fields exactly as read from the card. The remaining seven lines are the results achieved after each of the seven passes. The output reflects in no way the difference between the two routines. However, when the program is run on an IBM 1620, the difference in processing time is readily noticeable. When using SORT 2, each pass is completed more quickly than the preceding one, since fewer comparisons are made with each succeeding pass.

The output from SORT 3 (Figure 13–14) for the first case is identical to that of SORT 1 and SORT 2. Since these fields were initially arranged in descending sequence, seven passes were required to rearrange them, and the program broke out of the loop by the same means used in SORT 1 and SORT 2. However, in the case of the other two runs, processing was completed in fewer than seven runs. When the fields had been arranged in proper sequence, one more run was required to turn the switch off and allow the computer to break out of the loop.

```
01 010      *              SORT 2
01 020      *
01 030   START  SW  0001        0181
01 040   READ   R
01 050          MCW 0080        0280
01 060          W
01 070          MCW A280        TEST
01 080   LOOP1  MCW A220        LOOP2 +003   INITALIZE ADRESS
01 090          MCW A220        REPLCE+006   FOR NEXT PASS
01 100   LOOP2  MCW 0220        0200         ACCESS A PAIR OF
01 110          C   0200        0190         FIELDS AND TEST
01 120          B   EXCHGE                U
01 130          B   INSEQ                    IF THE FIRST OF
01 140   EXCHGE MCW 0200        HOLD         THE PAIR IS
01 150          MCW 0190        0200         LARGER,EXCHANGE
01 160          MCW HOLD        0190         THEM
01 170   REPLCE MCW 0200        0220
01 180   INSEQ  SW  LOOP2 +001  REPLCE+004   INCREMENT THE
01 190          C   LOOP2 +003  TEST         ADDRESSES FOR
01 200          A   TEN         LOOP2 +003   NEXT PAIR . IF
02 010          A   TEN         REPLCE+006   ALL PAIRS HAVE
02 020          CW  LOOP2 +001  REPLCE+004   NOT BEEN TESTED
02 030          B   LOOP2                  / THEN RETURN
02 040          W
02 050          C   TEST        A220         IF ALL TESTED,
02 060          S   TEN         TEST         DECREMENT TEST
02 070          B   LOOP1                  / ADDRESS FOR THE
02 080          H                            NEXT PASS
02 090          B   READ
02 100 03 A280  DCW *           280
02 110 03 A220  DCW *           220
02 120 03 TEST  DCW *
02 130 02 TEN   DCW *           10
02 140 10 HOLD  DCW *
02 150          END START
```

Figure 13–11. Source Program for Sort 2

```
01 010    *                 SORT 3
01 020    *
01 030    START  SW  0001         0181
01 040    READ   R
01 050           MCW 0080         0280
01 060    W
01 070           MCW A280         TEST
01 080    LOOP1  MCW A220         LOOP2 +003  INITALIZE ADRESS
01 090           MCW A220         REPLCE+006  FOR NEXT PASS
01 100           MCW OFF          SWITCH      SET SWITCH FOR
01 110    LOOP2  MCW 0220         0200        LATER USE
01 120           C   0200         0190        ACCESS FIELDS
01 130           B   EXCHGE                   UIF FIRST OF PAIR
01 140           B   INSEQ                    IS LARGER ,THEN
01 150    EXCHGE MCW 0200         HOLD        EXCHANGE THEM.
01 160           MCW 0190         0200        WHENEVER FIELD
01 170           MCW HOLD         0190        OUT OF SEQUENCE
01 180    REPLCE MCW 0200         0220        RESET SWITCH
01 190           MCW ON           SWITCH      FOR ANOTHER PAS
01 200    INSEQ  SW  LOOP2 +001   REPLCE+004  INCREMENT THE
02 010           C   LOOP2 +003   TEST        ADDRESSES FOR
02 020           A   TEN          LOOP2 +003  NEXT PAIR . IF
02 030           A   TEN          REPLCE+006  ALL PAIRS HAVE
02 040           CW  LOOP2 +001   REPLCE+004  NOT BEEN TESTED
02 050           B   LOOP2                    / THEN RETURN
02 060    W
02 070           C   TEST         A220        IF 7 PASSES OR
02 080           S   TEN          TEST        IF ALL FIELDS
02 090    SWITCH B   LOOP1                    / IN SEQUENCE
02 100    H                                   THEN HALT
02 110           B   READ
02 120 03 A280   DCW *        280
02 130 03 A220   DCW *        220
02 140 03 TEST   DCW *
02 150 02 TEN    DCW *        10
02 160 01 ON     DCW *        B
02 170 01 OFF    DCW *        N
02 180 10 HOLD   DCW *
02 190           END START
```

Figure 13–12. Source Program for Sort 3

```
88888    77777    66666    55555    44444    33333    22222    11111
77777    66666    55555    44444    33333    22222    11111    88888
66666    55555    44444    33333    22222    11111    77777    88888
55555    44444    33333    22222    11111    66666    77777    88888
44444    33333    22222    11111    55555    66666    77777    88888
33333    22222    11111    44444    55555    66666    77777    88888
22222    11111    33333    44444    55555    66666    77777    88888
11111    22222    33333    44444    55555    66666    77777    88888


JONES     ANDERSON  JOHNSON   MILES     ARCHER    BAKER     SMITH     PRATT
ANDERSON  JOHNSON   JONES     ARCHER    BAKER     MILES     PRATT     SMITH
ANDERSON  JOHNSON   ARCHER    BAKER     JONES     MILES     PRATT     SMITH
ANDERSON  ARCHER    BAKER     JOHNSON   JONES     MILES     PRATT     SMITH
ANDERSON  ARCHER    BAKER     JOHNSON   JONES     MILES     PRATT     SMITH
ANDERSON  ARCHER    BAKER     JOHNSON   JONES     MILES     PRATT     SMITH
ANDERSON  ARCHER    BAKER     JOHNSON   JONES     MILES     PRATT     SMITH


222      111      333      444      555      666      777      888
111      222      333      444      555      666      777      888
111      222      333      444      555      666      777      888
111      222      333      444      555      666      777      888
111      222      333      444      555      666      777      888
111      222      333      444      555      666      777      888
111      222      333      444      555      666      777      888
111      222      333      444      555      666      777      888
```

Figure 13–13. Sample Output for Sort 1 and 2

```
88888    77777    66666    55555    44444    33333    22222    11111
77777    66666    55555    44444    33333    22222    11111    88888
66666    55555    44444    33333    22222    11111    77777    88888
55555    44444    33333    22222    11111    66666    77777    88888
44444    33333    22222    11111    55555    66666    77777    88888
33333    22222    11111    44444    55555    66666    77777    88888
22222    11111    33333    44444    55555    66666    77777    88888
11111    22222    33333    44444    55555    66666    77777    88888
```

```
JONES      ANDERSON   JOHNSON    MILES      ARCHER     BAKER      SMITH      PRATT
ANDERSON   JOHNSON    JONES      ARCHER     BAKER      MILES      PRATT      SMITH
ANDERSON   JOHNSON    ARCHER     BAKER      JONES      MILES      PRATT      SMITH
ANDERSON   ARCHER     BAKER      JOHNSON    JONES      MILES      PRATT      SMITH
ANDERSON   ARCHER     BAKER      JOHNSON    JONES      MILES      PRATT      SMITH
```

```
222      111      333      444      555      666      777      888
111      222      333      444      555      666      777      888
111      222      333      444      555      666      777      888
```

Figure 13–14. Sample Output for Sort 3

STATISTICAL COMPUTATIONS

Although the subject of statistics is in the field of mathematics, almost all disciplines use statistical methods to interpret the meanings of experimental data. Among the more common quantities computed are the *mean* and the *standard deviation*. The mean of a set of values is merely the average; that is, the sum total of all the data divided by the number of data values. The standard deviation is an indication of the data spread, and is somewhat more complex to calculate. For instance, three test scores of 25, 50, and 75 would have a mean of 50, and so would three scores of 49, 50, and 51. The means are identical, but the standard deviations would be considerably different, thus reflecting the spread of the first data set.

Equations

Since computation of the standard deviation requires that a square root be calculated, we shall determine the mean and *variance* of a set of data. The variance is also an indication of the data spread, since it is the square of the mean.

The equations that form the basis for this type of program are

$$m = \frac{\sum x}{n} \qquad v = \frac{\sum x^2 - (\sum x)^2/n}{n-1}$$

The symbols used are defined in Table 13–7.

In computing variance, note that we can express the square of the sum divided by n as

$$\frac{(\sum x)^2}{n} = \frac{\sum x}{n} \sum x = m \sum x$$

The result is the following equation for variance, which we shall use in writing the program:

$$v = \frac{\sum x^2 - m\sum x}{n - 1}$$

Table 13–7

SYMBOLS AND MNEMONICS FOR CALCULATING MEAN AND VARIANCE

ITEM	EQUATION	MNEMONIC
The variable	x	X
Identification number		NUM
Sample size	n	SIZE
Sum of the variable	$\sum x$	SUMX
Sum of the square of the variable	$(\sum x)^2$	SUMSQ
Mean	m	MEAN
Variance	v	VAR

Program Planning

The input data for this program will be punched one to a card, and the output will be printed with the format described in Table 13–8.

As each card is read, values for SUMX and SUMSQ will be computed and retained until all data cards have been processed. Then the final computations will be performed. Figure 13–15 is a program flowchart which illustrates the logic involved. As required, during the loop the desired quantities are read and summed until all cards have been processed, and then the mean and variance are calculated.

Table 13–8

INPUT/OUTPUT FORMAT

FIELD	CARD COLUMN OR PRINT POSITION	FORMAT
	INPUT	
Identification number	1–3	xxx
Not used	4–10	
Data	11–15	xxx$_\wedge$xx
	OUTPUT	
Mean	2–7	xxx.xx
Blank	8–13	
Variance	14–22	xxxx.xxxx
Blank	23–27	
Sample size	28–30	xxx

The Program

Figure 13–16 is the program written to perform the calculation of mean and variance. Both the program and program logic are reasonably straightforward and comments in the source program are adequate. The student is advised to pay particular attention to decimal alignment during various phases of the calculations, which heavily tax the subroutine work areas.

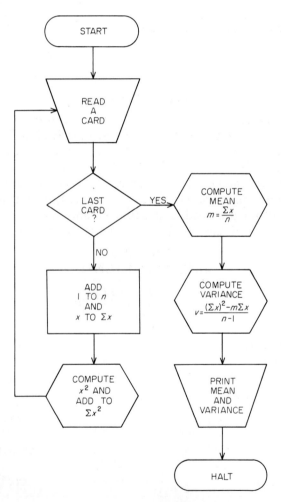

Figure 13–15. Program Flowchart for Calculation of Mean and Variance

```
01 010    *              MEAN AND VARIANCE
01 020    *
01 030    START  SW  0001        0010
01 040           MCW  ZERO        PROD        INITIALIZE
01 050           MCW  ZERO        MULTR       NECESSARY WORK
01 060           MCW  ZERO        SUMX        AREAS FOR
01 070           MCW  ZERO        SIZE        ANOTHER RUN
01 080           MCW  ZERO        SUMSQ
01 090    READ   R                            IF DATA CARD
01 100           C    NUM         NINE99      LAST THEN BRNCH
01 110           B    OUT                     S TO COMPUTE MEAN
01 120           A    ONE         SIZE        AND VARIANCE
01 130           A    X           SUMX        OTHERWISE SUM NO
01 140           MCW  X           MULTD       OF CARDS AND X
01 150           MCW  X           MULTR       THEN COMPUTE
01 160           MCW  RETRN1-  1  MULTX +  3  SQUARE OF X AND
01 170           B    MULT                    SUM IN PROD
01 180           B    RETRN1                  AREA AND RETURN
01 190    RETRN1 B    READ                    FOR NEW CARD
01 200    *              AFTER ALL DATA CARDS READ COMPUTE
02 010    *                   MEAN AND VARIANCE
02 020    OUT    MCW  SIZE        0231        FOR OUTPUT
02 030           MCW  PROD        SUMSQ       SAVE SUM OF X
02 040           MCW  ZERO        DIVD        INITIALIZE
02 050           MCW  ZERO        DIVR         MULTIPLY
02 060           MCW  ZERO        QUOT          WORK AREAS
02 070           MCW  SUMX        DIVD        DIVIDE DATA SUM
02 080           MCW  SIZE        DIVR        BY NUMBER OF
02 090           MCW  RETRN2-  1  DIVX +   3  DATA TO OBTAIN
02 100           B    DIV                     MEAN
02 110           B    RETRN2
02 120    RETRN2 MCW  QUOT        MEAN        MOVE QUOTIENT TO
02 130           MCW  POINT       MEAN  -  2  OUTPUT WITH
02 140           MCW  QUOT  -  2  MEAN  -  3  DECIMAL
02 150           MCW  ZERO        PROD
02 160           MCW  SUMX        MULTD       MOVE DATA SUM TO
02 170           MCW  RETRN3-  1  MULTX +  3  MULTD,MEAN
02 180           B    MULT                    ALREDY IN MULTR
02 190           B    RETRN3                  THEN COMPUTE
02 200    RETRN3 SW   PROD  - 12              PROD AND SUBTR
03 010           S    PROD        SUMSQ       FROM SUMSQ
03 020           CW   PROD  - 12
03 030           MCW  SUMSQ       DIVD        MOVE SUMSQ TO
03 040           MCW  ZERO        DIVR        DIVD,ZERO OTHER
03 050           MCW  ZERO        QUOT        WORK AREAS THEN
03 060           MCW  SIZE        DIVR        MOVE NUMBER OF
03 070           S    ONE         DIVR        DATA,SIZE,TO
03 080           MCW  RETRN4-  1  DIVX +   3  DIVR AND SUBTR
03 090           B    DIV                     ONE. THE QUOT
03 100           B    RETRN4                  IS VARIANCE SO
03 110    RETRN4 MCW  QUOT        VAR         MOVE TO OUTPUT
03 120           MCW  POINT       VAR   -  4  AND WRITE.IF
03 130           MCW  QUOT  -  4  VAR   -  5  DESIRED,PUSH
03 140           W                            START TO PROCES
03 150           H    START                   NEW DATA DECK
03 160 03 SIZE   DCW  *
03 170 08 SUMX   DCW  *
03 180 13 SUMSQ  DCW  *
03 190 01 ONE    DCW  *           1
03 200 01 POINT  DCW  *           .
04 010 03 NINE99 DCW  *           999
04 020 13 ZERO   DCW  *           0000000000000
04 030    NUM    DS   0003
04 040    X      DS   0015
04 050 06 MEAN   DCW  0207
04 060 09 VAR    DCW  0222
04 070    *              DIVIDE SUBROUTINE FOLLOWS ON
04 080    *                 CARDS 04 090 THROUGH 05 170
05 180    *              MULTIPLY SUBROUTINE FOLLOWS ON
05 190    *                 CARDS 05 200 THROUGH 07 010
07 020           END  START
```

Figure 13-16. Source Program for Calculation of Mean and Variance

PRIME NUMBERS

More than 2200 years ago, the great mathematician Euclid wrote his *Elements*, an amazing work that consisted of thirteen volumes on such mathematical subjects as geometry and number theory. In his works he introduced the concept of the *prime number*, a number divisible only by itself and by one. For instance, 21 is not a prime number since it can be factored to 3×7, whereas 19 is a prime number since it has no such factors. Euclid further set forth a surprisingly simple proof for an infinite number of primes. The next logical step would appear to be developing a formula for all primes. Euclid was not able to do this and, in fact, no such formula has been developed to this day.

Much has been written of prime numbers and considerable time has been devoted to the study of them. During the last two centuries, prizes have been offered for certain mathematical proofs, many of which involved primes. Many methods have been devised for calculating prime numbers, and computers have turned out long lists of them. We shall now undertake to write a modest program for computing prime numbers.

The Problem

Quite obviously, 2 is the only even prime number, since all other even numbers are divisible by 2. Also, 3 is a prime, so we will begin by assuming both 2 and 3 to be primes. The number 5 is neither divisible by 3 nor by 2 so it is a prime. Similarly 7 is not divisible by 3 or 5, so it is a prime. Finally we come to the odd number 9, which is divisible by 3 and therefore not a prime. If we continued in this manner, we would compile a table of primes and also discover the following two points:

1. In testing whether or not a number is prime we need only test by using previously determined primes as quotients, not all odd numbers.

2. We need only test until all trial divisors not exceeding the square root of the suspected prime have been exhausted.

The second point warrants further comment here. Suppose we are testing the number 143. Since the square of 12 is 144, which is the first perfect square exceeding 143, we need only use trial divisors that are less than 12. Clearly, given two integers whose product is 143, one of them must exceed 12 and the other must be less. In this case the factors are 11 and 13. As we will discover, this fact saves considerable computing time.

Program Planning

The primary program requirements are outlined in the problem definition. In the interest of simplifying computations, we will type out each prime as it is determined and not retain it in storage. As a result, the trial divisors used in testing for a prime will consist of all odd numbers whose squares do not exceed the number being tested. Although this is somewhat inefficient from a computational point of view, it will greatly simplify programming. The program flowchart is shown in Figure 13–17.

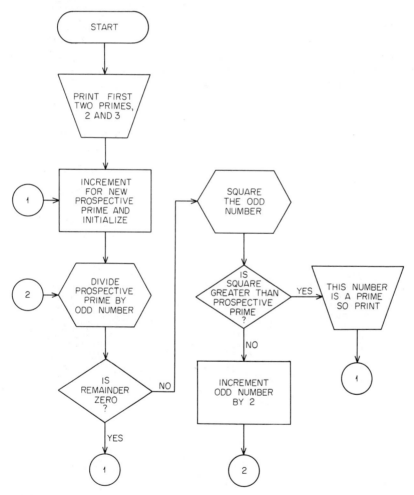

Figure 13–17. Program Flowchart for Computation of Prime Numbers

The Program

Figure 13–18 is a program that will compute all prime numbers up to four digits. The first prime, 2, is printed from the constant TWO, which is used to increment; the second, 3, is printed (after appropriate zero suppression) directly as it is defined by the assembler. From that point the number TSTPRM (test prime) is incremented by two and tested by odd numbers, beginning with 3, and using the working area ODD. If a zero remainder is detected, the number TSTPRM is not a prime number and a new one is tested. Whenever the square of ODD exceeds TSTPRM, TSTPRM is printed as a prime number. The remainder of documentation and program description is clearly set forth by the comments area in the program.

It is interesting to note that the main program consists of 33 cards and requires 201 storage positions, but the three subroutines require 67 cards and 335 storage positions.

```
01 010    *              PRIME NUMBERS
01 020    *
01 030    START   MCW  TWO          0215        FIRST PRIME IS
01 040            W                             TWO THEN THE
01 050            B    OUTP                      NEXT IS THREE
01 060    NEWPRM  A    TWO          PRIME       INCREASE NUMBER
01 070            MCW  THREE        ODD          BY TWO AND
01 080    NEWTST  MCW  PRIME        DIVD        INITIALIZE DIVR
01 090            MCW  ODD          DIVR         TO 3 THEN DIVID
01 100            MCW  RETRN1-  1 DIVX  +  3    AND CHECK FOR
01 110            B    DIV                       FOR A REMAINDER
01 120            B    RETRN1                    OF ZERO.  IF
01 130    RETRN1  C    DIVD         THREE  -  4  ZERO THEN NO.
01 140            B    NEWPRM                   S NOT A PRIME SO
01 150            MCW  MULTD        MULTR        RETURN AND TRY
01 160            MCW  THREE  -  4 PROD          ANOTHER
01 170            MCW  RETRN2-  1 MULTX  +  3   OTHERWISE SQUAR
01 180            B    MULT                      DIVISOR AND IF
01 190            B    RETRN2                    GREATER THAN
01 200    RETRN2  C    PROD         PRIME       NUMBER
02 010            A    TWO          ODD          INCREMENT DIVR
02 020            MCW  THREE  -  1 PROD          ZERO PROD AREA
02 030            B    NEWTST                   UIF SQUARE LESS
02 040    OUTP    MCW  PRIME        SZARG        THAN NUMBER TRY
02 050            MCW  RETRN3-  1 SUPZRX+  3    ANOTHER DIVISOR
02 060            B    SUPZR                     OTHERWISE
02 070            B    RETRN3                    SUPPRESS ZEROES
02 080    RETRN3  MCW  SZARG        0215        THEN MOVE TO
02 090            W                             OUTPUT SINCE
02 100            B    NEWPRM                    NUMBER IS PRIME
02 110 04 PRIME   DCW  *            0003
02 120 03 ODD     DCW  *
02 130 07 THREE   DCW  *            0000003
02 140 01 TWO     DCW  *            2
02 150    *              MULTIPLY SUBROUTINE FOLLOWS ON
02 160    *                 CARDS 02 170 THROUGH 03 180
03 190    *              DIVIDE SUBROUTINE FOLLOWS ON
03 200    *                 CARDS 04 010 THROUGH 05 090
05 100    *              SUPPRESS ZERO SUBROUTINE FOLLOWS ON
05 110    *                 CARDS 05 120 THROUGH 06070
06 080            END  START
```

Figure 13–18. Source Program for Computation of Prime Numbers

SQUARE ROOT

Although a square root subroutine is not included in this text, one could easily be written; in fact, perhaps some of the more mathematically inclined students have already written one. One method for computing square root, although not particularly suited for use as a subroutine, is Newton's method of successive approximations.

Newton's Method

To illustrate the principle of Newton's method we will compute the square root of 256. If we think of 256 as being the area of a square, then the length of a side is $\sqrt{256}$.

$$
\boxed{A = 256}\ \ \sqrt{256}
$$

$$
\sqrt{256}
$$

Let us make the guess that $\sqrt{256}$ is $256/2 = 128$. For our rectangular figure to have an area of 256, the other side must be $256/128 = 2$.

$$
\boxed{A = 256}\ \ 2
$$

$$
128
$$

Obviously this is not a square, but we can average these two sides and obtain a better approximation. The second estimate, e_2, would be

$$
e_2 = \frac{128 + 2}{2} = 65
$$

The new figure will have one side of length 65 and the other $256/65 = 3.9$ (truncated to the nearest tenth).

$$
\boxed{A = 256}\ \ 3.9
$$

$$
65
$$

Continuing in this manner, our figure assumes the following dimensions with each estimate:

TRIAL	ESTIMATE	COMPUTED SIDE
4	34.5	7.4
5	20.9	12.2
6	16.5	15.5
7	16.0	16.0

or

$$A = 256 \qquad \sqrt{256} = 16$$

$$\sqrt{256} = 16$$

Note that, in spite of a very poor first estimate, the calculations converged to the final answer of 16 very rapidly. In general, if we wish to make a better first guess, we should use an estimate consisting of half the number of digits in the number. For larger numbers the calculations would converge much faster this way, but, from the point of view of simplicity, the method illustrated appears to be better. This approach is diagrammed in the flowchart of Figure 13–19 and programmed in Figure 13–20.

Computing the Average

Since the principles involved are described above and the comments in Figure 13–19 are reasonably descriptive, we shall go on to the source program for discussion. The DIVIDE subroutine of the program could have been used to obtain half the number for the first estimate and for the following averaging. However, this was done by using a short open subroutine in which the number was added to itself five times and the decimal shifted one place to the left through address adjusting. Frequently it is convenient to write and use such a short subroutine to accommodate special cases.

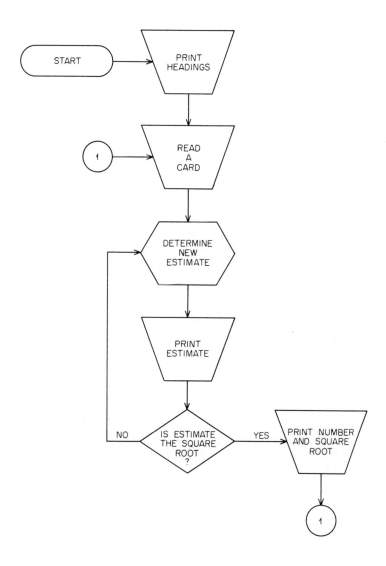

Figure 13–19. Program Flowchart for Computing Square Root

```
01 010    *            SQUARE ROOT BY NEWTONS METHOD
01 020    *
01 030    START   SW   0001
01 040            MCW  HEAD1       0240            PRINT
01 050            W
01 060            MCW  HEAD2       0240            HEADINGS
01 070            W
01 080    NEWNO   CS   0240
01 090            MCW  ZEROES      DIVR
01 100            W                                THEN READ INPUT
01 110            W                                CARD WITH SEVEN
01 120            MCW  HEAD3       0218            DIGIT NUMBER IN
01 130            R                                CC 1 THROUGH 7
01 140            MCW  NUMBER      0232            AND PRINT
01 150            W                                NUMBER XXXXXXX
01 160            CS   0225
01 170            MCW  HEAD4       0245
01 180            W
01 190            CS   0245
01 200            W
02 010            MCW  NUMBER      DIVR  - 1       FOR FIRST TRIAL
02 020    TEST    A    QUOT        DIVR            FOR NEW ESTIMATE
02 030            MCW  DIVR        QUOT            ADD QUOT TO
02 040            A    DIVR        DIVR            DIVR TO GET
02 050            A    DIVR        DIVR            AVRAGE,I.E.FIVE
02 060            A    QUOT        DIVR            TIMES SUM
02 070            MCW  DIVR  - 1   DIVR            SHIFTED ONE
02 080            MCW  ZEROES      DIVR  - 8       PLACE TO RIGHT
02 090            MCW  DIVR  - 1   0240            THEN TYPE THIS
02 100            W                                ESTIMATE OUT
02 110            MCW  ZEROES      QUOT            INITIALIZE THEN
02 120            MCW  ZEROES- 7   DIVD            DIVIDE NUMBER
02 130            MCW  NUMBER      DIVD  - 2       BY ESTIMATE
02 140            MCW  RETRNI- 1   DIVX  + 3
02 150            B    DIV
02 160            B    RETRNI                      IF QUOT=DIVR THE
02 170    RETRNI  C    DIVR  - 1   QUOT  - 1       ESTIMATE IS SQ
02 180            B    TEST                       / ROOT,OTHERWISE
02 190            CS   0240                        NOT SO RETURN
02 200            W                                TO TEST
03 010            MCW  HEAD3       0218
03 020            MCW  NUMBER      0232
03 030            W
03 040            MCW  HEAD4 - 10  0220
03 050            MCW  DIVR  - 1   SZARG
03 060            MCW  RETRN2- 1   SUPZRX+ 3
03 070            B    SUPZR
03 080            B    RETRN2
03 090    RETRN2  MCW  SZARG       0232
03 100            W
03 110            B    NEWNO
03 120 29 HEAD1   DCW  *           SQUARE ROOT BY NEWTONS METHOD
03 130 29 HEAD2   DCW  *           OF SUCCESSIVE APPROXIMATIONS
03 140 06 HEAD3   DCW  *           NUMBER
03 150 18 HEAD4   DCW  *           SQ. ROOT ESTIMATES
03 160 09 ZEROES  DCW  *           000000000
03 170 00 NUMBER  DS   0007
03 180    *                        DIVIDE SUBROUTINE FOLLOWS ON
03 190    *                           CARDS 03 200 THROUGH 05 080
05 090    *                        SUPPRESS ZERO SUBROUTINE FOLLOWS ON
05 100    *                           CARDS 05 110 THROUGH 06 060
06 070            END  START
```

Figure 13–20. Source Program for Computing Square Root

Program Usage

This program can be used to compute the square root of a number of up to seven digits punched in card columns 1–7 of an input data card. Because COMPARE and CONDITIONAL BRANCH instructions are used, it is necessary that leading zeros be punched on the input card. The square root will be computed to the nearest whole number; the output form is shown in Figure 13–21. Note that the square root of 3 is determined to the nearest whole number in the first run, and is given as 1. In successive runs, more accuracy was obtained by positioning the number on the input data card.

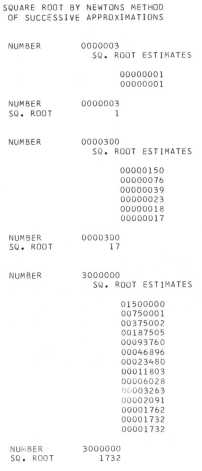

```
SQUARE ROOT BY NEWTONS METHOD
OF SUCCESSIVE APPROXIMATIONS


NUMBER        0000003
              SQ. ROOT ESTIMATES

              00000001
              00000001

NUMBER        0000003
SQ. ROOT            1


NUMBER        0000300
              SQ. ROOT ESTIMATES

              00000150
              00000076
              00000039
              00000023
              00000018
              00000017

NUMBER        0000300
SQ. ROOT           17


NUMBER        3000000
              SQ. ROOT ESTIMATES

              01500000
              00750001
              00375002
              00187505
              00093760
              00046896
              00023480
              00011803
              00006028
              00003263
              00002091
              00001762
              00001732
              00001732

NUMBER        3000000
SQ. ROOT         1732
```

Figure 13–21. Sample Output of Square Root

THE PERFECT GAS LAW

In studying mathematics and science we frequently marvel at the contributions that have been made by the many outstanding men in history. Even more astonishing is the versatility they have shown. For instance, Blaise Pascal, the inventor of the first mechanical calculating machine, is not nearly as well known for that invention as for a multitude of accomplishments in the field of mathematics. He was unquestionably one of the great mathematicians of his time.

As if his mathematical works were not enough, he also performed extensive experiments on fluids, both liquids and gases; in fact, Pascal's principle deals with the transmission of pressures in a fluid. In his studies of vacuums he observed that air was compressible, and only a few years later Robert Boyle determined a relationship between pressure and temperature. More than 150 years later Joseph L. Gay-Lussac included the effect of temperature. We now commonly call this the *perfect gas law*, which is expressed algebraically as

$$PV = kT$$

that is, pressure times volume is equal to some constant times temperature.

The Problem

We shall now consider a program to compile a table of pressures, temperatures, and volumes using the perfect gas law. Given a value for k (which, in this case, includes the mass of the gas), it is possible to assume values for any two of the variables and calculate the third. For instance, if we chose a value of 30 psi (pounds per square inch) for P and a temperature of 32° for T, we could determine the volume V. (It is always necessary to pay heed to the system of units; in particular, pressure and temperature must be in absolute units.) By applying the appropriate constants and using 1 cu ft of gas at standard pressure and temperature, the law may be put in the form

$$PV = 0.0299 \, (T + 460)$$

where

P = pressure in psi
V = volume in cubic feet
T = temperature in °F.

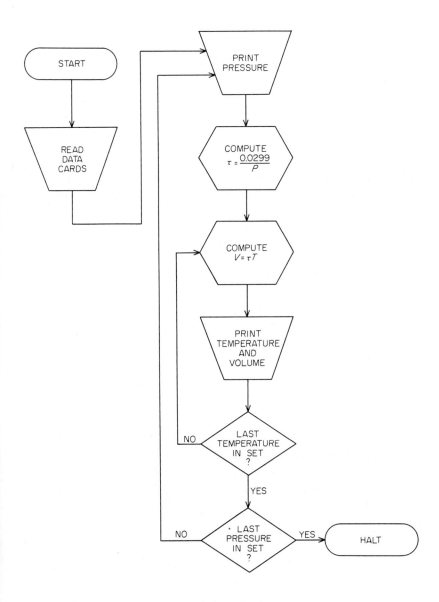

Figure 13–22. Program Flowchart for Perfect Gas Law Computations

Program Planning

Assuming that a set of up to ten input values for each P and T will be given, we will solve for corresponding values of V, using the equation

$$V = \frac{0.0299}{P}\,(T + 460)$$

Thus, if the input consists of three pressures and four temperatures, the output will consist of 12 volumes; that is, all combinations of P and T.

This involves a program consisting of a loop within a loop, as shown in the flowchart of Figure 13–22. Since the program requires both multiplication and division, the multiplication is performed in the inner loop and the division in the outer loop. That is, the gas law will be divided into the two following equations and solved accordingly:

$$\tau = 0.0299/P \qquad \text{(outer loop)}$$
$$V = \tau\,(T + 460) \qquad \text{(inner loop)}$$

INPUT CARD FORMAT

FIELD	CARD COLUMN	FORMAT
First card (Pressure)		
Number of pressures	1–2	xx
P_1 (first pressure)	3–7	xxx$_\wedge$xx
P_2	8–12	xxx$_\wedge$xx
.	.	.
.	.	.
.	.	.
P_{10}	48–52	xxx$_\wedge$xx
Second Card (temperature)		
Number of temperatures	1–2	xx
T_1 (first temperature)	3–7	xxx$_\wedge$xx
T_2	8–12	xxx$_\wedge$xx
.	.	.
.	.	.
.	.	.
T_{10}	48–52	xxx$_\wedge$xx

If only three input pressures are used, card columns 1–2 will contain 03 and columns 3–17 will contain the three pressures. Output will consist of each pressure followed by the table of temperatures and volumes. The output format is shown in the sample run included in this section.

The Program

A program that will perform the calculations as outlined is shown in Figure 13–23. The input pressures contained on the first card are retained in the PUNCH area of storage, and the temperatures are stored in the READ area. The outer loop in which τ is calculated begins with the instruction labeled PRLOOP (pressure loop), and the inner loop in which each volume is computed begins with the instruction TMLOOP (temperature loop). Details of the program are contained in the comments of Figure 13–23.

Note that the HALT instruction terminating the program contains an I address. Thus, if we wish to run several sets of data, it is only necessary to stack the input cards in pairs of pressure and temperature. When one table is complete, calculation of the next one will begin merely by restarting the computer.

```
01 010    *              PERFECT GAS LAW
01 020    *
01 030    START   SW   0001
01 040    READ    R                          READ AND STORE
01 050            MCW  0052      0152           PRESSURE TABLE
01 060            R                          READ TEMP TABLE
01 070            MCW  ZERO      COUNTN       INIALIZE FOR NEW
01 080            MCW  INITAL    PRES  +  3     INPUT VALUES
01 090    *
01 100    *              OUTER LOOP (PRESSURE)
01 110    PRLOOP  CS   0249
01 120            W
01 130            W
01 140    PRES    MCW  P         WORK         READS NEW PRES
01 150            MCW  WORK      0217           THEN MOVE WITH
01 160            MCW  POINT     0215           DECIMAL TO
01 170            MCW  WORK   -  2 0214         WRITE AREA
01 180            MCW  HEAD1     0210           AND WRITES
01 190            W                             PRESSURE
01 200            S    QUOT      QUOT
02 010            S    DIVD      DIVD
02 020            MCW  WORK      DIVR
02 030            MCW  CONST     DIVD         QUOTIENT OF
02 040            MCW  RETRN1-   1 DIVX  +  3   CONST AND PRES
02 050            B    DIV                      GIVES TAU
02 060            B    RETRN1
02 070    RETRN1  MCW  ZERO      COUNTM
02 080            MCW  INITAL    TMLOOP+  3
02 090            CS   0217
02 100            W
02 110            SW   0243                   PREPARES WRITE
02 120            MCW  HEAD2     0216           AREA TO OUTPUT
02 130            MCW  HEAD3     0241           HEADING WITH
02 140    *
02 150    *              INNER LOOP (TEMPERATURE)
02 160    TMLOOP  MCW  T         WORK         TEMP AND VOL
02 170            MCW  WORK      0223           THEN MOVE TEMP
02 180            MCW  POINT     0221           TO WRITE WITH
02 190            MCW  WORK   -  2 0220             DECIMAL
02 200            S    PROD      PROD
03 010            A    FOUR60    WORK
03 020            MCW  WORK      MULTD        MOVE NEW TEMP TO
```

Figure 13–23. Source Program for Perfect Gas Law Computations

```
03 030          MCW RETRN2-  1 MULTX +  3     MULTD, MULTR
03 040          B   MULT                      CONTAINS TAU
03 050          B   RETRN2                     FROM DIVIDE
03 060   RETRN2 MCW PROD   -  6 0249          MOVE COMPUTED
03 070          MCW POINT       0246          VOLUME TO
03 080          MCW PROD   -  9 0245            WRITE AREA
03 090          W                             AND WRITE
03 100          SW  TMLOOP+  1
03 110          A   FIVE         TMLOOP+  3
03 120          CW  TMLOOP+  1
03 130          A   ONE          COUNTM
03 140          C   N            COUNTM       COMPLETED THEN
03 150          B   TMLOOP                   / RETURN . IF
03 160          SW  PRES   +  1               COMPLETED THEN
03 170          A   FIVE         PRES   +  3  INCREMENT FOR
03 180          CW  PRES   +  1               NEXT PRESSURE
03 190          A   ONE          COUNTN       IF ALL PRES NOT
03 200          C   M            COUNTN       COMPLETED THEN
04 010          B   PRLOOP                   / RETURN, IF DONE
04 020          H   READ                      THEN HALT
04 030 02 COUNTN DCW *
04 040 02 COUNTM DCW *
04 050 02 ZERO   DCW *        00
04 060 01 ONE    DCW *        1
04 070 01 FIVE   DCW *        5
04 080 01 POINT  DCW *        .
04 090 02 INITAL DCW *        07
04 100 05 WORK   DCW *
04 110 05 FOUR60 DCW *        46000
04 120 08 CONST  DCW *        29900000
04 130 10 HEAD1  DCW *        PRESSURE =
04 140 13 HEAD2  DCW *        TEMPERATURE =
04 150 08 HEAD3  DCW *        VOLUME =
04 160    P      DS  0107
04 170    T      DS  0007
04 180    M      DS  0102
04 190    N      DS  0002
04 200    *          MULTIPLY SUBROUTINE FOLLOWS ON
05 010    *             CARDS 05 030 THROUGH 06 040
06 040    *          DIVIDE SUBROUTINE FOLLOWS ON
06 050    *             CARDS 06 070 THROUGH 07 150
07 150    END START
```

Figure 13-23. Continued

A Sample Run

The input cards for the sample run are shown in Figure 13-24. The first card contains pressures beginning in card column 3 (columns 1 and 2 contain 04, telling how many pressures follow); the second card contains temperatures, also beginning in column 3 (again columns 1 and 2 tell how many temperatures follow). The output for this run follows as Figure 13-25, which consists of all input pressures and temperatures plus the calculated volumes.

■ REMARKS

The example programs of this chapter show the versatility of the 141 system with its limited storage and instruction capabilities. They have also served to illustrate many commonly encountered programming techniques.

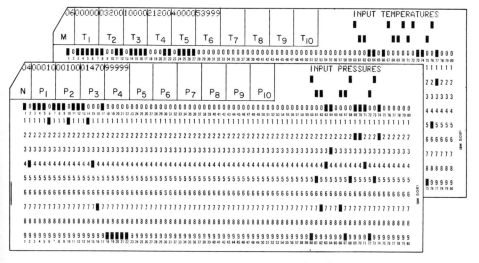

Figure 13–24. Data Cards for Perfect Gas Law Computations

```
PRESSURE = 000.10

        TEMPERATURE = 000.00            VOLUME = 137.540
        TEMPERATURE = 032.00            VOLUME = 147.108
        TEMPERATURE = 100.00            VOLUME = 167.440
        TEMPERATURE = 212.00            VOLUME = 200.928
        TEMPERATURE = 400.00            VOLUME = 257.140
        TEMPERATURE = 539.99            VOLUME = 298.997


PRESSURE = 001.00

        TEMPERATURE = 000.00            VOLUME = 013.754
        TEMPERATURE = 032.00            VOLUME = 014.710
        TEMPERATURE = 100.00            VOLUME = 016.744
        TEMPERATURE = 212.00            VOLUME = 020.092
        TEMPERATURE = 400.00            VOLUME = 025.714
        TEMPERATURE = 539.99            VOLUME = 029.899


PRESSURE = 014.70

        TEMPERATURE = 000.00            VOLUME = 000.935
        TEMPERATURE = 032.00            VOLUME = 001.000
        TEMPERATURE = 100.00            VOLUME = 001.139
        TEMPERATURE = 212.00            VOLUME = 001.366
        TEMPERATURE = 400.00            VOLUME = 001.749
        TEMPERATURE = 539.99            VOLUME = 002.033


PRESSURE = 999.99

        TEMPERATURE = 000.00            VOLUME = 000.013
        TEMPERATURE = 032.00            VOLUME = 000.014
        TEMPERATURE = 100.00            VOLUME = 000.016
        TEMPERATURE = 212.00            VOLUME = 000.020
        TEMPERATURE = 400.00            VOLUME = 000.025
        TEMPERATURE = 539.99            VOLUME = 000.029
```

Figure 13–25. Sample Output of Perfect Gas Law Computations

■ EXERCISES

13.1 Each employee of a certain company submits a time card for every day of the week, Monday through Friday. If he does not work one of the weekdays, his card will be submitted with a zero for hours worked. Thus, there will always be five cards. The input card format is

CARD COLUMN	FIELD
1–4	Employee number
5–16	Last name
17–23	First name
24	Middle initial
25–32	not used*
33–35	Hourly rate
36–67	not used*
68–70	Hours worked
71–80	not used*

* These columns cannot be assumed blank.

The hourly rate and hours worked will be specified in the form

$$x_\wedge xx \quad \text{(hourly rate)}$$
$$xx_\wedge x \quad \text{(hours worked)}$$

The deck of cards for each employee will consist of five cards arranged in order from Monday through Friday, and the complete deck consists of the individual decks. Compute the gross pay for each employee. Use time and a half (that is, the specified hourly rate $\times 1\frac{1}{2}$) for anything over 8 hours per day. Punch a new card with the following information:

CARD COLUMN	FIELD
1–67	Same as input card
68–70	Total hours
72–74	Overtime hours
76–80	Gross pay

$$xx_\wedge x \quad \text{(hours)}$$
$$xx_\wedge x \quad \text{(overtime hours)}$$
$$xxx_\wedge xx \quad \text{(gross pay)}$$

The gross pay may be half-adjusted to the nearest cent.

13.2 In Exercise 13.1, assume that the employee may work Saturday. If he does, a sixth card will be submitted with his deck for Saturday. Thus there will always be either five or six cards. Pay overtime for all day Saturday. Compute gross pay as required in Exercise 13.1.

13.3 A common method for determining overtime hours is to consider as overtime only those hours that exceed 9 hours in a given day or 40 hours in a given week. Thus, if an employee worked 10 hours per day but only 4 days that week, he would receive 36 hours straight time and 4 hours overtime. On the other hand, if he worked 10 hours per day, 5 days per week, he would receive 40 hours straight time and 10 hours overtime. Using the formats specified in Exercise 13.1, compute gross pay.

13.4 Example 9–3 (flowcharting techniques) describes the processing of a deck of cards to determine equivalent sick leave as calculated by a predefined process. The predefined process is (1) day-for-day credit through 120 days, (2) two-thirds of a day for each day between 121 and 180, (3) one-half day for each day exceeding 180. Card fields to be used in this program are:

FIELD	*CARD COLUMNS*
Employee number	1–4
Age	27–28
Length of service (years)	29–30
Sick leave (days)	37–39
Blank	73–75

Write the program for this problem as indicated in Chapter 9. Punch a new card with the contents of the old one and equivalent accumulated sick leave in columns 73–75.

13.5 A deck of employee cards contains, among other information, the following:

FIELD	*CARD COLUMNS*
Employee name	1–19
Telephone extension	31–33

The name field contains the last name followed by a blank, the first name, a blank, and the middle initial. Write a program that will print a list of names and telephone extensions with the following format:

FIELD	PRINT POSITIONS
First name and middle initial	beginning 4
Last name	beginning 20
Extension	40–42

13.6 The program of Problem 3 (Money and Interest) is written to compute an amortization table. Modify it to print subtotals for interest and premium payments every twelfth month and complete totals after the loan is repaid. It will probably be necessary to delete the EDIT subroutine.

13.7 A deck of salesman cards contains information concerning sales for each of eight salesmen numbered 1–8. Card contents and format are:

FIELD	CARD COLUMN	FORMAT
Salesman number	1	x
Amount of sale	6–11	xxxx∧xx
Salesman's commission	16–20	xxx∧xx

The input cards will be in random order; that is, they will *not* be ordered by salesman number. Write a program that will compute total sales and total commissions for each salesman and print a report with the following information (use the EDIT subroutine):

FIELD	PRINT POSITION	FORMAT
Salesman number	4	x
Total sales	ending in position 16	$xx,xxx.xx
Total commission	ending in position 28	$x,xxx.xx

At the end of the report, print grand totals for sales and commissions. Assume that the last card of the data deck is blank.

13.8 A common entry in the sports page of the daily newspaper is a "sports log." Typically, such a log summarizes results as the season progresses by listing all scores and opponents for each team. For instance, the season record for a team, let's say the Eagles, appears as:

Eagles	21	Pirates	7
	31	Beavers	30
	3	Bears	24
	17	Indians	17
	21	Vikings	3
	93	(3–1–1)	81

Each line contains the results of one of the Eagles' games, with their score on the left, and the opponent and the opponent's score on the right. The last line consists of total points scored by the Eagles, their season won-lost-tied record in parentheses, and total points scored by the opposition. The record of each team is punched in an input data deck, one game per card, according to the following format:

FIELD	CARD COLUMNS
Team	1–12
Points scored	14–15
Opponent	19–30
Opponent points scored	32–33

The complete deck consists of decks for each team. Write a program that will process a deck of cards and print a record for each team as shown in the above example. Format planning is left to the student.

13.9 Using the input data of Exercise 13.8, print a list of team standings based on the won-lost percentages, ignoring games that ended in ties. Output should include each team and its season record. Assume that the league consists of eight teams.

13.10 In coding for internal storage a binary system is used. Referring to Table 3–3, all nine nonzero digits may be coded, using the four digits 8, 4, 2, and 1. Another way of representing this table is shown below:

| | BIT | | | |
DIGIT	8	4	2	1
1	0	0	0	1
2	0	0	1	0
3	0	0	1	1
4	0	1	0	0
5	0	1	0	1
6	0	1	1	0
7	0	1	1	1
8	1	0	0	0
9	1	0	0	1

Thus the zero represents an off bit and the one an on bit. If we understand the value of each position starting from the right to be 1, 2, 4, ...n in the binary system, then we can represent the number 9 in binary as 1001. Similarly, if desired, we could represent 15 as 1111, and by adding more significant positions, 16 as 10000 (thus it can be seen that the value of each place in a binary number is a power of 2). Since $61 = 32 + 16 + 8 + 4 + 1$, its binary equivalent would be

32	16	8	4	2	1
1	1	1	1	0	1

or 111101.

Write a program that will read a card consisting of a four-digit number, convert it to its binary equivalent, and punch a new card with the original number and the binary equivalent.

13.11 A mass suspended from a spring will oscillate with a frequency as determined by the equation

$$f = \frac{1}{2\pi}\sqrt{\frac{k}{m}}$$

where

f = frequency in cycles per second
k = spring constant in pounds per inch
m = mass in lb-sec^2/in.

Another form of the equation is

$$f^2 = 9.8\,\frac{k}{W}$$

where

W = weight of the mass in pounds
f^2 = square of frequency.

Write a program that will print a table of f^2 (square of frequency) for up to ten values of each k and W. The output should consist of all values for k on the first line and on each succeeding line the value for W followed by the appropriate entry for f^2. Thus to find f^2 for any required value of k and W it would be necessary to find the corresponding row and column.

13.12 Data or output from a computer program can easily be plotted as a graph with the printer by including the proper instructions in the program. Commonly the ordinate runs across the top of the page from left to right (when viewing the printer) and the abscissa down the left edge from top to bottom. Thus if the square function

$$y = x^2$$

were being plotted, the point $x = 0$, $y = 0$ would be printed in the upper left-hand corner using any desired printing character, such as a plus sign. The selected character could, for instance, be printed from print position 10, thus corresponding to $y = 0$. The point $x = 1$, $y = 1$ would then be printed on the next line ($x = 1$) and from print position 11 ($y = 1$). The point $x = 2$, $y = 4$ would be printed on the third line from print position 14, and so on. Write a subroutine that will perform this plotting function and use it, in open or closed form, to plot the function

$$y = x^2$$

with values for x from zero through nine.

13.13 Whenever a round is fired from a gun at an angle with the horizontal as shown in Fig. 13–26, the projectile will follow a path as indicated by the broken line. For an ideal case the motion is described by the equations

$$x = v_x t$$
$$y = v_y t - 16t^2$$

where v_x is the beginning speed or velocity in the x direction, v_y is the beginning velocity in the y direction (they do not change with time), and t is time in seconds.

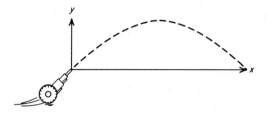

Figure 13–26

Write a program that will compute the path of the projectile second by second and print a table. Formats are

	FIELD	CARD COLUMNS OR PRINT POSITIONS
Input		
	v_x	1–3
	v_y	5–7
Output		
First line	v_x	1–3
	v_y	7–9
Second line blank		
succeeding lines	t (in sec)	3–4
	x	7–11
	y	15–19

Chapter Fourteen

THE LOAD
ROUTINE

Every object deck assembled by the computer consists of one card for each source card, preceded by three cards necessary to clear storage and load the program. Since the routine punched in these three cards performs no functions that are pertinent to the actual program, it is frequently referred to as a *utility routine*. The utility routine for loading an object deck is a very interesting and sophisticated programming application and the one we shall study next.

AN ADDITIONAL INSTRUCTION

In Chapter 10 it was pointed out that the 141 system included one additional instruction which would be discussed later and which is necessary to the load routine. The instruction, LOAD CHARACTERS TO A WORD MARK, is similar to the MOVE CHARACTERS TO A OR B WORD MARK, but word marks are treated differently. The MOVE instruction is terminated by the first word mark sensed in either the A or B field; the word mark is not affected. However, the LOAD instruction requires that the A field have a word mark since this is the one that terminates the operation. As with the MOVE instruction, the A field is transferred to the corresponding positions of the B field, but, unlike the MOVE instruction, word marks in the B field are cleared and the A field word mark is placed in the B field. The formal definition of this instruction is as follows.

LOAD CHARACTERS TO A WORD MARK (LCA)

Op code	A Address	B Address
L̲	aaa	bbb

Description. The LOAD CHARACTERS TO A WORD MARK instruction moves the characters and word mark from the A field to the B field. The A field remains undisturbed.

Word Marks. The A field must contain a word mark to terminate the transmission of data. All word marks in the B field are cleared and a word mark is placed in the B field corresponding to that in the A field.

Use of the LCA instruction is illustrated by the following example:

Contents of storage *before* execution of LCA instruction:

$$\underline{\quad\quad {}_|\underline{1}{}_|2{}_|3{}_|4{}_|5{}_|\quad\quad\quad}$$
$$0\,_1\,_5$$

$$\underline{\quad\quad\quad {}_|\underline{E}{}_|7{}_|5{}_|\underline{3}{}_|2{}_|0{}_|\quad}$$
$$5\,_4\,_2$$

Instruction: L̲015542

Contents of storage *after* execution of LCA instruction:

$$\underline{\quad\quad {}_|\underline{1}{}_|2{}_|3{}_|4{}_|5{}_|\quad\quad\quad}$$
$$0\,_1\,_5$$

$$\underline{\quad\quad\quad {}_|\underline{E}{}_|\underline{1}{}_|2{}_|3{}_|4{}_|5{}_|\quad}$$
$$5\,_4\,_2$$

LOADING THE OBJECT PROGRAM

The Object Program

Some of our initial exposures to programming were provided by a 5-instruction routine to reproduce cards. A complete object deck listing is shown in Figure 14–1, and the storage contents after it has been loaded are shown in Figure 14–2. These are familiar cards; the first

```
,008015,022026,030034,041,045,053,0570731026
L072116,110106,105117B101/999,027A074028)027B0010270B026/0991,001/00111710
,008015,022029,056063/056029                           ,0240671056
01010 4START SW 0001                                   L0703361056,001
01020 1READ  R                                         L06733710561
01030 7      MCW0080            0180                    L0733441056M080180
01040 1      P                                         L06734510564
01050 4      B  READ                                    L07034910568337
0106022HEADNGDCW*           CONSTANT WITH WORDMARK      L0453711056
0107014TITLE DC *            BUT NONE HERE              M0373851056
0108008      DC 0220        CONSTANT                    M0312201056
01090 3ADRES DSA*           337 READ                    L0263881056
01100  NAME  DS 0022                                    N00105610560022
01110  *            THIS IS ALL                         N0010561056
01120        ENDSTART                                   /333080
```

Figure 14–1. Source Program Listing

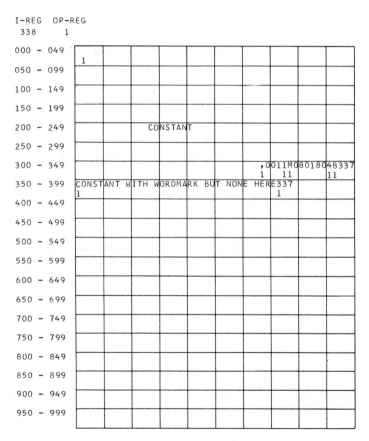

Figure 14–2. Storage Dump

three contain loading instructions and were punched from the assembler. The next five cards contain the original SPS program on the left, and the machine-language equivalent, together with necessary loading instructions, on the right. Following these are five SPS pseudo instructions and a COMMENTS card, which are included only to illustrate how they are accommodated during loading. Finally, the last card is the END statement, which is necessary to complete the assembly process.

We shall approach our study of the loading routine by starting with the first program instruction and progressing through the END card. Then we will consider the first three cards in reverse order. In taking this "reverse look" at what takes place, the conditions remaining from processing of the preceding card will be stated. For instance, when the first card of the object program (01 010 in Figure 14–1) is read into storage, word marks exist at locations 024, 056, 063, and 067, and the computer has been directed to branch to 056.

Loading Instructions

After the card containing the first instruction has been read, the READ area of storage will appear as shown in Figure 14–3. Execution

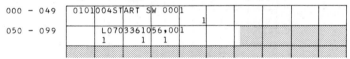

```
000 - 049   | 0101004START SW 0001 |
                                  1
050 - 099   |     L07033610 56,001 |
                  1        1  1
```

Figure 14–3

of the instruction at 056 causes the field at 070, together with its word mark, to be loaded into storage positions 333–336 (to verify this, refer to Figure 14–2). The next instruction, 1056, is a READ AND BRANCH, so 056 is placed in the I register for future use and the instruction executed. This causes the next card to be placed into the READ area of storage as shown in Figure 14–4, and the computer again goes to 056 for its next instruction.

```
000 - 049   | 0102001READ  R |
                           1
050 - 099   |     L06733710561 |
                  1        1  1
```

Figure 14–4

The LOAD instruction transmits the one-position field and word mark at 067 to 337, then the following READ AND BRANCH causes the next card to be read, executed, and the computer to branch to 056. This process continues through the last instruction (01 050).

Loading Constants

The next card in the object deck contains a DCW which, when read, will appear in storage as shown in Figure 14–5. Note that location 024, which contains a word mark, is the first position of the constant as defined in the SPS program. Thus, when the instruction at 056 is executed, the constant with its word mark is placed in storage immediately following the instruction from card 01 050.

```
000 - 049   0106022HEADNGDCW*        CONSTANT WITH WORDMARK
                                     1
050 - 099        L04537110 56
                 1      1   1
```

Figure 14–5

The next line, 01 070, consists of a DC, so the loading portion on this card differs from the previous one in that the constant field is placed in storage with an MCW rather than an LCA, resulting in no word mark in the machine-language version of the program. Another DC is used in line 01 080, but this time with an actual instead of an asterisk address. As a result, the MCW instruction at 056 is given a B address of 220. The student is referred to Figure 14–2 to verify the proper loading of each constant.

The DSA Card

When using a DSA instruction, the programmer specifies the symbolic address by placing it in the B address of the DSA instruction.

During assembly, this address is punched in columns 24–26 of the object deck. When loaded, it is treated in the same manner as a DCW and loaded from position 026, as is evident by loading instruction in Figure 14–1. In the example, an asterisk address is used in the A operand, so the address (337) is stored in the first available storage positions, which in this case are 386–388.

The DS and COMMENT Cards

The DS pseudo instruction is used to reserve areas in storage and to define mnemonics for input quantities. It causes nothing to be loaded into storage and causes no word marks to be set. Once the assembly is complete, the purpose of the DS has, in essence, been served. This is reflected by an N in card column 56 (Figure 14–1), which causes the computer to proceed to the next instruction. The COMMENT card is treated in the same manner, since its only purpose is to provide the programmer with information when he is studying the object listing. An inspection of Figure 14–2 verifies that these card contents are not placed in storage.

The END Card

In the past, it has been emphasized that the END card results in no machine-language instruction in the program. However, an instruction from the END card is used to clear the remainder of storage and begin execution of the program. After the END card is read into storage, the READ area will appear as shown in Figure 14–6.

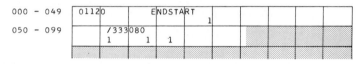

Figure 14–6

Prior to execution of this CLEAR STORAGE AND BRANCH instruction, the I address of 333 is placed in the I register, then storage is cleared from 080 down through 000, thus erasing all trace of the loading routine. Since the I register contains 333, the first instruction of the program will be executed.

THE "BOOTSTRAP" CARD

The next portion of the loading routine to be discussed concerns the third card in the object deck, or the *bootstrap card* as it is frequently called. Again we will begin with the following conditions, which existed immediately prior to reading this card: (1) there is a word mark in 001, (2) the last instruction executed from the second card was READ AND BRANCH to 001. After the card is read, the storage contents will appear as shown in Figure 14–7.

Since the seven-position SW instruction requires no word mark after the last character of its B address, it is executed, thus setting word

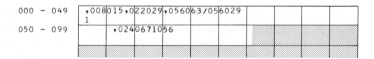

Figure 14–7

marks for the operation codes of the next two instructions. These instructions, in turn, set the other necessary word marks, which will be used before and during loading. At this point, the READ area appears as shown in Figure 14–8.

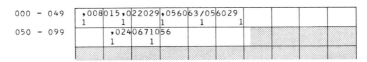

Figure 14–8

Once the required word marks have been set at 056 and 063, the computer executes the CLEAR STORAGE AND BRANCH instruction at 022, thus clearing itself and the preceding instructions, and then branches to 056. At this point, the READ area of storage appears as shown in Figure 14–9. Execution of these instructions sets the remaining two word marks, reads a card and branches to 056.

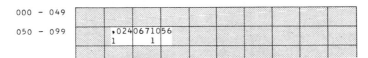

Figure 14–9

These are the conditions that were discussed as existing prior to reading the first object program card. Once again, they were (1) word marks at 024, 056, 063 and 067, and (2) READ AND BRANCH to 056.

"CLEAR STORAGE" CARDS

In the 141 system, it is of utmost importance that storage be cleared prior to loading, since existing word marks could interfere with loading of constants from DC instructions and with eventual execution of the program. The clearing of storage is accomplished by executing the first two cards of the object deck.

The First Card

In order to read the first card into storage and execute it, the following three operations must be performed:

1. The READ area cleared.
2. A word mark set in 001.
3. READ AND BRANCH to 001.

These three functions are performed on the 1401 by depressing the LOAD key and on the 1620 by typing the word "LOAD." After the first card is read, the contents are stored in the READ area as shown in Figure 14-10. The READ area now contains seven SET WORD MARK

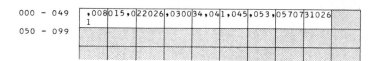

000 - 049
050 - 099

Figure 14-10

instructions, whose sole function is to set up the READ area for the next card. After execution of these seven instructions, the READ area will appear as shown in Figure 14-11.

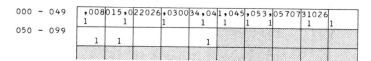

000 - 049
050 - 099

Figure 14-11

The Second Card

Execution of the instruction at 041 will cause the computer to read the second card and branch to 026. The READ area will now contain the information shown in Figure 14-12.

000 - 049
050 - 099

Figure 14-12

Of first interest to us is that portion of storage from 026–056 and the two positions 073 and 074, all of which are not shaded. The first instruction to be executed is at 026 and it clears storage from 999–900. The next three instructions modify the A address of the CLEAR STORAGE instruction to 899. This is done by adding 10 (whose numerical equivalent is 90) at 074 to 99 at 028. A first impression might suggest that the address be modified by subtracting 1 from position 027. Although both methods result in the desired modification, the latter is not compatible with the 1401.

This process is repeated until all storage positions down to 100 have been cleared, at which time the eight-position branch causes the next instruction to be taken from 001. The portion of the program which is of interest now is shown as the unshaded areas of Figure 14–13.

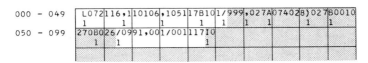

000 - 049	L072	116,1 1	10106 1	,1051 1	1781 1	01/999 1	,027A 1	074028 1	)027B 1	0010
050 - 099	2708	026/09 1	91,00 1	1/001 1	117I0 1				

Figure 14–13

Execution of the instruction at 001 loads the field at 072, together with the word mark at 057, to storage positions 101–116. The instructions which follow, beginning at 008, set word marks at 105, 106, 110, and 117, and cause the program to branch to 101. The instruction at 101 immediately clears all positions from 099 through 000, after which the storage contents of positions 100–149 appear as shown in Figure 14–14.

000 - 049									
050 - 099									
100 - 149	/099 1	1,001 11	/0011 1	117 1					

Figure 14–14

Following this, a card is read and a word mark is set in position 001. It should be recognized that these final instructions perform the same operations as the LOAD key. The final function of these remnants from the second CLEAR STORAGE card is to clear the storage positions from 100–117 (thus erasing itself) and to branch back to 001 for the next instruction. This then satisfies the conditions which are necessary to reading the bootstrap card, that is, (1.) a word mark in 001, (2.) READ AND BRANCH to 001.

REVIEWING THE LOAD OPERATION

The object deck, which we have considered as a unit, consists of four distinct parts that can be categorized according to their functions; they are

1. Two clear storage cards.
2. The bootstrap card.
3. The object program.
4. The END card.

Depression of the LOAD key on a 1401 or typing of LOAD on a 1620 causes the READ area to be cleared, a word mark to be set at 001, the first card to be read, and execution of instructions to begin at 001. After word marks are set by the first CLEAR STORAGE card, the second proceeds to clear the storage from 000–999, sets a word mark at 001, reads the bootstrap card, and branches to 001. The function performed by the bootstrap card is to set the four word marks required to load the program, read the first object program card, and branch to 056. Each succeeding card loads its portion of the machine language, reads another card, and branches to 056. Finally, the instruction on the END card clears the READ area and causes a branch to the address specified on the END card to begin execution of the program.

PROCESSOR CONTROL OPERATIONS

With the introduction of SPS in Chapter 5, two types of pseudo instructions were described. The declarative statements consist of DCW, DC, DS, and DSA, all of which have been used in example programs. The only processor control statement that we have used is the END, which signifies the end of the source deck and includes the address of the first instruction to be executed. In addition to this the 141 system includes two other control statements, which, although not so widely used as the END statement, are useful SPS tools.

The ORIGIN Statement

In preceding sections we discussed how the object program is loaded into storage. The positions that each instruction occupies were determined by the assembler; the first instruction was assigned position 333 and the others followed. Normally, the actual positioning of the program in storage is of little concern to the programmer. Occasionally, however, it is desirable to locate the program or a portion of it beginning at locations other than 333.

Provided for this purpose is the ORIGIN statement, which consists of the symbolic operation code ORG and an absolute address in the A operand portion of the instruction. An ORG statement may be placed at the beginning of a source deck, causing the entire program to be stored at other than 333, or several may be used throughout the program to separate constants, working areas, and subroutines from the main program.

Figure 14–15 is a listing of two object decks (excluding the first three cards in each) in which the ORG statement has been used. In the first, the program origin is defined as 201, so the loading instruction places the first instruction in 201–204, with the remainder of the program following. In the second program, the assembler was allowed to place the main program at 333, but the constants were assigned locations beginning with 500. This is evident from inspection of the loading instruction.

```
01010         ORG0201                          N0010561056
0102004START  SW  0001                         L0702041056,001
0103001READ   R                                L06720510561
0104007       MCW0080          0180            L0732121056M080180
0105001       P                                L06721310564
0106004       B   READ                         L07021710568205
01070         ENDSTART                         /201080


0101004START  SW  0001                         L0703361056,001
0102001READ   R                                L06733710561
0103007       MCW0080          0180            L0733441056M080180
0104001       P                                L06734510564
0105004       B   READ                         L07034910568337
01060         ORG0500                          N0010561056
0107014       DCW*             FIRST CONSTANT  L0375131056
0108015       DCW*             SECOND CONSTANT L0385281056
01090         ENDSTART                         /333080
```

Figure 14–15. The ORG *Statement*

The EXECUTE Statement

Occasionally we will find the 1000 storage-position capacity of the 141 system insufficient for a program we desire to assemble and run. In many such instances, it is possible to divide the program into several sections to be executed separately. For instance, extensive headings for a report could be printed, and the main portion of the program loaded in the positions occupied by the printing routine.

Another common use is to compile a table prior to actual program calculations. For example, a standard table might be loaded with the object deck. However, each run would use values, specified by an input card, that are to be determined from the original table by predefined mathematical methods. Once the new table is determined for a given run, the original table and the program for calculating the new one can be discarded, so the main program may be loaded over the previous one. For obvious reasons, this is frequently called an *overlay*.

The functions described above are usually accomplished by use of an SPS EXECUTE statement, which is provided in the 141 system specifically for such needs. By placing EXECUTE statements in proper positions of the source program, the programmer can divide his program into several sections, each of which is executed prior to loading the following section.

In using the EXECUTE statement the programmer must provide the following:

1. The symbolic operation code EX in the operation field.
2. A symbolic or actual address in the A operand that designates the first instruction to be executed.
3. A READ AND BRANCH instruction at the end of the section to be executed. This will provide for loading of the remainder of the program after the initial portion has been executed.

Use of an EX is illustrated in Figure 14–16. Line 110 contains the EX statement and directs that, during loading of the object program, loading be discontinued and that portion of the program beginning with the instruction labeled PRELIM be executed. After this has been completed, the instruction on line 090 will cause the next card of the object deck to be read, thus continuing the loading process. The NOP insures that a word mark follows the READ AND BRANCH instruction.

In some instances the initial operations to be performed may require considerable use of the READ area, so the four word marks used by the loading routine must be cleared. In such a situation, the first instruction of the initial program section would probably clear storage addresses 000–080. However, it is important that these word marks be set before continuing the loading operation, or it will be impossible to execute the loading instructions. In such a situation the additional instructions shown in Figure 14–17 are required for clearing and resetting word marks.

The ORG and EX statements provide additional flexibility for the 141 system. Although infrequently used, they provide a means for programming problems that are otherwise too large for the 1000 storage positions of the 141.

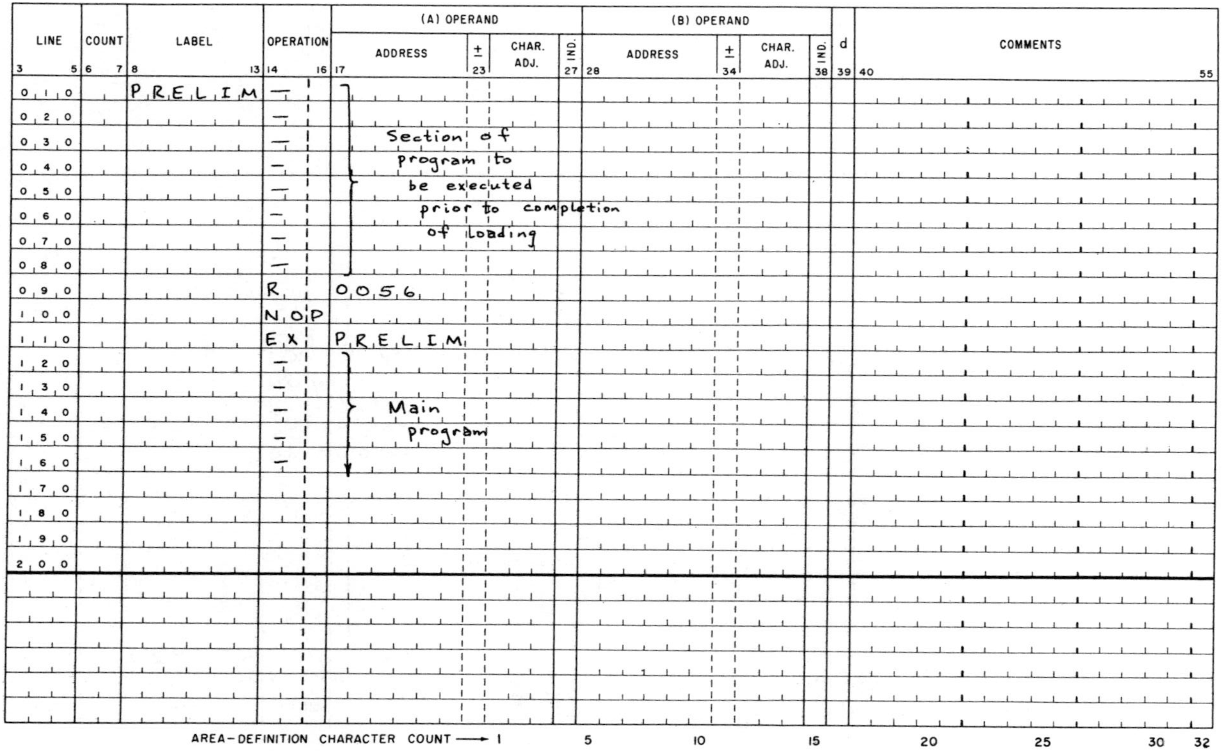

Figure 14–16. The EXECUTE Statement

IBM 1401 SYMBOLIC PROGRAMMING SYSTEM
CODING SHEET

LINE	COUNT	LABEL	OPERATION	(A) OPERAND ADDRESS	±	CHAR. ADJ.	I/ND	(B) OPERAND ADDRESS	±	CHAR. ADJ.	I/ND	d	COMMENTS
010		PRELIM	CS	0080									
020				Section of program									
030				to be executed									
040				prior to completion									
050				of loading									
060													
070													
080													
090			SW	0024				0056					
100			SW	0063				0067					
110			R	0056									
120			NOP										
130			EX	PRELIM									
140				Main									
150				program									
160													
170													
180													
190													
200													

AREA-DEFINITION CHARACTER COUNT ⟶

Figure 14–17. The EXECUTE Statement

Chapter Fifteen

THE IBM 1401 DATA PROCESSING SYSTEM

By using the 141 concept we have learned the basic elements of computer programming. We have intentionally de-emphasized the hardware aspects of any real computer on the basis that these details would only detract from the greater objective—understanding programming. Now with the learning of programming fundamentals behind us, it is time to examine those parts of the 1401 that the 141 has omitted. However, it is still not the intent to present 1401 programming in detail.

IBM 1401 ADDRESSES

The IBM 1401 is available with six different storage capacities; 1400, 2000, 4000, 8000, 12,000, and 16,000 characters. The last four sizes are the most common and are frequently referred to as having 4K, 8K, 12K, or 16K storages, with the letter K standing for *kilo*, or 1000. The 1460, which is a more powerful version of the 1401, is available only with 8K, 12K, and 16K storage capacities.

The forms of 1401 instructions are identical to those of the 141, including the addresses, which are three characters in length. We saw in the 141 that the first thousand addresses run from 000–999. It is obvious that if the addresses above 999 are to remain only three characters in length, they cannot be purely numeric. A three-character address not only contains three numeric digits but also has three zones. Each zone is made up of an A bit and a B bit. The addresses for a 4K machine, 0000–3999, can be represented by the three digits and one of the zones. For this the leftmost (or hundreds position) zone is used. These addresses take the form of

$$Z_2 \times 1000 + d_2 d_1 d_0$$

Where $d_2 d_1 d_0$ are the three digits and Z_2 is the zone over the hundreds digits. As before, the three-digit number $d_2 d_1 d_0$ has the range 000–999, and Z_2 can have the values 0, 1, 2, or 3. The values of Z are given below with their corresponding A bit and B bit configurations and the corresponding zone punches:

Z	ZONE BITS	ZONE PUNCHES
0	None	None
1	A bit only	0 zone
2	B bit only	11 zone
3	A bit, B bit	12 zone

The address 2345 would then be

$$2 \times 1000 + 345$$

A value for Z of 2 is represented by a B bit in storage or an 11 zone on a card. Since this is the zone of the hundreds position, the address digits would be B3, 4, and 5, or, as we will represent it here, $\overset{B}{3}45$.

However, $\overset{B}{3}$ is equivalent to an 11–3 punch or the letter L. Hence the address 2345 would appear in a 1401 storage dump as L45. This clever use of alphabetic characters in 1401 addresses greatly increases the effectiveness of storage by keeping the addresses to three characters instead of using four or even five. The cost of this trick is paid for in decreased readability. For additional examples, here are the IBM 1401 three-character addresses for 0736, 1529, 2481, and 3999.

$$0736 = 0 \times 1000 + 736 = 736$$

$$1529 = 1 \times 1000 + 529 = \overset{A}{5}29 = V29$$

$$2481 = 2 \times 1000 + 481 = \overset{B}{4}81 = M81$$

$$3999 = 3 \times 1000 + 999 = \overset{AB}{9}99 = I99$$

High Addresses

When addresses exceed 3999 it is necessary to go to a new device. This time Z_0, the zone of the units position of the address, is used. Z_0 also can have the values of 0, 1, 2, and 3, and is a multiplier for a factor of 4000. Adresses ranging all the way from 0000 to 15,999 can be represented by:

$$Z_0 \times 4000 + Z_2 \times 1000 + d_2 d_1 d_0$$

For example, 7186 is converted as

$$7186 = 1 \times 4000 + 3 \times 1000 + 186 = \overset{AB}{1} 8 \overset{A}{6} = A8W$$

and 15,999 becomes

$$15,999 = 3 \times 4000 + 3 \times 1000 + 999 = \overset{AB}{9} 9 \overset{AB}{9} = I9I$$

Notice that the zone of the middle digit, or tens position, of the address has not been used. The design engineers did not ignore it, however. It is used to designate index locations, which we will discuss shortly. Thus any or all of the three characters of an IBM 1401 address may be alphabetic. In addition to the 26 letters of the alphabet, four special characters are needed to bring the total to 30 non-numeric characters. One of these is the familiar slash mark (/); the others are not so familiar. The four special characters used in addresses are

ZONE BITS	ZONE PUNCH	DIGIT	CHARACTER
A	0	0	$\neq$ record mark
A	0	1	/
B	11	0	$\bar{0}$ or !
A and B	12	0	$\overset{+}{0}$ or ?

ARITHMETIC OPERATIONS

The arithmetic operations of addition and subtraction are slightly more complex in the IBM 1401 than in the 141. One difference is in the handling of overflows. In the 141, if $\underline{7}4$ is added to $\underline{5}8$ the result is $\underline{3}2$, since a carry out of a too-small field (overflow) is simply lost. In the 1401 carries beyond the high-order position appear as zone bits over the high-order position. The first overflow, such as that which occurs when $\underline{7}4$ is added to $\underline{5}8$, will appear as an A bit over the high-order position. Hence the result will be $\overset{A}{\underline{3}}2$ or $\underline{T}2$. At the time the overflow occurs, an OVERFLOW INDICATOR is turned on. This indicator can be tested by the program with one of the forms of the BRANCH IF INDICATOR ON instruction.

If further addition is performed on a field that already has an A bit in the high-order position and a second overflow occurs, it will appear as a B bit. A third overflow will appear as an A and B bit and a fourth overflow will be lost, returning the zone back to no A bit and no B bit. The usefulness of this feature appears in address modification. For example:

$$\underline{7}36 + \underline{7}93 = \overset{A}{\underline{5}}\ 2\ 9 = \underline{V}29$$

$$\underline{V}29 + \underline{9}52 = \overset{B}{\underline{4}}\ 8\ 1 = \underline{M}81$$

$$\underline{M}81 + \underline{5}18 = \overset{AB}{\underline{9}}\ 9\ 9 = \underline{I}99$$

This overflow system will permit address modification from 0000 to 3999 by the direct use of the ADDITION instruction. The SUBTRACTION instruction, however, cannot be used in address modification.

For machines larger than 4K, a special instruction, MODIFY ADDRESS, must be used in order to place the proper zone bits over the units position as well as over the high-order position. For example, without the MODIFY ADDRESS instruction, we have

$$\underline{I}99 + \underline{0}03 = \underline{0}02$$

But with the MODIFY ADDRESS instruction, we have

$$\underline{I}99 + \underline{0}03 = \underline{0}\ 0\ \overset{A}{2} = \underline{0}0S$$

which has the proper address equivalent of 4002.

Sign Control

In the 141 system, if the result of an ADDITION or a SUBTRACTION is negative, it will be represented by a B bit over the units position (alphabetic characters J–R); if it is positive, it will be represented by no zone over the units position. In other words, the result will either have a minus sign or no sign (NS). In the 1401, a negative result from an addition or subtraction operation will also have a B bit over the units position, but a positive result may have either no sign bits or it may have both an A bit and a B bit, depending upon the original sign of the B field and whether or not there was a change in the sign of the B field. Table 15–1 summarizes the sign control of the 1401.

Table 15–1
IBM 1401 SIGN CONTROL

	B			+B			−B		
	$A<B$	$A=B$	$A>B$	$A<B$	$A=B$	$A>B$	$A<B$	$A=B$	$A>B$
ADD A	NS	NS	NS	+	+	+	−	−0	+
ADD +A	NS	NS	NS	+	+	+	−	−0	+
ADD −A	+	+0	−	+	+0	−	−	−	−
SUB A	+	+0	−	+	+0	−	−	−	−
SUB +A	+	+0	−	+	+0	−	−	−	−
SUB −A	NS	NS	NS	+	+	+	−	−0	+

Arithmetic Instructions

Two additional arithmetic operations are standard features of the 1401. They are ZERO AND ADD (ZA) and ZERO AND SUBTRACT (ZS). They are similar to ADD and SUBTRACT, respectively, except that the entire B field is set to zero before the addition or subtraction takes place.

Multiplication and division are available as special features on the IBM 1401, but for standard machines without these features, MULTIPLY and DIVIDE subroutines are used.

CHAINING INSTRUCTIONS

There are several sets of registers in the IBM 1401, two of which are already familiar to us. They are the op register, which holds the operation code of the instruction in progress for the duration of the operation, and the I address register, which contains the storage location of the next instruction character to be used by the program. Two other registers that the IBM 1401 contains are the A address register and the B address register. These registers contain the storage addresses of the characters of data that are being acted upon. For example, if the instruction M076154 is being executed, the registers will stand initially at

OP REG = M   A ADD REG = 076   B ADD REG = 154

This will cause the character in location 076 to be moved to location 154. As soon as this is done, the contents of both the A address register and the B address register will be decreased by 1. The register will then stand at

OP REG = $\underline{M}$ A ADD REG = 075   B ADD REG = 153

This will cause the character in location 075 to be moved to location 153. This process will continue until a character with a word mark is found in either the A field or the B field. If the shorter of the two fields in this example consisted of five characters, the register would contain the following during the execution of the instruction:

	OP REG	A ADD REG	B ADD REG
1. Initial	$\underline{M}$	076	154
2.	$\underline{M}$	075	153
3.	$\underline{M}$	074	152
4.	$\underline{M}$	073	151
5. Character found with word mark	$\underline{M}$	072	150
6. Final	$\underline{M}$	071	149

If the next task to be performed by the program is to move an adjacent field, such as 068–071, to locations 146–149, and following that move the next field, 066 and 067, to locations 144 and 145, a shortened instruction form called *chaining* may be used. Because the A-address and B-address registers are already set to 071 and 149, respectively, it is not necessary to reset them for the next instruction. Instead, the next instruction may consist of only the operation code $\underline{M}$. Similarly the A-address and B-address registers will already be set at 067 and 145, respectively, for the third instruction. Again only the op code of $\underline{M}$ is needed. The three consecutive instructions would be

$$\underline{M}076154\underline{M}\ \underline{M}$$

Both execution time and storage space are saved when chaining is used. Chained instructions do not necessarily have to use the same operation codes.

INPUT/OUTPUT

Instructions

Another method by which the 1401 saves space is the use of combination input/output instructions, in which two, or even three, operations are designated by a single character. The clever choice of the

READ, WRITE, and PUNCH operation codes of 1, 2, and 4 respectively permits the addition of two, or all three, of these codes into a single-digit multiple-operation code. For example, the combined operations of WRITE and PUNCH can be designated by a 6 (2 for WRITE plus 4 for PUNCH). The combined operation of WRITE, READ, and PUNCH can be designated by a 7 (2 for WRITE, plus 1 for READ, plus 4 for PUNCH). Table 15–2 shows the one-digit input/output operation codes of the 1401.

Table 15–2
IBM 1401 MULTIPLE INPUT/OUTPUT OPERATIONS

OPERATION	MNEMONIC	OP CODE
READ	R	1
WRITE	W	2
WRITE, PUNCH	WR	3
PUNCH	P	4
READ, PUNCH	RP	5
WRITE, PUNCH	WP	6
WRITE, READ, PUNCH	WRP	7

Each of the combination input/output instructions can be further combined with a BRANCH operation in the same manner as the single input/output instructions. It is therefore possible to combine as many as four operations into a single instruction. For example,

SPS	ABSOLUTE
W	2
R	1
P	4
B NEXT	B345

can be combined into the single instruction

WRPNEXT   7345

A special instruction is provided on the 1401 to print word marks as ones. This is primarily used for printing storage dumps. The operation code for the WRITE WORD MARKS instruction is the usual code for WRITE, but it is modified by a d character of □, thus making a two-character instruction. If an I address is inserted between the op code and the d character, a WRITE WORD MARKS AND BRANCH instruction is formed.

The 1402 card read-punch unit that is used with the 1401 for card input and output operations has five pockets into which cards may be dropped (see Figure 15–1).

From left to right they are designated as NP, 4, 8/2, 1, NR. Cards from the punch feed fall into the NP (normal punch) pocket unless they are directed by the program to fall into pocket 1 or 2. The center pocket is both pocket 8 for punch operations and pocket 2 for read operations, hence the designation of 8/2. However, card merging can be accomplished only under certain, very limited conditions.

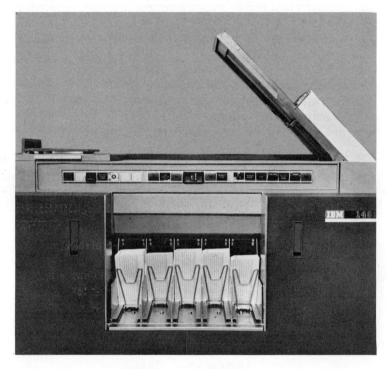

Figure 15–1. Card Stackers

The instruction SELECT STACKER is used to direct cards into pockets other than NP and NR. This instruction is a two-character instruction with an operation code of $\underline{K}$ (the SPS mnemonic is SS) and a d character that designates which stacker pocket is selected. The possible d characters are as follows:

d CHARACTER	FEED	STACKER POCKET
1	READ	1
2	READ	8/2
4	PUNCH	4
8	PUNCH	8/2

The SELECT STACKER instruction may also be combined with a BRANCH by inserting an I address.

The 1403 printer that is used with the 1401 system (see Figure 2–4) has a paper carriage-control tape synchronized with the continuous paper used. A punched hole in any one of 12 possible positions, known as channels, can be read by a reading brush, and will cause skipping of the paper to begin or end. A punch in channel 1 is traditionally used to indicate the position of the first line to be printed on a new page. Punches in channels 2, 3, 4, . . . n are used to indicate subsequent skip stops within the body of the page. A punch in channel 12 usually indicates the last line to be printed. Sensing a channel-12 punch can, under program control, initiate overflow skipping to the next page. Channel 9 is used in a somewhat similar manner to initiate skips within the same page.

An instruction is provided on the 1401 to control the carriage on the 1403 printer. The operation code for the CONTROL CARRIAGE instruction is F (the SPS mnemonic is CC), and a d character designates whether the action is to take place before or after printing the line and whether a skip to a channel or a space of 1, 2, or 3 lines is called for. The d characters in Table 15–3 may be used and have the indicated significance. The CONTROL CARRIAGE instruction may also be combined with a BRANCH by inserting an I address.

BRANCHING OPERATIONS

In the 141 the BRANCH IF INDICATOR ON instruction was demonstrated with four possible d characters. Namely, /, S, T, and U for unequal, equal, low, and high COMPARE results, respectively. In the 1401 a great many d characters can be used to test other indicators and switches. Some of the more significant ones are discussed below.

Printer Indicators

When a punch in channel 9 or 12 in the carriage-control tape of the 1403 printer is sensed, special indicators are turned on. These indicators can be tested with a BRANCH IF INDICATOR ON instruction, with a d character of 9 or @, respectively.

Table 15–3
CONTROL CARRIAGE *d* CHARACTERS

IMMEDIATE			*AFTER PRINTING*		
d CHARACTER		*CHANNEL*	*d CHARACTER*		*CHANNEL*
1	skip to	1	A	skip to	1
2		2	B		2
3		3	C		3
4		4	D		4
5		5	E		5
6		6	F		6
7		7	G		7
8		8	H		8
9		9	I		9
0		10	?		10
#		11	.		11
@		12	◻		12
d CHARACTER		*LINES*	*d CHARACTER*		*LINES*
J	space	1	/	space	1
K		2	S		2
L		3	T		3

Last-Card Indicator

When the last card in the read hopper of the 1402 has been read, a special LAST CARD indicator is turned on. This indicator can be tested with a BRANCH IF INDICATOR ON instruction with a *d* character of A. The programmer can therefore write the program to print a message, or calculate totals, when the last card has been detected.

Sense Switches

The 1401 console may have, as a special feature, six toggle switches known as SENSE SWITCHES B, C, D, E, F, and G. These switches are very useful as a means of communication between the operator and the program. For example, the programmer might choose to let SENSE SWITCH E control the output of his program. A BRANCH IF INDICATOR ON instruction with a *d* character of E might cause the output to be printed if SENSE SWITCH E is off, and punched if it is on. The decision of which output is wanted would not have to be made until the program is actually run. Since each switch can cause a two-way branch, the various combinations of six switches will permit the writing of a program with a main path and up to 63 alternative paths.

Overflow

Another special indicator is the OVERFLOW indicator. Whenever an overflow bit is carried into the zone of the high-order digit during an ADD or SUBTRACT operation, this indicator is turned on. The indicator can be tested with a BRANCH IF INDICATOR ON instruction with a *d* character of Z.

Summary of Indicators

Table 15–4 shows valid *d* characters, for use with the BRANCH IF INDICATOR ON instruction, which have been discussed to this point. Additional *d* characters are used with certain error conditions and with various special features.

Table 15–4
BRANCH IF INDICATOR ON *d* CHARACTERS

d CHARACTER	*BRANCH CONDITION*
A	LAST CARD
B	SENSE SWITCH B ON
C	SENSE SWITCH C ON
D	SENSE SWITCH D ON
E	SENSE SWITCH E ON
F	SENSE SWITCH F ON
G	SENSE SWITCH G ON
/	UNEQUAL COMPARE $(B \neq A)$
S	EQUAL COMPARE $(B = A)$
T	LOW COMPARE $(B < A)$
U	HIGH COMPARE $(B > A)$
Z	OVERFLOW
9	CARRIAGE CHANNEL 9
@	CARRIAGE CHANNEL 12

Word Marks and Zone Bits

An instruction is provided in the 1401 to test for the presence (and absence) of word marks and zone bits. The BRANCH IF WORD MARK AND/ OR ZONE instruction has a familiar form of code, an I address, a B address, and a *d* character. The operation code is $\underline{V}$ and the SPS mnemonic is BWZ. This instruction will cause a branch to the location specified by the I address if the single character specified by the B address has a word mark or zone bits as specified by the d character. The possible d characters and their meanings are shown in Table 15–5.

Table 15–5
BRANCH IF WORD MARK AND/OR ZONE d CHARACTERS

d CHARACTER	BRANCH CONDITION
1	Word Mark
2	No Zone (no A or B bit)
B	12 Zone (A and B bits)
K	11 Zone (B bit only)
S	0 Zone (A bit only)
3	Word Mark or no Zone
C	Word Mark or 12 Zone
L	Word Mark or 11 Zone
T	Word Mark or 0 Zone

For example, the instruction V456076K would cause a branch to 456 if the character in location 076 has a B bit but no A bit. Since this character is in the READ area, the instruction could mean branch to 456 if column 76 has an X punch. This instruction is also very useful in determining whether the result of an arithmetic operation is positive or negative, since signs are stored as zones over the units position of the B field.

DATA MOVEMENT

Two instructions are included in the 1401 that move less than a whole character. The MOVE ZONE instruction has an operation code of Y (the SPS mnemonic is MZ), an A address, and a B address. This instruction causes the A bit and the B bit of the character specified by the A address to replace the A bit and the B bit at the B address.

The MOVE NUMERIC instruction has an operation code of D (the SPS mnemonic is MN), an A address and a B address. This instruction causes the 8, 4, 2, and 1 bits of the character specified by the A address to replace the 8, 4, 2, and 1 bits of the character specified by the B address.

Another data-movement instruction is the MOVE CHARACTERS AND SUPPRESS ZEROS. This instruction has an operation code of Z (the SPS mnemonic is MCS), an A address, and a B address. The data field specified by the A address is moved to the location specified by the B address, and the high-order zeros are replaced by blanks. This is particularly useful in preparing numeric results for output.

Editing

A very powerful editing instruction, MOVE CHARACTERS AND EDIT, is provided as a standard feature of the 1401. With this single instruction, a data field can be moved into the print output area; desired commas, decimals, dollar signs, asterisks, credit symbols, and minus signs can be inserted; and leading zeros can be suppressed. The operation code for this instruction is $\underline{E}$ and its SPS mnemonic is MCE. The A address specifies the data field to be edited, and the B address specifies the location in which the resultant edited field should be placed. Prior to the execution of the MCE operation, an edit-control word is moved into the B field by an LCA instruction. This control field designates, character-by-character, what editing is desired.

For example, a numeric field in location 632 is to be placed in the print area, at location 241, with a dollar sign, comma, and decimal point, and leading zeros are to be suppressed. The EDIT word is in location 618. The coding for this would be

LCA0618	0241
MCE0632	0241

The contents of these locations would be as follows.

Contents of storage initially:

$\underline{\,|1_|2_|3_|4_|5_|6_|5_|4_|3_|2_|1_|\,}$

$\overset{2}{\underset{1}{4}}$

$\underline{\,|\$_|b_|b_|b_|\,,_|b_|b_|0_|\,._|b_|b_|\,}$

$\overset{6}{\underset{8}{1}}$

$\underline{\,|0_|0_|3_|7_|9_|5_|6_|2_|\,}$

$\overset{6}{\underset{2}{3}}$

Contents of storage after execution of LCA instruction:

| $ | b | b | b | , | b | b | 0 | . | b | b |
2
4
1

| $ | b | b | b | , | b | b | 0 | . | b | b |
6
1
8

| 0 | 0 | 3 | 7 | 9 | 5 | 6 | 2 |
6
3
2

Contents of storage after execution of MCE instruction:

| $ | b | b | 3 | , | 7 | 9 | 5 | . | 6 | 2 |
2
4
1

| $ | b | b | b | , | b | b | 0 | . | b | b |
6
1
8

| 0 | 0 | 3 | 7 | 9 | 5 | 6 | 2 |
6
3
2

The field at locations 231 through 241 would print as

$ 3,795.62

With a special feature, EXPANDED PRINT EDIT, even fancier editing can be accomplished, including floating signs and check-protective asterisks.

INDEXING FEATURE

When address modification is used in a program, it is more than likely that several addresses must all be stepped by the same increment. In fact, in some applications, such as processing blocked records from magnetic tape, it may be necessary to modify upwards of 100 addresses at a time. The 1401 indexing feature makes it as easy to modify 100 addresses as it is to modify one.

When an instruction having an indexed address is executed, the address used is an *effective* address, which is automatically calculated. This effective address is equal to the actual address plus the contents of an index location.

There are three index locations. Each is a three-character field located in the little-used portion of storage between the READ area and the PUNCH area. Each is specified by a tag, which is a unique A bit and B bit combination placed over the tens position of every address to be modified by it. Table 15–6 shows the storage locations of each index location, the A bit and B bit configuration, and the zone equivalent.

Table 15–6
INDEX LOCATIONS

INDEX LOCATION	*STORAGE*	*TAG*	*ZONE*
1	087–089	A bit	0
2	092–094	B bit	11
3	097–099	A bit, B bit	12

The programmer tags an address in SPS by placing a 1, 2, or 3 in column 27 of the coding sheet if an A address is to be tagged, or in column 38 if a B address is to be tagged. For example, to modify the A address of a SET WORD MARK instruction with index location 2, the programmer would write as shown in Figure 15–2. Since index location

				(A) OPERAND				(B) OPERAND				d	
LINE	COUNT	LABEL	OPERATION	ADDRESS	±	CHAR. ADJ.	IND.	ADDRESS	±	CHAR. ADJ.	IND.		
3	5 6 7 8		13 14 16 17		23		27 28		34		38	39 40	
0 1 0			S W	0 5 7 4			2						

Figure 15–2

2 is indicated by a B bit over the tens position, the SPS would assemble the instruction as

,5P4

When this instruction is executed, the current value in index location 2 will be added to 574 and a word mark will be set at that location.

Suppose that storage location 092–094 contains 015. Then a word mark will be set at 574 + 015 or 589. The actual address in the SW instruction, however, remains as 574. If 005 is then added to location 094 and the instruction is executed again, the word mark will be set at 574, plus the new contents of index location 2—namely 574 + 020, or 594. This has little or no advantage if only one address is modified by index location 2, but if many addresses are modified, *every one* will be automatically stepped by 5 when 5 is added to the index location. Because the actual instruction is never modified within storage, all instructions modified by index location 2 will automatically be reinitialized if index location 2 is set at zero.

MAGNETIC TAPE

Thus far we have considered only card-oriented computer systems. The addition of magnetic tape extends the capacity of the computer in two ways. First, magnetic tape can be used as an extension of the computer's storage. Data, intermediate results, and portions of the program can be written out on tape when not needed and called back in at a later time, thereby freeing much of the computer's main core storage for other portions of the program. The processes of writing information out on tape and reading it back in can be done very rapidly. For example, the entire storage of a 4000-character 1401 can be obtained from magnetic tape in less than 0.1 sec.

The second way magnetic tape can extend the capacity of the computer is as a high-speed input/output device. Entire large-volume files can be stored on magnetic tape instead of cards. One reel of tape can hold as much information as fifty file drawers of cards. When these files are processed by the 1401, the information is read from tape at a rate equivalent to 45,000 cards per minute. The exact values of tape capacity and input/output speeds are dependent upon the model of the tape drive, the recording density, and the blocking factor.

Three different types of tape drives can be used with the 1401. They are the 7330 tape unit (see Figure 2–4), the Model II 729 tape unit, and the Model IV 729 unit. Each has the capability of recording and reading information at either of two densities—200 characters per inch or 556 characters per inch. Table 15–7 is a summary of their information-handling characteristics.

Table 15–7
TAPE UNIT OPERATING CHARACTERISTICS

	7330	*729–II*	*729–IV*
Tape speed (in in. per sec)	36	75	112.5
Character rate at 200 char/in.	7,200	15,000	22,500
(in characters			
per second) at 556 char/in.	20,016	41,667	62,500
Inter-record gap (in in.)	¾	¾	¾

Coding on Tape

The magnetic tape for the tape units in Table 15–7 is a continuous strip of oxide-coated plastic (see Figure 15–3). It is 2400 ft long and ½ in. wide, and is wound on a reel 10½ in. in diameter. Seven channels of information are recorded on the tape—one for each of the bits in a character, namely, the C, B, A, 8, 4, 2, and 1 bits. The character-coding on tape is exactly the same as in storage (see Appendix II) except that the C bit reflects an even parity rather than an odd parity. This is because the new parity bit is recorded when the tape is written, rather than using the one from storage. This new C bit is written such that the number of x's in a character will always be an even number, and the number of x's is checked for being even every time the tape is read.

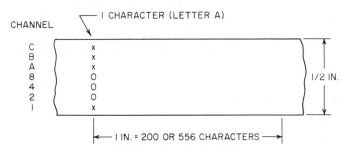

Figure 15–3. Magnetic Tape

Records

When using cards the record length is always 80 characters, since even blank columns are read. With magnetic tape this restriction is removed; records may be any size. They can be less than 80 characters, but more often they are made as large as the available storage will permit, which may be as large as 5000 characters.

Large records save time because of fewer starts and stops of the tape, and make more efficient use of the tape itself. When the tape is written, the tape motion stops between every record, and a ¾ in. gap of unrecorded tape is left between records. If the records are short, such as the 80 characters of a card, the amount of tape used for gaps far exceeds the amount of tape used for information. With 80-character records, tape recorded at 200 characters per inch is approximately ⅓ information and ⅔ gap; at 556 characters per inch it is approximately ⅙ information and ⅚ gap. By using long records the portion lost by inter-record gaps becomes trivial.

Blocking

The advantages of long records can be gained for short records by a technique called *blocking*. For example, twenty 80-character records might be placed end-to-end in core storage and written as one 1600-character record. It is then said to have a blocking factor of 20. When the tape is read, the entire 1600–character record is placed in core storage and the individual records are usually processed by instructions that are indexed. When the processing of the first record is completed, adding 80 to the appropriate index location will automatically modify every instruction to process the second record. If the indexing feature is not available, other techniques must be used. The most common is to move the particular record being processed to a special work area.

The very nature of magnetic tape requires for efficient operation that records be processed in the same order that they appear on the tape. If an application requires that records in a file be processed in a random order, the capabilities of random access can be added to the 1401 by the attachment of either the 1405 (see Figure 2–4), or the 1311 disk storage units.

Details for programming the 1401, with all of its special features including magnetic tape and disk storage, can be found in IBM reference manuals.

BASIC AUTOCODER

In addition to the SPS assembly language, the 1401 has another assembly language available to it called *autocoder*. For a small card 1401, *autocoder* has little to offer over SPS, but with longer tape systems the difference becomes significant. In Figure 15–4, the honor roll program from Example 9–2 has been rewritten in basic autocoder.

The major difference that will be noticed is the format. The operand field is what is known as a *free-field* format. The A operand, B operand, and *d* character are written one after the other, separated only by commas. Comments can then be written after the last operand, separated by at least two blanks. Both the A operand and the B operand may consist of a symbolic address or an absolute address followed immediately by whatever address adjustment and indexing is needed. If the address is absolute, leading zeros may be omitted.

Honor-Roll Problem

With these differences in mind, let us compare the autocoder program in Figure 15–4 with the SPS program in Figure 9–12. Lines 01, 02, and 03 of the autocoder program set five word marks. Line 04 is a simple

Line	Label	Operation	OPERAND
0 1	START.	S W	7,1,9 DEFINE FIELDS
0 2		S W	2,6,2,5,5
0 3		S W	2,5,7
0 4		MLC	TITLE,2,4,6 WRITE
0 5		W	HEADING
0 6		C S	2,4,6 AND
0 7		W	SPACE
0 8		MLC	@.@,2,5,6 PLACE DECIMAL POINT
0 9	CARD.	R	READ STUDENT CARD
1 0		C	7,4,@,1,2,@ TEST
1 1		BU	CARD GRADE
1 2		C	6,4,@,1,5,0,@ TEST NUMBER
1 3		BL	CARD
1 4		C	6,7,@,3,2,0,@ TEST OF UNITS
1 5		BL	CARD
1 6		MLC	2,5,2,2,6 GRADE POINT AVERAGE
1 7		MLC	2,6,2,2,8 MOVE
1 8		MLC	1,8,2,4,1 NAME
1 9		MLC	6,5,2,5,5 AND
2 0		MLC	6,7,2,2,5,8 GRADE POINT AVERAGE
2 1		W	TO PRINT AREA
2 2		B	CARD WRITE HONOR ROLL ENTRY
2 3	TITLE.	DCW	@SENIOR HONOR ROLL@
2 4		END.	START.
2 5			

Figure 15-4. Honor Roll Problem in Autocoder

MOVE instruction, but the autocoder mnemonic is MLC instead of MCW. Lines 05, 06, and 07 write a line, clear storage, and write another line, respectively. On line 08 an alphabetic literal is used in the A operand field. This permits a short cut for the programmer. If the field to be moved is five characters or less of constant information, he merely writes the actual character between two @ signs. The autocoder processor automatically generates a DCW of the proper size and value at the end of the program. The programmer does not need to write the DCW or think up a label for the field.

On line 09 a READ instruction is given, and on line 10 a COMPARE is written, with an alphabetic literal in the B operand. On line 11 the operation code is BU. This stands for BRANCH ON UNEQUAL COMPARE and is equivalent to an SPS operation code of B with a d character of /. Lines 12 and 13 and lines 14 and 15 are a pair of COMPARE AND BRANCH operations. The BL operation codes stands for BRANCH ON LOW COMPARE, and is equivalent to an SPS operation code of B and a d character of T. Lines 16–20 are all regular MOVE instructions, and lines 21 and 22 are the WRITE and UNCONDITIONAL BRANCH instructions.

If a literal, alphabetic or numeric, is longer than five characters it must be written as a DCW in basic autocoder. On line 23 a long alphabetic literal is needed. The label, the DCW operation code, and the constant are written in the usual way except that the constant is preceded and followed by an @ sign. This eliminates the need for the COUNT field that was required with SPS. The END card on line 24 is the same as in SPS.

The assembled machine-language program produced from this autocoder program will be identical to that produced by the SPS program, except that the automatically assigned literal will follow the DCW-produced alphabetic constant.

FULL AUTOCODER

With a tape 1401 system, a more advanced autocoder known as *tape autocoder* or *full autocoder* may be used. With this system, some of the restrictions on lengths of literals have been removed, but the real increase in power comes from its area defining statement and its macro capabilities.

DEFINE AREA Statement

In the honor roll example just discussed the input was from cards, so the exact numeric address of each field was easily determined. The programmer could, if he wanted, give each field a symbolic name by using DS statements. In a tape system, the tape record might be read into almost any location and it might be blocked.

Suppose that the same program is to be written for a tape system with the same input format except that the 80-character records are to be blocked with a factor of 20. Index location 3 is to be used to step from one record to the next within the block. The coding shown in Figure 15–5 will set up the storage area for the twenty 80-character records, give each input field a symbolic name, and index all instructions using symbolic names with index location 3.

Line 3 5	Label 6	Operation 15 16 20	OPERAND 21 25 30 35 40 45
0 1	S,T,U,D,C,D	D,A	2,0,X,8,0,,3,X,
0 2	L,A,S,T,N,		7,,,1,8,
0 3	F,I,R,S,T,N		1,9,,,2,5,
0 4	I,N,I,T,L		2,6,,,2,6,
0 5	U,N,I,T,S,		6,2,,,6,4,
0 6	G,P,A,		6,5,,,6,7,
0 7	G,R,A,D,E,		7,3,,,7,4,
0 8			

Figure 15–5

The first line in Figure 15–5 is called the DA (DEFINE AREA) header line. It gives the records a symbolic name, has an operation code of DA, and designates the blocking factor, the record length, and the associated index location, if any. The subsequent lines are called DA entries. They give symbolic names to fields within the record.

The operation code is left blank, and the operand field contains the first and last character positions of the field within the record. For example, each record in the block is called STUDCD and characters 7–18 of each record are referred to as LASTN. Whenever LASTN, as well as the other symbols of lines 02–07, are used in the main program, it will be automatically tagged with index location 3.

Macro Instructions

In SPS each symbolic instruction assembles into one, and only one, machine-language instruction. In Full Autocoder several macro instructions are provided that generate into a group of machine-language instructions. For example we learned in Chapter 14 that, preceding an EX instruction, we must write the instruction necessary to continue the loading of the OVERLAY instruction. This is a set of four instructions (although fewer may be used if the READ area word marks are not disturbed), and hence in autocoder a single symbol can signal the processor to generate them. Figure 15–6 shows the OVLAY macro and the instruction it generates. The programmer can write lines 03–06, or get the same results by writing only line 01.

In addition to six standard macro instructions available in the autocoder processor, the facility is provided for the programmer to write his own macro instructions.

Line 3 5	6	Label	Operation 15 16 20	21 25	30	35	40	OPERAND 45
0 1			O V L A Y				M A C R O I N S T R U C T I O N	
0 2								
0 3			C S	8 0		I N S T R U C T I O N S		
0 4			S W	2 4 5 6			G E N E R A T E D B Y	
0 5			S W	6 3 6 7			O V L A Y M A C R O	
0 6			R	5 6			I N S T R U C T I O N	
0 7								
0 8								

Figure 15–6

■ **REMARKS**

As stated at the beginning of this chapter, the purpose here is not to teach 1401 programming. An entire text could be devoted to each of the several topics which have been discussed. This chapter is intended to give the student a very brief description and introduction to the 1401. Manuals and study materials are available from IBM covering each of the items discussed here.

■ **EXERCISES**

15.1 What are the 3-character 1401 addresses for (*a*) 1806? (*b*) 12,345? (*c*) 13,727?

15.2 What are the numeric equivalents of the following 1401 addresses? (*a*) X34. (*b*) F75. (*c*) A5A.

15.3 What is the numeric equivalent, including index location tag, for your three initials (assuming you have three initials)?

15.4 What relation exists between the multiple input/output operation codes and the binary number system?

15.5 How many branch possibilities exist with two sense switches? With three sense switches? With five sense switches? What is the general relationship between the number of switches and the number of branches?

15.6 Verify the approximate 1 to 2 and 1 to 5 ratios between a tape used for information and a tape used for gaps, with unblocked 80-character records at 200 and 556 characters per inch, respectively.

15.7 What percentage of tape is used for information with a record size of 1000 characters and a recording density of 200 characters per inch? At 556 characters per inch?

Chapter Sixteen

HIGHER-LEVEL LANGUAGES

As soon as the first electronic digital computers were built, it became obvious that the means by which man could communicate with the machine were inadequate and that better methods had to be found. In the beginning man had to learn the machine's language and prepare his instructions to the machine in *exactly* that language. Over the next twenty years, through the use of what has become known as programming systems (often informally referred to as *software* in contrast to the machine *hardware*), the situation has become reversed to the point where the machine, in a sense, understands man's languages of English and mathematics. The development of these higher-level languages has been a major factor in the advancement of computer technology.

ASSEMBLERS

We have been using an assembly language, SPS, since Chapter 5, but in order to relate assemblers in general to the more advanced languages, let us review their development and advantages. The term *assembler*, or *assembly programs*, has its origin in the function of these programs to assemble the various parts of an instruction, such as an operation code, one, two, or three addresses, index register tags, flags or indicators, and so on, into a single machine-language instruction. In the case of binary computers they are extremely helpful in converting decimal addresses and constants written by the programmer to the binary values needed by the machine.

Next, assemblers were written that permitted the use of symbolic operation codes and symbolic addresses. By no means the first of this type, but significant because of its widespread use, was the Symbolic Optimal Assembly Program (*Soap*) for the IBM 650 data processing system. This program was written in 1956 by Stan Poley of IBM's Service Bureau Corporation, and like most assemblers greatly decreased the time required to write a program, simplified the debugging of the program, and provided better documentation.

Programming time was improved through the use of this symbolic system; with symbolic operation codes, it was easier to remember that multiply was MPY rather than 19; using symbolic addresses, it was easier to remember that a constant 5 had been stored in location FIVE rather than at some numeric address such as 1732; and it was certainly much simpler to use blanks in places where the assembly program could assign addresses much more easily than the programmer.

Debugging, or checking of a program, was simplified because the symbolic program was easier to follow and because no erroneous duplication of address assignments could occur since the bookkeeping was performed by the assembler. Documentation was greatly improved by the use of remarks and comment cards, and even the mnemonic symbolic addresses were very helpful.

In addition to these functions, which are common to almost all assemblers, *Soap* also optimized the program. Because the IBM 650 had its main storage on the surface of a revolving drum, gaining access to data or the next instruction was much like catching the brass ring on a merry-go-round. If you reach without looking you might catch the ring immediately or you might just miss it, and have to wait almost a whole revolution. Similarly, a 650 program would be fast or slow depending upon whether the data and instructions were placed in good or poor locations. The *Soap* program automatically placed them in near optimum locations.

The development of programming systems has been greatly influenced by computer users' groups. These are organizations of computer installations that use the same type of computer and find it advantageous to share their programs. When the largest of these groups, aptly named *Share* (sometimes said to stand for the Society to Help Alleviate Redundant Effort) was formed, it found that its members could not communicate with each other. Although they all used IBM 704 computers, they were using different symbolic assembly languages. For example, General Electric had its *Cage* (Compiler and Assembler for General Electric), United Aircraft had its *Sap* (Symbolic Assembly Program), and IBM had its *Nyap*1, the first assembly program written by the New York group. It was obvious that the organization needed to settle on a single language, and a vote by the members selected United Aircraft's *Sap*, written by Roy Nutt.

COMPILERS

A compiler is a much more powerful programming tool than an assembler. In an assembler one symbolic instruction must be written for each machine-language instruction assembled, but in a compiler one statement will produce a multitude of machine-language instructions. A macro assembler, such as the 1401 Autocoder described in the last chapter, can be thought of as a combination of the two. Another difference between an assembler and a compiler is that the assembler language is so closely tied to the computer's machine language that it is impossible to use the assembler language of one computer on any other computer. This is not the case with compiler languages, which are generally considered *problem-oriented* rather than *machine-oriented*.

The first compiler was the A-O compiler written by Dr. Grace Murray Hopper for Univac in 1952. This program compiled subroutines from a magnetic tape library into complete computer programs. In or about 1957 the IT (Internal Translator) language of A. J. Perlis, J. W. Smith, and H. R. Van Zoeren was made available for both the IBM 650 and the Burroughs 205 Datatron computers. Here for the first time was a computer language that not only ran on two different machines but cut across manufacturer's lines as well.

In summary the compiler has all the features of the assembler plus multiple instruction per statement and machine independence. This latter quality permitted systems programmers to take the concept one step further. Why couldn't this machine-independent language be algebra or English?

FORTRAN

In 1954 John W. Backus of IBM proposed the idea of a *FOR*mula *TRAN*slating compiler with statements that were as near to algebraic expressions as the key punch would permit. A working committee was formed, including Backus, R. A. Hughes of the University of California Radiation Laboratory at Livermore, R. Nutt of United Aircraft, and ten others from IBM. In early 1957 Fortran was running on the IBM 704. Since that time IBM has written a Fortran compiler for each of its new computers, and in September of 1960 Burroughs released a version of Fortran for its Datatron 205 which they called Fortocom.

This started a major trend in manufacturer-independent languages, leading to Fortran's becoming the most universally used scientific computer language.

The Fortran Language

Every computer programming language must provide the programmer with the means to do input/output operations, data manipulations, calculations, conditional and unconditional branching, and instruction modification. All of these types of operations can be coded in machine language or in an assembly language, but the programmer must write on the detailed instruction level. In a compiler language as much of the detail as possible is made automatic, and the language is either scientifically or commercially oriented, depending upon the notation used and upon which types of operation have been emphasized and which are limited in their capabilities. Fortran is a scientific-engineering language using a notation that is basically algebraic, and as we shall see with strong capabilities in the area of calculation and instruction modification, but somewhat limited in input/output and data manipulation operations.

The purpose here is to show several examples of programs written in Fortran to illustrate the language, but it is not intended to be complete enough for the reader to learn to program in Fortran.

EXAMPLE 16-1

Exercise 13.5 involved computing the mean and variance of a set of data; the purpose of this Fortran example program is also to compute the mean and variance of a set of data. The values of a variable x have been punched in columns 11–15 of a card and an identification number has been punched in columns 1–3 (the same format as used in Chapter 13). The only purpose, in this program, of the identification number is that the number 999 must be punched in, and only in, the card that follows the last value of x. Other columns of the cards are ignored in this program.

As the cards are read, the program must (1) count the cards to obtain the size of the sample, (2) obtain the sum of the variable ($\sum x$) for use in the calculation of the mean, and (3) obtain the sum of the square of the variable ($\sum x^2$) for use in the calculation of the variance. When the last card is identified by the number 999, the mean and the variance are computed by the following formulas:

$$\text{Mean} = \frac{\sum x}{n} \qquad \text{Variance} = \frac{\sum x^2 - (\sum x)^2/n}{n - 1}$$

Following are the symbols that have been used in the above formulas, and their equivalents that have been used in the Fortran program.

ITEM	FORMULA	FORTRAN
The variable	x	X
Identification number		NUM
Sample size	n	SIZE
Sum of the variable	$\sum x$	SUMX
Sum of the square of the variable	$\sum x^2$	SUMSQ
Mean	mean	XMEAN
Variance	variance	XVAR

Fortran Coding Sheet

A program for Example 16–1 is shown in Figure 16–1. It is written on a standard Fortran coding form, from which it will be key-punched as one card per coding-sheet line. It is desirable to have the symbols), +, (and = on the key punch, but if it does not have them the same holes are punched by keys marked □, &, %, and # respectively.

Columns 1–5 on the coding sheet are for the statement number. Statements in general are not numbered unless there is a need for referencing them within another statement of the program. The numbers need not be in any particular order. Columns 7–72 contain the actual Fortran statement. If the letter C appears in column 1, columns 2–72 may be used for any type of comment. The numbers and the letter L to the left of column 1 are not part of the program (for instance 1L), but have been placed there for easy reference to specific statements during this discussion. They can be considered as referring to line 1, line 2, and so on.

Fortran Symbols

The names of variables in Fortran can be from one to five characters long and, because they must be key-punched, they are written in capital letters. Names of variables that always have small whole-number values (integers) usually begin with the letter I, J, K, L, M, or N; names of variables that may take a wide range of values (floating-point numbers) must begin with a letter other than I, J, K, L, M, or N.

Input/Output Operations

Each input or output operation requires two Fortran statements. One is an executable statement that causes the particular READ, WRITE, PRINT or PUNCH operation to take place, and the other is a nonexecutable

Figure 16-1. Fortran Program to Calculate Mean and Variance

```
C  COMPUTATION OF MEAN AND VARIANCE
7      SIZE = 0.0
       SUMXI = 0.0
       SUMSIQ = 0.0
1      READ 2,NUM,X
       IF(999-NUM) 3,4,5
5      SIZE = SIZE+1.0
       SUMXI = SUMX+X
       SUMSIQ = SUMSQ+X**2
       GO TO 1
4      XMEAN = SUMX/SIZE
       XVAR = (SUMSQ-SUMX**2/SIZE)/(SIZE-1.0)
       PRINT 6,XMEAN,XVAR,SIZE
3      PAUSE
       GO TO 7
2      FORMAT (I3,7X,F5.2)
6      FORMAT (F7.2,5X,F10.4,5X,F5.0)
       END
```

statement that describes the *format* of the input or output record. Statement 2 on line 16L is the format statement that describes the input card of the program. The I3 tells us that the first three columns (1–3) of the card will contain a 3-digit integer. The 7X tells us that the next seven columns (4–10) are to be ignored, and the F5.2 tells us that the next five columns (11–15) will contain a five-digit floating-point number with two decimal places. Since the rest of the card is not used, it need not be described in the format statement.

The actual reading of the card is caused by statement number 1 on line 5L. This statement tells what operation is to take place (read a card), references the format statement (number 2) that describes the card, and lists the names that are to be given to the variables read (in this case, NUM and X).

In a similar manner the statement on line 13L and statement 6 on line 17L print the answers after they are calculated. The former indicates that the variables XMEAN, XVAR, and SIZE are to be printed in the form given in the format statement. The latter is format statement 6, which describes the output print line as three floating-point quantities, the first consisting of seven positions with two decimal places (F7.2), the next consisting of ten positions with four decimal places (F10.4), and finally the last of five positions with no decimal places (F5.0). Each of these numbers is to be separated by five blank spaces (5X).

Program Control

Fortran statements will be executed in sequence as they appear on the page until the sequence is altered by a GO TO or an IF statement or until it is halted by a PAUSE or a STOP statement. In Figure 16–1, the program begins with statement number 7 on line 2L and proceeds down the page to the GO TO statement on line 10L. At this point it unconditionally branches back to statement number 1 on line 5L. Statement number 1 is needed on this statement as the reference used by the GO TO statement. Statement number 1 causes a card to be read and, as long as the number in columns 1–3 is not a 999, the program continues in the loop between lines 5L and 10L.

An IF statement combines a test and a three-way branch. The expression in parentheses is evaluated and a branch is executed to the statement indicated by the first, second, or third number following the parenthesis, depending upon the current value of the expression. If the value of the expression is negative, the branch is to the first numbered statement; if it is zero, the branch is to the second numbered statement; and if it is positive, the branch is to the third statement.

On line 6L of this program, the expression 999–NUM is evaluated and tested. That is, the identification number from card columns 1–3 is subtracted from 999. Only when the number in the card equals 999, indicating the last card, will the value of the expression be zero. At all other times the number in the card will be less than 999, and the value of the expression will be positive. Hence the three numbers that follow the parenthesis, 3, 4, and 5 will cause branching to an error halt, to the computational portion of the program, or to continuance of the reading loop, respectively.

When all of the cards have been read and the IF statement has caused a branch to 4, the mean and variance are calculated and printed, and the PAUSE statement causes the program to halt. Pushing the START key of the computer will cause the program to continue to the next statement. In this case the next statement is a GO TO 7, which will start the whole program over again, reading a new set of data and calculating its mean and variance.

A STOP statement differs from a PAUSE in that depressing the START key will not execute the next statement, but rather will cause the computer to halt again immediately. Thus, a STOP is a permanent halt, while a PAUSE will permit the operator to continue the program if he so desires.

Calculations

Calculations in Fortran are performed by arithmetic statements. These statements are of the form of an expression on the right of an equal sign and a single variable on the left of the equal sign. The expression is evaluated and the variable on the left is given this value. For this reason it is more accurate to read the statement on line 8L as SUMX is "replaced by" SUMX plus X, rather than SUMX is "equal to" SUMX plus X. By the regular rules of algebra the latter would be true only when X equals zero. In the former sense, the old value of SUMX is added to X to give the new value of SUMX.

The right-hand portion of an arithmetic statement can be anything from simple constants, such as the zeros in the statements on lines 2L, 3L, and 4L, to expressions that are much more complex than that on line 12L. The key-punch symbols for the permitted operators are as follows:

+	Add
−	Subtract
*	Multiply
/	Divide
**	Raise to a power

Parentheses are used in the same manner as in algebra and may be nested to any depth. That is, a parenthesis may be used within a parenthesis, and a parenthesis may be used within that parenthesis, and so on. If an arithmetic statement is too long to fit on one card, a continuation number can be placed in column 6 and the statement continued on the next card.

In statement 7 of the mean and variance program, the quantity SIZE is set to zero, and each time a card is read the value of SIZE is increased by one by statement 5. At the end of the card reading, SIZE will equal the number of cards read, which is also the sample size. In a similar manner the statement on line 3L sets the value of SUMX to zero, and the statement on line 8L adds in each value of X as the cards are read. The statement on line 4L sets the value of SUMSQ to zero, and the statement on line 9L totals the values of x^2. After all the cards have been processed, statement 4 on line 11L and the statement on line 12L calculate the value of the mean and variance.

Functions

The more common mathematical functions are available in Fortran to the programmer by simply writing the name of the function followed by parentheses containing the argument. The argument may be a simple constant or a complex expression.

In Figure 16–2 the mean and variance program has been altered to calculate the mean and standard deviation by the use of one of the built-in Fortran library functions. In statistics the standard deviation is equal to the square root of the variance. The statement on line 12L of this program calculates the standard deviation by taking the SQRT function of the same expression that was used in Figure 16–1 to calculate the variance.

The following functions are available in all versions of Fortran:

Square root	SQRT
e to the x power	EXP
Sine	SIN
Cosine	COS
Arctangent	ATAN
Natural logarithm	LOG

In addition to these built-in library functions, the programmer is also given means by which he may define his own functions. The methods for doing this are beyond this simple discussion of Fortran.

C FOR COMMENT

STATEMENT NUMBER | Cont. | FORTRAN STATEMENT

```
C COMPUTATION OF MEAN AND STANDARD DEVIATION
    7 SIZE = 0.0
      SUMX = 0.0
      SUMSQ = 0.0
    1 READ 2,NUM,X
      IF(999-NUM) 3,4,5
    5 SIZE = SIZE+1.0
      SUMX = SUMX+X
      SUMSQ = SUMSQ+X**2
      GO TO 1
    4 XMEAN = SUMX/SIZE
      STDEV = SQRT((SUMSQ-SUMX**2/SIZE)/(SIZE-1.0))
      PRINT 6,XMEAN,STDEV,SIZE
    3 PAUSE
      GO TO 7
    2 FORMAT (I3,7X,F5.2)
    6 FORMAT (F7.2,5X,F7.2,5X,F5.0)
      END
```

Figure 16–2. Fortran Program to Calculate Mean and Standard Deviation

EXAMPLE 16-2

The ability of Fortran to handle scientific calculations is particularly well demonstrated in the use of subscripts and indexed loops. Figure 16–3 illustrates these types of statement. This program computes the volume of an ideal gas for a series of pressures and temperatures and prepares a table of the volumes. In the first of two data cards, 1–10 values of pressure are given to the program. The first two columns of the card contain an integer which tells how many pressures are contained in the card. Similarly the second card contains 1–10 values of temperature. For each value of pressure the volume is calculated for all the values of temperature; thus, if there were 4 pressures and 6 temperatures, a table of 24 volumes would result. In this program the pressure is given in pounds per square inch and the temperature is given in degrees Fahrenheit. The volume in cubic feet of a quantity of gas that occupies 1 cu ft at standard temperature and pressure is calculated by the formula

$$V = \frac{0.0299 \, (T + 460)}{P}$$

This problem should immediately be recognized as identical to calculating the perfect gas law in problem eight of Chapter 13.

Subscripts

In scientific computing it is common to have a series of values for the same variable, such as the four pressures in Example 16–2. They are usually considered to have a sequential order, much like the volumes of an encyclopedia set. Thus the values of pressure could be called the first pressure, the second pressure, the third pressure, and the fourth pressure. The mathematical notation for this is P_1, P_2, P_3, and P_4. The index numbers 1, 2, 3, and 4 are called *subscripts* (because they are written below the normal line of print), and the values of pressure are read "P sub 1," "P sub 2," and so on. The entire set of P's is called an *array*, and each P is called an *element* of the array. A subscript may be a constant and refer to a specific element, such as P_3 for the third element of the P array, or it may be a variable to refer to the elements in general, such as P_i. Of course, at any particular time, the general subscript i will have a specific value, so that if $i = 3$ then $P_i = P_3$.

```
C COMPUTATION OF THE VOLUME OF AN IDEAL GAS
      DIMENSION P(10),T(10)
   10 READ 1,N,P(1),P(2),P(3),P(4),P(5),P(6),P(7),P(8),P(9),P(10)
      READ 1,M,T(1),T(2),T(3),T(4),T(5),T(6),T(7),T(8),T(9),T(10)
      DO 20 I=1,N
      PRINT 2,P(I)
      TAU = 0.0299/P(I)
      DO 20 J=1,M
      TEMP = T(J)+460.0
      V = TAU*TEMP
   20 PRINT 3,T(J),V
      PAUSE
      GO TO 10
    1 FORMAT (I2,F5.2,F5.2,F5.2,F5.2,F5.2,F5.2,F5.2,F5.2,F5.2,F5.2)
    2 FORMAT (//11HPRESSURE = F7.2/)
    3 FORMAT (17H TEMPERATURE = F7.2,10X,9HVOLUME = F8.3)
      END
```

Figure 16–3. Fortran Program to Compute the Volume of an Ideal Gas

In the Fortran solution of the second example, two arrays, one for pressure and one temperature, are set up by the DIMENSION statement on line 2L. At the time the program is compiled it is not known how many pieces of data will appear on each data card, so the DIMENSION statement must provide for the maximum of ten elements in each array. The elements of these arrays are referred to in the statements on lines 7L and 9L for calculations, and in the statements on lines 6L and 11L for printing. In these statements the subscript I is used for indexing the values of P, and the subscript J is used for indexing the values of T.

The values of I and J, in turn, must be set and stepped by other statements within the program. Those may be simple arithmetic statements or a more powerful type of statement called the DO statement. If arithmetic statements are to be used, a set of statements that would start the value of I at one and step it by one until it passes ten might be the following printing loop:

$$I = 1$$
$$3 \quad \text{PRINT 2, P(I)}$$
$$I = I + 1$$
$$\text{IF } (I - 10) \ 3, 3, 5$$
$$5 \quad \text{continuation of program}$$

Here the variable I is called the index of this loop and its current value may be used as a subscript for another variable. In this example, the program would print P_1, P_2, P_3, ..., P_{10}, and then, having completed the loop, would progress to statement number 5.

DO Loops

Because indexed loops are so useful in Fortran, a more convenient way of writing them is provided in the form of the DO statement. The above print loop could be written

$$\text{DO 4 } I = 1, 10$$
$$4 \quad \text{PRINT 2, P(I)}$$
$$\text{continuation of program}$$

The DO statement says to execute all the following Fortran statements down to and including the one whose number appears after the word DO in the DO statement. In this case the number is 4 and the range from the DO statement to statement 4 includes only statement 4 itself. The second part of the DO statement says to use I as on index and repeat the loop over and over from the first time when $I = 1$ through the last time when $I = 10$. A third number after 10 would tell how much to step the value of I each time. If this third number, or parameter, is missing, it is understood to equal 1. These two Fortran statements would also print P_1, P_2, P_3, ..., P_{10}, and then continue on to the next statement.

In Example 16–2 one DO loop is nested inside another, with the outer loop starting on line 5L and proceeding through line 11L. The index of this loop is I, which takes on values from 1 through N, where N is the number of pressures read by the READ statement of line 3L. The value of N must not exceed 10, since the DIMENSION statement sets the maximum of the P array at 10, and the compiler sets aside storage space for only that number of values. The inner loop starts on line 8L and also proceeds through line 11L. Its index is J, which takes values from 1–M, where M (which is also limited to a maximum of 10) is the number of temperatures read by the READ statement on line 4L.

In order to clarify the above, refer to this same problem as programmed in Chapter 13. Recall that the quotient of the perfect gas law constant and the first pressure were computed; from this the values for volume using each of the six temperatures were obtained. Then the second pressure was used as the divisor, and the computations again were performed, using each temperature. This was continued until calculations were completed, using each of the volumes.

In a similar fashion the inner DO loop of the Fortran program will compute volumes for each of the temperatures, while the outer DO loop provides for each pressure. In executing this program, the value for I, the pressure index, is set to 1 at line 5L, and the first pressure is printed. Continuing on, the value for J is also set to 1 at line 8L. Computations follow to obtain the volume V_1 for P_1 and T_1, and these values are printed out at statement 20. But statement 20 is also the one referred to by the inner DO statement (line 8L), so a return is made to this point and the value of J is incremented to two and the operation repeated, this time producing V_2. This is repeated until $J = 6$ and the inner DO loop is satisfied (that is, until J equals the value given M). Then, and only then, does the program return to the outer DO statement (line 5L), increment the value of I to two, and repeat the inner loop. In each pass of the outer loop, the inner loop is re-entered and cannot be left until its index J reaches its limit M (in this case 6). Finally, at the end of the last pass through the outer loop, I reaches its limit N (in this case 4) at the same time that J reaches M.

Now both DO loops are satisfied and the program can proceed to line 12L. The total number of times that the volume of the ideal gas is computed will be N times M, or in this case 24, as can be seen in the sample output of this program in Figure 16–4 (this may be compared to Figure 13–25).

COBOL

In May 1959 the U.S. Department of Defense called together representatives from government agencies and computer manufacturers to discuss the possibility of adopting a common language for business data processing. At this meeting the Conference On Data Systems Languages (Codasyl) was established, and in January 1960 this group completed its specifications for a COmmon Business-Oriented Language (Cobol).

1. The new language was to be machine-independent and written in English.

2. Automatic documentation was to be provided by a program that could be read by a nonprogrammer. No longer would the

```
PRESSURE =      .10

    TEMPERATURE =      0.00        VOLUME =   137.540
    TEMPERATURE =     32.00        VOLUME =   147.108
    TEMPERATURE =    100.00        VOLUME =   167.440
    TEMPERATURE =    212.00        VOLUME =   200.928
    TEMPERATURE =    400.00        VOLUME =   257.140
    TEMPERATURE =    539.99        VOLUME =   298.997


PRESSURE =     1.00

    TEMPERATURE =      0.00        VOLUME =    13.754
    TEMPERATURE =     32.00        VOLUME =    14.710
    TEMPERATURE =    100.00        VOLUME =    16.744
    TEMPERATURE =    212.00        VOLUME =    20.092
    TEMPERATURE =    400.00        VOLUME =    25.714
    TEMPERATURE =    539.99        VOLUME =    29.899


PRESSURE =    14.70

    TEMPERATURE =      0.00        VOLUME =      .935
    TEMPERATURE =     32.00        VOLUME =     1.000
    TEMPERATURE =    100.00        VOLUME =     1.139
    TEMPERATURE =    212.00        VOLUME =     1.366
    TEMPERATURE =    400.00        VOLUME =     1.749
    TEMPERATURE =    539.99        VOLUME =     2.033


PRESSURE =   999.99

    TEMPERATURE =      0.00        VOLUME =      .013
    TEMPERATURE =     32.00        VOLUME =      .014
    TEMPERATURE =    100.00        VOLUME =      .016
    TEMPERATURE =    212.00        VOLUME =      .020
    TEMPERATURE =    400.00        VOLUME =      .025
    TEMPERATURE =    539.99        VOLUME =      .029
```

Figure 16–4. Sample Output for Example 16–2

programmer have to write comments about what his program was doing. It could almost be said that he kept the comments and threw away the coding.

3. Communication between the business executive who requested the program and the programmer who wrote it was to be improved, since both could read the program.

4. The time required to write the program was to be decreased by leaving the detail code to the Cobol compiler.

5. The debugging time was to be decreased by having the Cobol compiler print diagnostic messages indicating possible programming errors.

6. Once written, the program should be able to run on a computer of another model or manufacture by recompiling after only minor changes.

7. The education of a Cobol programmer should be applicable to any computer.

These were all valuable objectives for the Department of Defense because of the variety of computers that it uses and the mobility of its programmers. These objectives are also valid, but perhaps to a lesser extent, for the entire computer industry.

The original Cobol specifications published in 1960 became known as Cobol 60. This version was implemented by both RCA and Sperry Rand's Univac Division. Most other manufacturers waited until Codasyl updated the language the next year and published it as Cobol 61. Since then, Cobol compilers have been written for almost every tape-oriented computer in operation.

The Cobol Language

Every Cobol program must contain four parts, known as *divisions*. These are the *identification* division, the *environment* division, the *data* division, and the *procedure* division. Each has its own function and each has its counterpart in the programming systems we have already examined. The identification division contains explanatory comments under the headings of PROGRAM ID, AUTHOR, INSTALLATION, DATE WRITTEN, DATE COMPILED, and SECURITY. Except for a PROGRAM ID, which is required, the programmer may write as little or as much about these items as he desires. Furthermore, one additional category, REMARKS, is available for additional comments. These entries correspond to the REMARKS fields and COMMENT cards of the other systems, and in no way affect the compiled program.

The environment division is divided into two sections, the *configuration* section and the *input/output* section. The configuration section describes both the computer upon which the program will be compiled and the computer upon which it will be run. The configuration section serves much the same function as the CTL (Control) card of 1401 Autocoder. The input/output section assigns specific input/output devices to each file used in the program. It is a real advantage to assign input/output devices this way rather than to use direct reference to them in the body of the main program, since, when it is necessary to use a different device, it is easier to change one sentence in this section than to search through the entire program, find all the references to the device, and change each of them. This flexibility is not available in SPS, Autocoder, or Fortran.

The data division is made up of three sections, the *file* section, the *working-storage* section, and the *constant* section. The file section describes such things about each file as whether the records are blocked or unblocked, whether or not the file has label records, and gives the names of the data records. Following the file descriptions are detailed descriptions of each item in each record, giving its name, size, decimal location, and so on. The functions performed by this section are accomplished by DS entries in SPS, by DA entries in Autocoder, and by FORMAT statements in Fortran. The WORKING-STORAGE SECTION and the CONSTANT SECTION provide for work areas and constants, as their names imply.

The two functions of machine-language computer instructions are (1) to tell the computer what to do, which is done by operation codes, and (2) what to do it to, which is done by one or more addresses. This is not at all unlike the English language (or any other language), where verbs tell what is to be done and nouns tell what it is to be done to. It therefore follows that simple English commentary, written under very restrictive rules and with a limited vocabulary, can be translated into a computer program. The procedure division is just such a commentary. It is a computer program and it reads like good English, but it is somewhat deceptive. Although the untrained person can read it, he can not write it. That is not to say that Cobol programming is difficult, but rather to point out that all Cobol is English (except perhaps in some other countries) but not all English is Cobol. For example it is perfectly correct to use the word COMPUTE in Cobol but the word CALCULATE can not be used in its place. A Cobol programming example will give a better understanding of the capabilities of the language.

EXAMPLE 16-3

We will use the same gross-to-net payroll computation used in Chapter 13. Although it is written for card input and output, it would not be difficult to alter it to use magnetic tape input and output.

In the identification division, lines 1010 and 1020 of Figure 16–5, the program is identified as GROSS-TO-NET. The first part of this name, GROSS, will appear in the heading of each page of the compilation output.

In the environment division, lines 1030–1100, it is stated that the program will be compiled on an IBM 1401 and it will be run on an 8K 1401. It further states that the file called PAYROLL-FILE will be read from the card reader, and the file called PAY-OUT-FILE will be punched on the card punch. Words connected by hyphens are all part of the same name. A Cobol name can be up to 30 characters long and must not contain any blanks. For example, PAYROLL-FILE is a single name but PAYROLL − FILE indicates that the quantity FILE is to be subtracted from another quantity PAYROLL.

The data division indicates that the records on the PAYROLL-FILE will be referred to by the name PAYROLL, and describes the items, or *elements*, of that record. The particular record described is a card record, but the description for a tape record would be the same, except that it would not be restricted to 80 characters. The first element in this record is the employee number, EMPLOYEE-NO, which is described by the PICTURE clause as being six numeric digits long. A 9 in a picture clause means that in the actual data this character will be any digit,

```
001010 IDENTIFICATION DIVISION.
001020 PROGRAM-ID.  GROSS-TO-NET.

001030 ENVIRONMENT DIVISION.
001040 CONFIGURATION SECTION.
001050 SOURCE-COMPUTER.  IBM-1401.
001060 OBJECT-COMPUTER.  IBM-1401 MEMORY SIZE 8000 CHARACTERS.

001070 INPUT-OUTPUT SECTION.
001080 FILE-CONTROL.
001090     SELECT PAYROLL-FILE ASSIGN TO 1402-R, O.
001100     SELECT PAY-OUT-FILE ASSIGN TO 1402-P, O.

002010 DATA DIVISION.
002020 FILE SECTION.
002030 FD  PAYROLL-FILE
002040     LABEL RECORDS ARE OMITTED
002050     DATA RECORD IS PAYROLL.
002060 01  PAYROLL.
002070     02 EMPLOYEE-NO PICTURE IS 999999.
002080     02 NAME PICTURE IS X(29).
002090     02 EXEMPTIONS PICTURE IS 9.
002100     02 YTD-GROSS PICTURE IS 99999V99.
002110     02 YTD-FICA PICTURE IS 999V99.
002120     02 YTD-WITHHOLDING-TAX PICTURE IS 99999V99.
002130     02 FILLER SIZE IS 19.

002140     02 GROSS PICTURE IS 9999V99.
002150 FD  PAY-OUT-FILE
002160     LABEL RECORDS ARE OMITTED
002170     DATA RECORD IS NEW-PAYROLL.
002180 01  NEW-PAYROLL.
002190     02 NEW-EMPLOYEE-NO PICTURE IS 999999.
002200     02 NEW-NAME PICTURE IS X(29).
```

Figure 16–5. Source Program for Example 16–3

0–9. The second element is the employee's name, NAME, and is pictured as X(29). The X means any character in the computer character set, and the 29 in parenthesis means that there are 29 of these characters. This is shorter than writing all 29 X's. The next element, EXEMPTIONS, is a one-digit code giving the number of exemptions. The year-to-date gross pay, YTD-GROSS, is described by its picture as a seven-digit number, with the decimal point, indicated by the V, understood to be between the second and third digits from the right. A decimal point implied by a V is not actually punched in the data card and hence does not require a column in the card, but the V is used to make it possible for the Cobol compiler to perform automatic decimal alignment. The next two elements, year-to-date *FICA*, YTD-FICA, and year-to-date withholding tax, YTD-WITHHOLDING-TAX, and the last element, gross pay, GROSS, follow the same rules as YTD-GROSS.

The positions of the entries within this list imply the positions of the data within the data record. Since EMPLOYEE-NO is first and is six characters long, it will be found in card columns 1–6. NAME is next,

```
002210    02 NEW-EXEMPTIONS PICTURE IS 9.
002220    02 NEW-YTD-GROSS PICTURE IS 99999V99.
002230    02 NEW-YTD-FICA PICTURE IS 999V99.
002240    02 NEW-WITHHOLDING-TAX PICTURE IS 99999V99.
003010    02 NET-PAY PICTURE IS 9999V99.
003020    02 FICA PICTURE IS 99V99.
003030    02 WITHHOLDING-TAX PICTURE IS 9999V99.
003040    02 FILLER SIZE IS 3.
003050    02 NEW-GROSS PICTURE IS 9999V99.


004010 PROCEDURE DIVISION.
004020 START.  OPEN INPUT PAYROLL-FILE, OUTPUT PAY-OUT-FILE.

004030 READ-IN.  READ PAYROLL-FILE RECORD AT END GO TO CLOSE-FILES.
004040     IF GROSS - EXEMPTIONS * 13.00 IS GREATER THAN ZERO THEN
004050     COMPUTE WITHHOLDING-TAX ROUNDED = 0.14 * (GROSS - EXEMPTIONS
004060     * 13.00) OTHERWISE MOVE ZEROES TO WITHHOLDING-TAX.

004070     IF 4800.00 - YTD-GROSS - GROSS IS GREATER THAN ZERO THEN
004080     COMPUTE FICA ROUNDED = 0.03625 * GROSS AND GO TO UP-DATE.

004090     IF 4800.00 - YTD-GROSS IS GREATER THAN ZERO THEN COMPUTE
004100     FICA ROUNDED = 0.03625 * (4800.00 - YTD-GROSS) OTHERWISE
004110     MOVE ZEROS TO FICA.

004120 UP-DATE.  ADD YTD-WITHHOLDING-TAX AND WITHHOLDING-TAX GIVING
004130     NEW-WITHHOLDING-TAX.  ADD YTD-GROSS AND GROSS GIVING
004140     NEW-YTD-GROSS.  ADD YTD-FICA AND FICA GIVING NEW-YTD-FICA.
004150     COMPUTE NET-PAY = GROSS - WITHHOLDING-TAX - FICA.

004160     MOVE EMPLOYEE-NO TO NEW-EMPLOYEE-NO, MOVE NAME TO NEW-NAME,
004170     MOVE EXEMPTIONS TO NEW-EXEMPTIONS.  MOVE SPACES TO NEW-GROSS.
004180     WRITE NEW-PAYROLL.  GO TO READ-IN.

004190 CLOSE-FILES.  CLOSE PAYROLL-FILE AND PAY-OUT-FILE.  STOP 99.
```

Figure 16–5. Continued

and will therefore be in columns 7–35. Similarly, EXEMPTIONS will be in column 36, YTD-GROSS in columns 37–43, YTD-FICA in columns 44–48, and YTD-WITHHOLDING-TAX in columns 49–55. GROSS is in columns 75–80, which leaves a gap of 19 columns between YTD-WITHHOLDING-TAX and GROSS. Those columns must be described as elements if the program uses them, or they may be lumped together and called FILLER if the program has no need to refer to them. The second file, the PAY-OUT-FILE, and its record, NEW-PAYROLL, are described in the same manner.

The procedure division describes the actual program logic. Here Cobol verbs are combined with the programmer-chosen names from the data division to make up clauses. Clauses are combined to make up sentences, and sentences are combined to make up paragraphs. Each paragraph must have a paragraph name. The first paragraph, START, initializes the input/output routines and processes the file labels. This is more significant for tape files than for card files.

The second paragraph, READ-IN, reads the input card, PAYROLL, and computes the withholding tax by taking 14 percent of the taxable income. If the taxable income is negative, it sets the withholding tax to zero. Next FICA is computed by taking $3\frac{5}{8}$ percent of gross until an accumulation of 4800 dollars for gross is reached. Extra testing is required for the pay period in which the 4800-dollar limit is reached, since only a fraction of this period gross pay enters into the calculation.

In the third paragraph, UP-DATE, year-to-date figures are brought up to date and constant information is moved from input card to output card. The output card, NEW-PAYROLL, is then punched. This card will be used to write the pay checks, and it also serves as the input card for the next pay period.

The last paragraph, CLOSE-FILES, writes the trailer labels, if it is a tape file, and ends the program.

This example can only serve to give a general outline of Cobol programming. Many features and capabilities have not been illustrated. For example, like Fortran, Cobol can handle subscripted variables and execute indexed-controlled loops. In areas of data manipulation and tape handling, Cobol far excels Fortran.

ALGOL

While Fortran was being developed in this country, a similar language, Algol (*AL*Gebraic *O*riented *L*anguage, or *ALGO*rithmic *L*anguage), was being developed in Europe. The function of the two languages are basically the same, although Algol is considered to be the more flexible.

It is interesting to note that, as new versions of Fortran (Fortran II and Fortran IV) have been released, the language has included more and more of the features of Algol that are missing in Fortran, the differences now being almost negligible.

CONCLUSION

Both Cobol and Fortran are constantly being expanded and improved by their respective committees, namely Codasyl and the Share-Fortran committee. Just as Algol and Fortran have become more similar, so have Cobol and Fortran. Finally, in March 1964, the Share organization announced its *Share Advanced Language*, which seems to indicate a trend toward a universal language based upon the experiences gained in the use of Fortran, Algol, and Cobol.

SUMMARY OF INSTRUCTIONS

141 INSTRUCTIONS

(Arranged in the alphabetic order of the SPS mnemonic.)

ADD *(A)*

Op code	A address	B address
A	aaa	bbb

Description. The ADD instruction causes the data in the A field to be added algebraically to the data in the B field. The A field is not disturbed and the resulting sum is stored in the B field.

Word Marks. The defining word mark of the B field terminates the operation. If the A field is shorter than the B field, the A field word mark will halt transmission of data from the A field, but any resulting carrys will be added to the B field until the B field word mark is sensed. If a carry results beyond the B field word mark, it is lost, or if the A field is longer, the high-order positions of the A field that exceed the limits imposed by the B field word mark are lost. These both represent overflow conditions.

ADD *(A)*

Op code	A address
A	aaa

Description. The four-position ADD instruction causes the A field to be added to itself, with the sum replacing the original A field.

Word Marks. The word mark is not affected.

BRANCH (B)

Op code	I address
B̲	iii

Description. The BRANCH instruction causes the program to branch to the instruction specified by the I address.

BRANCH IF INDICATOR ON (B)

Op code	I address	*d* character
B̲	iii	d

Description. The BRANCH IF INDICATOR ON instruction is a conditional branch. The *d* character specifies the indicator to be tested as a criterion for the branch. If the indicator is on, the program branches to the instruction specified by the I address. If the indicator is off, the next sequential instruction is executed. The indicators to be tested and their *d* character codings are

INDICATOR		*d* CHARACTER
EQUAL COMPARE	(B = A)	S
UNEQUAL COMPARE	(B ≠ A)	/
HIGH COMPARE	(B > A)	U
LOW COMPARE	(B < A)	T

Testing of an indicator does not affect its setting.

BRANCH IF CHARACTER EQUAL (B)

Op code	I address	B address	*d* character
B̲	iii	bbb	d

Description. The BRANCH IF CHARACTER EQUAL instruction causes the single character at the B address to be compared to the *d* character. If they are identical, the program branches to the instruction specified by the I address. If they are different, the program proceeds to the next instruction in the sequence.

Word Marks. Word marks at the B address are ignored and thus do not affect the comparison.

COMPARE (C)

Op code	A address	B address
C̲	aaa	bbb

Description. The COMPARE instruction causes the information in the B field to be compared with an equal number of characters in the A field. The bit configuration of each character of the two fields is compared, and appropriate indicators are set as described below.

Word Marks. The first word mark encountered terminates the operation. If the A field is longer than the B field, extra A field positions beyond the length of the B field will not be compared.

Indicators. If the two fields are identical character-by-character, an EQUAL COMPARE results and the EQUAL indicator is turned on. If the fields are not equal, an UNEQUAL COMPARE results and the UNEQUAL indicator is turned on. In addition, the HIGH indicator is turned on if the B field is greater than the A field, and the LOW indicator is turned on if the A field is greater than the B field. If the B field is longer than the A field, the UNEQUAL and HIGH indicators are turned on regardless of their contents. All indicators are reset *only* by another COMPARE instruction.

CLEAR STORAGE (CS)

Op code	A address
/	aaa

Description. The CLEAR STORAGE instruction causes the storage to be cleared to blanks, beginning at the location specified by the A address and continuing downward through the nearest hundreds position.

Word Marks. Both word marks and data are cleared by this instruction.

CLEAR STORAGE AND BRANCH (CS)

Op code	I address	B address
/	iii	bbb

Description. The CLEAR STORAGE AND BRANCH instruction causes the storage to be cleared (including word marks) to blanks, beginning at the location specified by the B address and continuing downward through the nearest hundreds position in the same manner as the CLEAR STORAGE instruction. Upon completion of the clearing operation, the program branches to the instruction specified by the I address.

CLEAR WORD MARK (CW)

Op code	A address	B address
☐ or)	aaa	
☐ or)	aaa	bbb

Description. The CLEAR WORD MARK instruction causes a word mark to be cleared from the location specified by the A address. If a B address is also used, word marks will be cleared from the locations specified by each address. If no word mark existed in either location prior to the instruction, there will be no change at that location. Data will not be disturbed.

HALT *(H)*

Op code

.̇.

Description. The HALT instruction causes the computer to stop. Depressing the start key will cause the program to proceed to the next instruction in the sequence.

HALT AND BRANCH *(H)*

Op code	I address
.̇.	iii

Description. The HALT AND BRANCH instruction causes the computer to stop. Depressing the start key will cause the computer to proceed to the instruction designated by the I address.

LOAD CHARACTERS TO A WORD MARK *(LCA)*

Op code	A address	B address
L	aaa	bbb

Description. The LOAD CHARACTERS TO A WORD MARK instruction causes the characters *and* word mark from the A field to replace the B field. The A field remains undisturbed.

Word Marks. The A field must contain a word mark to terminate the transmission of data. All word marks in the B field are cleared, and a word mark is placed in the B field corresponding to that in the A field.

MOVE CHARACTERS TO A OR B WORD MARK *(MCW)*

Op code	A address	B address
M	aaa	bbb

Description. The MOVE CHARACTERS TO A OR B WORD MARK instruction causes the field specified by the A address (A field) to be moved to corresponding positions of the B field. The A field remains undisturbed, but the B field is lost.

Word Marks. The first word mark encountered in either field stops the transmission of data. Existing word marks in neither field are disturbed.

NO OPERATION *(NOP)*

Op code

<u>N</u>

Description. The purpose of the NO OPERATION instruction is to cause the program to proceed to the next instruction in sequence. The instruction may have the format of any allowable instruction; that is, it may have an A address, an A address and a B address, and so on.

PUNCH A CARD *(P)*

Op code

<u>4</u>

Description. The PUNCH A CARD instruction causes information in storage locations 101–180 (PUNCH area) to be punched in columns 1–80, respectively, of a Hollerith-coded card. The machine coding is converted to Hollerith coding prior to punching. The information stored in the PUNCH area is undisturbed. This instruction punches only information from the PUNCH area of storage onto the card.

Word Marks. Word marks are not punched, are not affected by the PUNCH instruction, and do not affect punching in any manner.

PUNCH AND BRANCH *(P)*

Op code	I address
<u>4</u>	iii

Description. The PUNCH AND BRANCH instruction causes the computer to punch the contents of the PUNCH area (in the same manner as the PUNCH A CARD instruction), and branch to the instruction specified by the I address.

READ A CARD *(R)*

Op code

<u>1</u>

Description. The READ A CARD instruction causes the information in columns 1–80 of a Hollerith-coded card to be read into storage positions 001–080, respectively. The Hollerith code from each column is converted to the appropriate computer coding as it is read into the computer. The READ A CARD instruction *always* reads into positions 001–080 (the READ area).

Word Marks. Word marks that exist in the READ area prior to execution of the instruction are not disturbed, nor do they affect the reading of information.

READ AND BRANCH *(R)*

Op code	I address
1	iii

Description. The READ AND BRANCH instruction causes the computer to read one Hollerith-coded card (in the same manner as the READ A CARD instruction), and branch to the instruction specified by the I address.

SUBTRACT *(S)*

Op code	A address	B address
S	aaa	bbb

Description. The SUBTRACT instruction causes the data in the A field to be subtracted algebraically from the data in the B field. The A field is not disturbed, and the resulting difference is stored in the B field.

Word Marks. Word marks control the SUBTRACT operation in the same manner as the ADD instruction.

SUBTRACT *(S)*

Op code	A address
S	aaa

Description. The four-position SUBTRACT instruction causes the A field to be subtracted from itself, with zeros replacing the original A field.

Word Marks. The word mark is not affected.

SET WORD MARK *(SW)*

Op code	A address	B address
‚	aaa	
‚	aaa	bbb

Description. The SET WORD MARK instruction causes a word mark to be set at the location specified by the A address. If a B address is also used, word marks will be set at the locations specified by each address. Existing word marks are undisturbed. Data at the location (or locations) will not be disturbed.

WRITE A LINE *(W)*

Op code

2

Description. The WRITE A LINE instruction causes the information in storage locations 201–300 (the PRINT area) to be printed on the printer (or on the typewriter). The information will remain in the PRINT area of storage after execution of the instruction. This instruction *always* prints information from all 100 positions of the PRINT area.

Word Marks. Word marks are not printed, are not affected by the instruction, and do not affect printing in any manner.

WRITE AND BRANCH *(W)*

Op code	I address
2	iii

Description. The WRITE AND BRANCH instruction causes the computer to print the contents of the PRINT area (in the same manner as the WRITE A LINE instruction), and branch to the instruction specified by the I address.

SPS PSEUDO INSTRUCTIONS

The following instructions do not result in equivalent machine-language instructions but are directives to the assembler. They fall in two classes, area-definition statements (declaratives), and processor-control statements (control).

Declaratives

DEFINE CONSTANT WITH WORD MARK *(DCW)*

The symbolic operation code DCW causes a constant to be loaded into storage and sets a word mark in the high-order (leftmost) position of the constant field. The number of characters in the constant field is specified in the COUNT portion of the coding sheet (columns 6 and 7). The symbolic label by which the constant is referenced is placed in the LABEL area (columns 8–13). The code DCW is placed in columns 14–16. Column 17 must contain an asterisk to indicate to the assembler that it may choose the location of the constant field, or else columns 17–20 must contain the desired storage location of the low-order position (rightmost) of the constant field. The constant itself begins in column

24 and may extend through 55, giving a maximum of 32 characters. If the constant is to be a signed number, the sign must be placed in column 23.

DEFINE CONSTANT (DC)

The symbolic operation code DC causes a constant to be loaded into storage without a word mark. Otherwise, it is identical to the DCW.

DEFINE SYMBOL (DS)

The operation code DS causes the processor to assign equivalent addresses to labels or to assign storage for work areas. The DS differs from DC and DCW statements in that neither data nor word marks are included during loading. The number of positions to be reserved in storage is specified in the COUNT portion of the coding sheet. If it is desired to refer symbolically to the low-order position of the field reserved, a label must be placed in the LABEL field. If the assembler is to assign the address, an asterisk must be placed in column 17 of the coding sheet. If it is desired to equate the label to an actual address, that address is written beginning in column 17, and the COUNT field of the coding sheet is left blank. It is not possible to character-adjust DS statements.

DEFINE SYMBOLIC ADDRESS (DSA)

The DSA statement causes a three-character machine-language address, which the assembler has assigned to a label, to be stored as a constant when the program is loaded. The number of characters need not be specified in the COUNT area of the coding sheet, since it is automatically assigned three storage positions by the processor. If it is desired to refer to the address of the address field, a symbol may be written in the LABEL portion of the coding sheet. Column 17 may contain an asterisk, thus allowing the assembler to assign the storage positions, or else columns 17–20 may contain the desired storage locations of the low-order position for the address field. The symbol whose equivalent address is to be the address field is written beginning in column 28 of the B operand.

Control Statements

ORIGIN (ORG)

The ORG statement causes the assembler to assign addresses to the following instructions, beginning at the location specified by the statement. The symbolic operation code ORG must be placed in the operation field, and the absolute address at which storage assignment is to be made must be written in columns 17–20 of the coding sheet.

EXECUTE *(EX)*

The EX statement causes the computer to suspend loading of the object program and execute part of the program prior to continuing the loading process. The symbolic operation code EX must be placed in the operation field, and the symbolic or actual address of the first instruction to be executed when the loading process is suspended must be placed in the A operand portion of the coding sheet. The card containing the EXECUTE statement must be inserted at the point in the source program where suspension of loading is desired in order to execute the preceding portion.

END *(END)*

The END statement is an indication to the assembler that last card of the source program has been processed. The symbolic operation code END must be placed in the operation field and the address of the first instruction, either actual or symbolic, must be placed in the A operand area of the coding sheet.

THE 141 CHARACTER CODE CHART

The complete set of symbols available to the 141 system is summarized in Table II-1. The Hollerith coding used on cards and the seven-bit alphameric coding used in computer storage are given. In addition, the second column contains the numeric equivalent of each symbol if it is used in an arithmetic instruction. For instance, if the letter *D* appeared in the A or B operand of an ADD instruction, it would be treated as a +4 during the addition operation.

Table AII-1
141 CHARACTER CODES
(In Collating Sequence)

CHARACTER	NUMERIC VALUE	CARD CODE	SEVEN-BIT ALPHAMERIC CODE						
			C†	B	A	8	4	2	1
Blank	0	Blank	x						
√		12–3–8		x	x	x		x	x
☐ or)	√	12–4–8	x	x	x	x	x		
& or +	+0	12	x	x	x				
$	√	11–3–8		x		x		x	x
*	√	11–4–8		x		x	x		
−	−0	11		x					
/	+1	0–1	x		x				x
,	√	0–3–8	x		x	x		x	x
& or (	√	0–4–8			x	x	x		
# or =	√	3–8				x		x	x
@ or '	√	4–8				x	x		
? or 0̇	+0	12–0		x	x	x		x	
A	+1	12–1		x	x				x

Table AII–1   (Continued)

CHARACTER	NUMERIC VALUE	CARD CODE	SEVEN-BIT ALPHAMERIC CODE						
			C†	B	A	8	4	2	1
B	+2	12–2		x	x			x	
C	+3	12–3	x	x	x			x	x
D	+4	12–4		x	x	x			
E	+5	12–5	x	x	x		x		x
F	+6	12–6	x	x	x		x	x	
G	+7	12–7		x	x		x	x	x
H	+8	12–8		x	x	x			
I	+9	12–9	x	x	x	x			x
! or 0̄	−0	11–0		x		x		x	
J	−1	11–1	x	x					x
K	−2	11–2	x	x				x	
L	−3	11–3		x				x	x
M	−4	11–4	x	x			x		
N	−5	11–5		x			x		x
O	−6	11–6		x			x	x	
P	−7	11–7	x	x			x	x	x
Q	−8	11–8	x	x		x			
R	−9	11–9		x		x			x
S	+2	0–2	x		x			x	
T	+3	0–3			x			x	x
U	+4	0–4	x		x	x			
V	+5	0–5			x		x		x
W	+6	0–6			x		x	x	
X	+7	0–7	x		x		x	x	x
Y	+8	0–8	x		x	x			
Z	+9	0–9			x	x			x
0	0	0	x			x		x	
1	1	1							x
2	2	2						x	
3	3	3	x					x	x
4	4	4					x		
5	5	5	x				x		x
6	6	6	x				x	x	
7	7	7					x	x	x
8	8	8				x			
9	9	9	x			x			x

√ Has no numeric meaning, invalid for arithmetic.
† Check bit to produce odd-parity. Table shows values for positions with no word mark. Reverse if word mark is present.

Appendix III

SUBROUTINES

Subroutines for the 141 system that are included in this appendix are MULTIPLY, DIVIDE, SUPPRESS ZEROS, and EDIT; the source listings are given for each subroutine.

In preparing these subroutines, the storage requirements, program length, and simplicity of use were among the primary considerations. In the interest of conserving storage, common work areas are used for all of the subroutines. Thus care must be exercised in clearing the work areas, especially if more than one is used in a given program. All work areas are set up during assembly by using DCW instructions. These areas as used by each subroutine, together with their symbolic addresses, are summarized below:

	SUBROUTINE			
ABSOLUTE ADDRESS	MULTIPLY	DIVIDE	SUPPRESS ZEROS	EDIT
081–089	MULTD	DIVR	not used	EDIN
091–099	MULTR	QUOT	SZARG	not used
181–196	PROD	DIVD	not used	EDOUT (181–191)

The mnemonics employed within each subroutine were chosen in an attempt to avoid labels that are frequently used. However, the student should exercise care so as not to use mnemonics in his program that are incorporated in the subroutines. In addition to labels required for linkage, the following symbols were used.

332

MULTIPLY	M3	M4	M6	M9	M16	M17	M18	M19
DIVIDE	D7	D8	D11	D13	D24	D25	D26	
SUPPRESS ZEROS	SZ3	SZ5	SZ13	SZ14	SZ15			
EDIT	ED9	ED11	ED19	ED20	ED21			

THE "MULTIPLY" SUBROUTINE

Title: Multiply

Mnemonic: MULT

Purpose: To provide the capability of multiplying a number containing up to 8 digits by a second number containing up to 8 digits to form a product up to 16 digits in length.

Storage Requirements.

Multiplicand	081–089
Multiplier	091–099
Product	181–196
Additional work areas	197–200
Program	100 additional locations as assigned by assembler

Linkage. Move the multiplicand of *m* digits to MULTD. This field will then occupy storage positions (090—*m*) through 089. Move the multiplier of *n* digits to MULTR. This field will then occupy storage positions (100—*n*) through 099. Move the return BRANCH instruction to MULTX + 3. Branch to MULT. The linkage is illustrated in Figure AIII–1.

0						
0			M,C,W	(multiplicand)		M,U,L,T,D
0			M,C,W	(multiplier)		M,U,L,T,R
0			M,C,W	R,E,T,U,R,N,−,0,0,I		M,U,L,T,X, +,0,0,3
0			B,	M,U,L,T,		
0			B,	R,E,T,U,R,N,		
0	R,E,T,U,R,N			(next instruction in program)		

Figure AIII–1

After completion of the operation, the product of *m* + *n* digits will be in PROD. Both the multiplicand and multiplier remain in their respective areas.

Word Marks. Word marks are placed in locations 081, 091, and 181 with DCW's during assembly, and care must be exercised to insure that they are not cleared during execution of the main program.

Clearing. Initially, all three work areas will be zero, and further clearing is left to the programmer. Blanking or zeroing of the multiplicand and multiplier areas will only be necessary if the new values contain fewer digits than the previous quantities that used these areas. Zeroing of the product accumulator will always be necessary unless it is desired to sum products. If the accumulator is not zeroed after prior use, the product will be summed with the quantity which was originally in this area.

Scaling. Decimal alignment is the responsibility of the programmer. The number of decimal places in the product is equal to the sum of the number of decimal places in the multiplicand and the multiplier.

```
M1 010    MULT    MCW M16          M3   + 3
M1 020            MCW M17          M6   + 6
M1 030    M3      MCW MULTR -  7 M19   - 1
M1 040    M4      C   M19   -  1 M18   - 1
M1 050            B   M9                        U
M1 060    M6      A   MULTD        PROD  - 7
M1 070            S   M18          M19
M1 080            B   M4
M1 090    M9      SW  M3    +  1 M6    + 4
M1 100            A   M18   -  1 M3    + 3
M1 110            A   M18   -  1 M6    + 6
M1 120            CW  M3    +  1 M6    + 4
M1 130            C   M3    +  3 M16   - 2
M1 140            B   M3                        /
M1 150    MULTX   B   0000
M1 160 03 M16     DCW *         092
M1 170 02 M17     DCW *          89
M1 180 02 M18     DCW 0198      10
M1 190 02 M19     DCW 0200      00
M1 200 09 MULTD   DCW 0089      000000000
M1 210 09 MULTR   DCW 0099      000000000
M1 220 16 PROD    DCW 0196      0000000000000000
```

Figure AIII–2. Source Listing for the MULTIPLY *Subroutine*

THE "DIVIDE" SUBROUTINE

Title: Divide

Mnemonic: DIV

Purpose: To provide the capability of dividing a number containing up to 16 digits by a second number containing up to 8 digits to form a quotient of up to 8 digits.

Storage Requirements:

Dividend	181–196
Divisor	081–089
Quotient	091–099
Program	154 additional locations as assigned by assembler

Linkage: Move the dividend of m digits to DIVD. This field will then occupy storage positions (197—m) through 196. Move the divisor of n digits to DIVR. This field will then occupy storage positions (090-n) through 089. Move the RETURN BRANCH instruction to DIVX + 3. Branch to DIV. The linkage is illustrated in Figure AIII–3.

	MCW	(dividend)	DIVD	
	MCW	(divisor)	DIVR	
	MCW	RETURN-001	DIVX	+003
	B	DIV		
	B	RETURN		
RETURN		(next instruction in program)		

Figure AIII-3

After completion of the operation, the quotient will be located at QUOT and the remainder at DIVD. The divisor remains in DIVR but the dividend is lost.

Word Marks: Word marks are placed in locations 081, 091, and 181 with DCW's during assembly, and care must be exercised to insure that they are not cleared during execution of the main program.

Clearing: Initially, all three work areas will contain zeros, and further clearing is left to the programmer. Zeroing of the dividend and divisor areas will be necessary if new values contain fewer digits than previous quantities that used these areas. The high-order position (081) of the divisor *must contain zero* or the subroutine will not function properly. Zeroing of the quotient accumulator will always be necessary unless it is desired to sum quotients. If the accumulator is not zeroed after prior use, the quotient will be summed with the quantity that was originally in this area.

Scaling: Decimal alignment is the responsibility of the programmer. Rules to follow are

1. Multiply the dividend and divisor by the appropriate power of ten to clear decimals from divisor.
2. Multiply the dividend and the expected quotient by the same power of ten to obtain greater accuracy.
3. The upper eight digits (181–188) of the dividend must be less than the divisor or the subroutine will not function properly.

The following examples illustrate scaling in the divide subroutine:

$$\frac{38}{1.2} = \frac{380}{12}$$

		NUMBER	LOCATION OF LOW-ORDER POSITION
(1)	Before division	380	DIVD
		12	DIVR
	After division	31	QUOT
		8 (remainder)	DIVD
(2)	Before division	380∧0	DIVD
		12	DIVR
	After division	31∧6	QUOT
		0∧8 (remainder)	DIVD
(3)	Before division	380∧00	DIVD
		12	DIVR
	After division	31∧66	QUOT
		0∧08 (remainder)	DIVD

```
D1 010   DIV    MCW  D24        D7   +  3
D1 020          MCW  D25        D11  +  6
D1 030          MCW  D24        D13  +  6
D1 040          C    DIVR       DIVD -  8
D1 050          B    D7                    T
D1 060          H    DIVX
D1 070   D7     MCW  DIVD  -  7 D26   -  1
D1 080   D8     C    D26   -  1 DIVR
D1 090          B    D13                    U
D1 100          S    DIVR  +  1 D26
D1 110   D11    A    D24   -  2 QUOT  -  7
D1 120          B    D8
D1 130   D13    MCW  D26   -  1 DIVD  -  7
D1 140          SW   D7    +  1 D11   +  6
D1 150          SW   D13   +  4
D1 160          C    D24        D11   +  6
D1 170          A    D24   -  2 D7    +  3
D1 180          A    D24   -  2 D11   +  6
D1 190          A    D24   -  2 D13   +  6
D1 200          CW   D7    +  1 D11   +  6
D2 010          CW   D13   +  4
D2 020          B    D7                    /
D2 030   DIVX   B    0000
D2 040 03 D24   DCW  *        189
D2 050 01 D25   DCW  *        2
D2 060 10 D26   DCW  *        0000000000
D2 070 09 DIVR  DCW  0089     000000000
D2 080 09 QUOT  DCW  0099     000000000
D2 090 16 DIVD  DCW  0196     0000000000000000
```

Figure AIII–4. Source Listing for the DIVIDE *Subroutine*

THE "SUPPRESS ZERO" SUBROUTINE

Title: Suppress Zero

Mnemonic: SUPZR

Purpose: Given a numeric field of 9 digits or fewer, to suppress leading zeros (that is, change high-order zeros to blanks).

Storage Requirements:
Work area   091–099 (addressed as SZARG)
Program   82 additional locations as assigned by assembler

Linkage: Move the numeric field of *m* digits to SZARG. The field will then occupy storage positions (100—*m*) through 099. For example, a three-digit field would occupy positions 097–099. Move the return BRANCH instruction to SUPZRX + 3. Branch to SUPZR. The linkage is illustrated in Figure AIII–5.

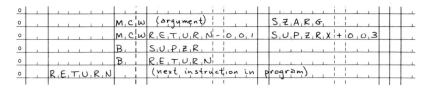

Figure AIII–5

After completion of the operation, the field with leading zeros suppressed will remain in its original location. If the entire field is zero, one zero will remain.

Word Marks: A word mark is set at location 091 during processing by the assembler. If cleared during execution of the main program, it should be reset.

Clearing: Initially, the work area will be zero, and further clearing is left to the programmer. Zeroing will always be necessary if the new field contains fewer digits than the previous quantity that used this area.

```
S1 010    SUPZR   MCW SZ15        SZ3   +   3
S1 020            MCW SZ15        SZ5   +   6
S1 030    SZ3     C   SZARG -  8  SZ13  -   1
S1 040            B   SUPZRX                      T
S1 050    SZ5     MCW SZ14        SZARG -   8
S1 060            SW  SZ3   +  1  SZ5   +   4
S1 070            A   SZ13        SZ3   +   3
S1 080            A   SZ13        SZ5   +   6
S1 090            CW  SZ3   +  1  SZ5   +   4
S1 100            C   SZ3   +  3  SZ15  -   1
S1 110            B   SZ3                         /
S1 120    SUPZRX  B   0000
S1 130 02 SZ13    DCW *           01
S1 140 01 SZ14    DCW *
S1 150 02 SZ15    DCW *           91
S1 160 09 SZARG   DCW 0099        000000000
```

Figure AIII–6. Source Listing for the SUPPRESS ZERO *Subroutine*

THE "EDIT" SUBROUTINE

Title: Edit

Mnemonic: EDIT

Purpose: To provide the capability to edit a field of up to 8 digits consisting of dollars and cents. Leading zeros are suppressed, and a decimal point, a comma (if needed), and a floating dollar sign are placed in appropriate positions of the field.

Storage Requirements:

Input field	081–089
Output field	181–191
Program	127 additional locations as assigned by assembler

Linkage: Move the field of m digits to be edited to EDIN. This field will then occupy positions (090—m) through 089. Move the RETURN BRANCH instructions to EDITX + 3. Branch to EDIT. The linkage is illustrated in Figure AIII–7.

Figure AIII–7

After completion of the operation, the edited field will be located at EDOUT. The original field remains in EDIN.

Word Marks: Word marks are placed in locations 081 and 191 with DCW's during assembly, and care must be exercised to insure that they are not cleared during execution of the main program.

Clearing: Initially, both work areas will be zero, and further clearing is left to the programmer. Zeroing of the input area (EDIN) will be necessary if the new argument contains fewer digits than previous quantities that used this area. The output area (EDOUT) is self-clearing.

Scaling: Quantities that are edited must consist of a dollar and cent amount. The following examples illustrate scaling in the EDIT subroutine:

INPUT FIELD	OUTPUT FIELD
12345678	$123,456.78
12345	$123.45
123	$1.23
12	$0.12

```
E1 010      EDIT    MCW  ED20        ED9   +  3
E1 020              MCW  ED20        ED11  +  6
E1 030              MCW  EDIN        EDOUT
E1 040              MCW  ED21        EDOUT -  2
E1 050              MCW  EDIN   -  2 EDOUT -  3
E1 060              MCW  ED21   -  1 EDOUT -  6
E1 070              MCW  EDIN   -  5 EDOUT -  7
E1 080              MCW  ED21   -  2 EDOUT - 10
E1 090      ED9     C    EDOUT  -  9 ED19  -  1
E1 100              B    EDITX                   T
E1 110      ED11    MCW  ED21   -  2 EDOUT -  9
E1 120              SW   ED9    +  1 ED11  +  4
E1 130              A    ED19        ED9   +  3
E1 140              A    ED19        ED11  +  6
E1 150              CW   ED9    +  1 ED11  +  4
E1 160              C    ED9    +  3 ED20  -  1
E1 170              B    ED9                     /
E1 180      EDITX   B    0000
E1 190 02   ED19    DCW  *        01
E1 200 02   ED20    DCW  *        82
E1 210 04   ED21    DCW  *        $,.
E1 220 11   EDOUT   DCW  0191     00000000000
E1 230 09   EDIN    DCW  0089     000000000
```

Figure AIII–8. Source Listing for the EDIT Subroutine

OPERATING
PROCEDURES

A special package of programs is available from the IBM 1620 program library that will permit the assembly and execution of 141 programs on the IBM 1620 data processing system.[1] Because so many 1620's have been installed in high schools and colleges for the purpose of computer instruction, it seems desirable to place the operating procedures for those 1620 programs here for easy reference.

Four versions of the 141 SPS assembler and the 141 simulator are available in order to permit maximum use of computer hardware. These are identified as

Non-Monitor Versions
    Version A—Basic 1620.
    Version B—1620 with 1443 Printer.

Monitor Versions
    Version C—1620 with 1311 disk storage drive and indirect
        addressing.
    Version D—1620 with 1443 printer, 1311 disk storage drive,
        and indirect addressing.

Letters preceding each procedure statement below identify the versions to which they apply.

---

[1] K. P. Swallow and R. E. Gentry, *An Educational Computer for Instruction in Basic Programming.* Version A, IBM File No. 13.0.015; Version B, IBM File No. 13.0.016; Version C, IBM File No. 13.0.017; Version D, IBM File No. 13.0.018.

141 SPS ASSEMBLER

Prepare Console

Version

AC	1. Set left typewriter margin at 10 and right margin at 95.
ABCD	2. Set parity switch and input/output switch at STOP.
ABCD	3. Set overflow switch at PROGRAM.
CD	4. Set disk switch at PROGRAM.
ABCD	5. Set program switches 1 and 2 according to the program switch options.

Assemble SPS Programs

Version

AB	1. Place the 141 SPS assembler deck in the reader hopper in the 9-edge face-down position.
CD	2. Place the following monitor cards in the reader hopper: COLD START, + + JOB, and + + XEQ 141 SPS.
ABCD	3. Place SPS source program decks in the reader hopper. Any number of programs may be stacked for assembly. The last card of each deck must be an END statement.
ABCD	4. With the machine in MANUAL mode, press the LOAD key on the 1622 reader-punch unit.

Program Switch Options

Version

ABCD	1. Switch 1 and 2 off—object deck will be punched and program will be listed.
ABCD	2. Switch 1 off and switch 2 on—object deck will be punched but program listing will be suppressed except for incorrect statements. A program listing can be prepared from the object program cards on an IBM 407 accounting machine. This option will greatly reduce assembly time for versions A and C.
ABCD	3. Switch 1 on and switch 2 off—object deck will be suppressed and program will be listed on the console typewriter (or printer).
ABCD	4. Switch 1 and 2 on—object deck and program listing will be suppressed. This combination can be used as an edit run. Programs from an entire class can quickly be scanned for errors with only incorrect statements being listed. The particular op code or address that is erroneous will appear as the symbol =. For easy recognition, be sure that the

source cards are numbered in columns 1–5 and that the identification field, columns 76–80, is punched.

Long Programs

Version

AB 1. An SPS assembly is a two-pass operation, but the 141 SPS assembler only requires that the cards be fed through once if the number of cards in the source program does not exceed 100. This reduces the amount of card handling and permits the stacking of programs. If the number of cards in a source program is greater than 100, images of the first 100 cards are held in storage and copies of the remaining cards are punched for a second pass. These cards are removed from the PUNCH stacker and placed in the READ hopper at the end of pass 1. Only those statements in excess of 100 need be processed twice.

CD 2. Images of the source cards are stored on the disk; therefore, the length of the program does not affect the operating procedures.

141 SIMULATOR

Prepare Console

Version

AC 1. Set left margin at 10 and right margin at 95.
ABCD 2. Set parity switch and input/output switch at STOP.
ABCD 3. Set overflow switch at PROGRAM.
CD 4. Set disk switch at PROGRAM.
ABCD 5. Set program switches 1, 2, 3, and 4 according to the options listed at the end of this section.

Load Simulator

Version

AB 1. Place the 141 simulator deck in the reader hopper in the 9-edge face-down position.

CD 2. Place the following monitor cards in the reader hopper: COLD START, + + JOB, and + + XEQ 141 SIM.

ABCD 3. With the machine in MANUAL mode, press the LOAD key on the 1622 reader-punch unit. When the simulator is loaded, the typewriter will automatically begin typing a list of the functions that the simulator will perform and the request words that will initiate these functions.

FUNCTIONS PERFORMED	REQUEST BY TYPING
Load Program from card reader	LOAD
Clear 141 storage	CLEAR
Alter storage from typewriter	ALTER
Dump contents of 141 storage	DUMP
Begin execution of program	EXECUTE
Return to 1620 monitor	EXIT (C and D only)

Select the Desired Function

Each function, except EXIT, is available in all versions. (*a*) The typewriter will type the words, REQUESTED FUNCTION IS, and then stop. (*b*) The operator then types the word LOAD, CLEAR, ALTER, DUMP, EXECUTE, or EXIT and presses the RELEASE and START keys on the console or the RS key on the typewriter. (*c*) If a function runs to completion, the simulator will automatically request the next function. If the function is interrupted by turning on program switch 1, the operator may return to the request statement by pressing, in order, the RESET, INSERT, RELEASE, and START keys on the console.

The LOAD Function

Programs that have been assembled by SPS can be loaded with this function. (*a*) Place the SPS object deck, including the two CLEAR STORAGE cards and the bootstrap card, in the hopper. (*b*) Type the request word LOAD and press the RELEASE and START keys. (*c*) Press READER START, if necessary.

The CLEAR Function

The 141 storage can be cleared (set to blanks) with this function. (*a*) Type the request word CLEAR and press the RELEASE and START keys. (*b*) When the clearing operation is completed, the typewriter will request the next function.

The ALTER Function

Instructions and data, including word marks, in the 141 storage can be altered with this function. This may be used for debugging a program or entering complete, small demonstration programs directly in machine language. (*a*) Type the request word ALTER and press the RELEASE and START keys. (*b*) The typewriter will type BEGINNING AT. (*c*) Type the three-digit 141 location at which the alteration is desired and press the RELEASE and START keys. (*d*) The typewriter will repeat this location to verify it. (*e*) Type the instructions and data in machine language, disregarding word marks. This is the only instance where the operator must use the typewriter shift key. For all other entries the typewriter will automatically be in the proper alphabetic or numeric shift. At any convenient place, at least one character before the end of the line, cease typing and press the RELEASE and START keys. (*f*) The typewriter carriage will return for a second line. This line will indicate the presence or absence of word marks. If the character above requires a word mark, type a one; if it does not, strike the space bar. Continue to type ones and spaces until the carriage has moved across the entire line above. In the first position after completion of the word mark line type a record mark (≠), and press the RELEASE and START keys. (*g*) The typewriter will now type the address of the next storage location that will be altered if steps (*e*) and (*f*) are repeated. (*h*) When altering is completed, press in order, the RESET, INSERT, RELEASE, and START keys. The EXECUTE function can be used to start the program.

The DUMP Function

When a 141 program is stopped, either by a programmed halt or by an error condition, it is desirable to be able to dump the instruction register (I REG), the operation register (OP REG) and the storage. The DUMP function will list the contents of the I REG, which will be the address of the next character to be accessed, the contents of the OP REG, which is the operation code of the last instruction to be executed, and the contents of the 141 storage as it stood when the program stopped. (*a*) Type the request word DUMP and press the RELEASE and START keys. (*b*) When the entire storage is dumped, the typewriter will request the next function.

The EXECUTE Function

Execution of 141 programs can be started with this function. (*a*) Type the request word EXECUTE and press the RELEASE and START keys. (*b*) The typewriter will type BEGINNING AT. (*c*) Type the three-digit 141 location of the first instruction to be executed and press the RELEASE and START keys.

The EXIT Function

In versions C and D this function returns control to the 1620 Monitor. (*a*) Type the request word EXIT. (*b*) Press the RELEASE and START keys.

Program Switch Options

1. *Program switch 1*—turning program switch 1 on will cause the program to halt at the end of the execution of the current 141 instruction. The operator may either press START to continue with the next

141 instruction, or he may press RESET, INSERT, RELEASE and START to request a new function.

2. *Program Switch 2*—when program switch 2 is off, the DUMP function will use the typewriter or printer. When it is on, the DUMP function will use the card punch. These cards can be listed on an IBM 407 accounting machine.

3. *Program Switch 3*—cards punched by the DUMP function can be reloaded with the LOAD function with program switch 3 on. With program switch 3 off, SPS self-loading cards can be loaded.

4. *Program Switch 4*—if program switch 4 is on at the time the simulator is loaded, the typing of the list of functions will be omitted.

Special Notes

1. *Restarting Programs*—If it is desired to interrupt a program during execution, it can be stopped, dumped, and later restarted by the following procedures: (*a*) Stop the program by turning program switch 1 on. (*b*) Dump the program on cards, using the DUMP function with program switch 2 on. (*c*) Prior to restarting, clear the 141 storage using the CLEAR function. (*d*) Load the storage dump with switch 3 on.

2. *Console Lights*—when a 141 program is stopped by a PROGRAM HALT, an ERROR HALT, or by turning on program switch 1, the operation code of the instruction just completed can be determined from the DIGIT AND BRANCH lights on the console. The 1620 display can be converted to a 141 operation code by using the following table:

DIGIT AND BRANCH	141 OP CODE	SPS OP CODE
03	$\dot{\underline{}}$	H
04	□ or $\underline{)}$	CW
21	$\underline{/}$	CS
23	$\underline{,}$	SW
41	$\underline{A}$	A
42	$\underline{B}$	B
43	$\underline{C}$	C
53	$\underline{L}$	LCA
54	$\underline{M}$	MCW
55	$\underline{N}$	NOP
62	$\underline{S}$	S
71	$\underline{1}$	R
72	$\underline{2}$	W
74	$\underline{4}$	P

The address of the next instruction to be executed can be determined by pressing the DISPLAY MAR key with the MEMORY ADDRESS REGISTER SELECTOR rotated to the OR-2 position. The 141 address of the next instruction will be displayed by the lights of the MEMORY ADDRESS REGISTER.

3. *Loading Machine-Language Programs*—machine-language programs can be loaded either by typing them under the control of the ALTER function or by key punching them in the card dump format and loading them using the LOAD function with program switch 3 on.

4. *Card Dump Format*—cards in this format must be sequentially numbered, with the odd-numbered cards containing the program and data characters, and the even-numbered cards containing the word marks.

COLUMNS	ODD	EVEN
1–2	Card number	Card number
4–6	Blank	Blank except for last card
9–11	Load address	Blank
20–69	Program or data	Ones for word marks

In an odd-numbered card, up to fifty characters to be loaded are punched, starting in column 20. In columns 9–11 is punched the address of the location in storage where the character in column 20 is to be stored. In columns 20–69 of an even-numbered card are punched ones for the word marks associated with the characters in columns 20–69 of the previous card. In columns 4–6 of the last card (even-numbered) is punched the address at which execution is to begin.

5. *Monitor END OF JOB cards*—in versions C and D, ≠ ≠ ≠ ≠ END OF JOB cards may be used to facilitate continuous operation. In an SPS assembly, if the last source program deck is followed by an END OF JOB card, control automatically causes a return to request a new function. This may be any 141 simulator function, including the EXIT function, that will return control to the 1620 Monitor.

Index

A address, 37, 38
A address register, 1401, 281
Abacus, 2, 3
ADD instruction, 98, 162, 321
Addition, 92–98
Address adjustment, 166–168
Address arithmetic (*see* Address adjustment)
Addressing, 1401, 277–280
Aiken, Howard, 11
Algol, 319–320
Amortization of a loan, example program, 225–231
Analog computer, 1
Analytic engine, 7–9
Arithmetic unit, 19
Argument, 170, 200, 201
Assembler, 65, 84, 202, 300, 301
141 SPS, 340–342
Assembling, 65, 67, 84–87
Autocoder, 1401, 294–298

B address, 37, 38
B address register, 1401, 281
Babbage, Charles, 5–9, 19

Backus, John W., 302
Binary digit (bit), 30, 31
Binary representation, 29, 30
Block diagram (*see* Flowchart)
Blocking, 1401 magnetic tape, 294
Boole, George, 10
Boolean algebra, 10, 11
Bootstrap card, 268, 269
BRANCH IF CHARACTER EQUAL instruction, 163, 164, 322
BRANCH IF INDICATOR ON instruction, 121, 322
BRANCH instruction, 56, 322
Branching operations, 1401, 285–288
Burks, A. W., 11

Carries (arithmetic), 93–95, 279, 280
Central processing unit, 19–22
Chaining, 1401, 281, 282
Character adjustment, 166–168
CLEAR STORAGE AND BRANCH instruction, 160, 161, 323
CLEAR STORAGE instruction, 70–73, 323

Clear storage routine, 87, 269–271
CLEAR WORDMARK instruction, 46–48, 158, 323
Closed subroutine, 169, 170
Cobol, 314–319
Cobol language, 315–319
  data division, 315, 317–319
  environment division, 315–317
  identification division, 315, 317
  procedure division, 315, 316, 319
Code, character, summary of, 330, 331
Coding, card, 26, 27
  internal storage, 29–32
  magnetic tape, 1401, 293
Collating sequence, 330, 331
Comments card, 134, 267, 268
COMPARE instruction, 116–121, 322, 323
Compiler, 302
Constant, 17, 18
Control statement, 90, 327
Control unit, 19
Controlled loop, 127, 130
Core plane, 35

d character, 121, 122, 126, 284–288
Data, 17, 18
Data division, Cobol, 315, 317–319
Data processing system (141), 20, 23, 24, 29–31
Debugging, 76, 146
Decimal alignment, 105, 106, 108
Declarative statement, 90, 327
Define area statement, 1401, 296, 297
DEFINE CONSTANT pseudo instruction, 75, 267, 328

DEFINE CONSTANT WITH WORD-MARK pseudo instruction, 69, 267, 327, 328
DEFINE SYMBOL pseudo instruction, 75, 76, 267, 328
DEFINE SYMBOLIC ADDRESS pseudo instruction, 179, 180, 267, 328
Difference engine, 5–7
Difference table, 6, 7
DIVIDE subroutine, 334–336
Documentation, need for, 132, 134
  program reports, 136
Dump, storage, 88–90

Eckert, J. Presper, 11
Edit, 153, 289, 290
EDIT subroutine, 338, 339
Edsac, 12
Edvac, 11, 189
END card, 268
END pseudo instruction, 65–67, 329
Eniac, 11
Environment division, Cobol, 315–317
Equal compare, 122
Euclid, 241, 242
EXECUTE pseudo instruction, 273, 274, 329

Field, 39–41
Flowchart, 15, 16, 136–145
  detail, 143
  program, 137
  symbols, 137–140
  system, 137
  template, 143, 144
  use of, 145

Fortran, 302–314
  arithmetic statements, 307, 308
  coding sheet, 304, 305
  control statements, 306, 307
  DO loop, 312–314
  format statements, 305
  functions, 308
  input/output operations, 304, 305
  subscripts, 310
  symbols, 304
Function, 200, 201

Goldstine, H. H., 11
Grade-point average, example program, 214–220

Half-adjusting, 108, 110–112
HALT AND BRANCH instruction, 160, 324
HALT instruction, 54, 324
Hardware, 300
Header card, 130
High compare, 122
Hollerith card, 9, 10, 26
Hollerith code, 26, 27, 96
Hollerith, Herman, 10
Hopper, Grace Murray, 302

I address, 56
I register, 90, 281
IBM 650, 301
  701, 12
  1401, 12, 20, 21, 277–298
  1620, 12, 22, 340

IBM card (*see* Hollerith card)
Identification division, Cobol, 315, 317
Imperative statements, 90
Index register, 211, 212
Indexing, 1401, 290–292
Indicators, compare (141), 116–122
  1401, 287
Input/output, 17, 18, 20–22, 49
Input/output instructions, 1401, 282–285
Instruction register, 90, 281

Jacquard loom, 9

Key punch, 28, 29

Label, 60–63
Label table, 84, 86, 202
Last-card indicator, 1401, 286
Linkage, subroutine, 169, 170
Listing, program, 148
LOAD CHARACTERS TO A WORDMARK instruction, 264, 324
Loading, 264–272
  constants, 267
  instructions, 266
Low compare, 122

Machine language, 37
Macro instructions, 1401, 297, 298
Magnetic core, 32–35
Magnetic tape, 1401, 292–294

Mark I, 11
Mauchly, John W., 11
Mean, 238–241, 303
Memory (*see* Storage)
Mnemonic operation code, 41
Modification of addresses, 189, 192
Morse code, 25
MOVE CHARACTERS TO A OR B WORDMARK instruction, 41, 324, 325
Movement of data, 17, 18, 37–45
MULTIPLY subroutine, 175–178, 332–334

Napier, John, 3, 4
Negative numbers, 95–97, 112, 113
Newton's method (square root), example problem, 245–249
NO OPERATION instruction, 54, 325
used as a program switch, 182, 184–186
Numeric punches, 26
Nutt, Roy, 302

Object deck, 65, 67, 87
Open subroutine, 169
Operating procedures, 141 assembler, 341, 342
141 simulator, 342–346
Operation code, 37
Operation register, 90, 281
ORIGIN pseudo instruction, 272, 273, 328
Overflow, 95, 98, 279, 280
Overflow indicator, 1401, 287
Overlay, 273, 297, 298

Parity check bit, 31
Pascal, Blaise, 4, 5, 249
Payroll calculation, example program, 220–224, 316–319
Perfect gas law, example program, 250–254, 310
Poley, Stan, 301
Prime numbers, example program, 242–244
PRINT area, 49, 50
Printer carriage control, 1401, 285
Procedure division, Cobol, 315, 316, 319
Processor (*see* Assembler)
Processor control statement, 90
Program identification, 78
Program switch, 180–186, 235
Pseudo instruction, 65
PUNCH A CARD instruction, 52, 325
PUNCH AND BRANCH instruction, 160, 325
PUNCH area, 49–51
Punched card, 9, 10, 26

READ A CARD instruction, 49–52, 325, 326
READ AND BRANCH instruction, 159, 160, 326
READ area, 49–51

Sense switches, 1401, 286, 287
Sequence checking, 122
SET WORDMARK instruction, 46, 157, 158, 326
Shannon, Claude, 10
Sign control, 1401, 280, 281

Simulator (141), 340
  operating procedures, 342–346
Soap, 301
Software, 300
Sorting, example programs,
  231–238
Source deck, 65
Square root, computation of, ex-
  ample program, 245–249
Stackers, 1401, 284
Standard deviation, 238
Statistical computations, example
  program, 238–241
Storage, 18–24
  dump, 88–90
  map, 23
Stored program, 17, 189
Subroutine, 169–180
  closed, 169, 170
  linkage, 169–172, 179
  open, 169, 170
  placement of, 174
Subroutines, 141, DIVIDE, 334–336
  EDIT, 207, 338, 339
  MULTIPLY, 175–178, 193–199,
    333, 334
  SUPPRESS ZEROS, 171–173, 192,
    193, 337, 338
SUBTRACT instruction, 98–100, 326
Symbolic programming system,
  60–80
  assembler, 65, 69
  assembly, 65, 67, 82–91
  card, 63, 64, 78
  coding sheet, 61, 62, 78
  pseudo instructions, 65, 88

Table look-up, 200–211
  direct, 201–207
  search (random), 201, 207–211

Transition card, 86, 88
Truncation, 108, 109

Unequal compare, 122
Unit record, 26
  (*see also* Punched card)
Univac, 12
Utility routine, 263

Variable, 17, 18
Variable instruction length, 53
Variable word length, 53
Variance, 238–241, 303
Vaucouson, Jacques de, 9
von Leibniz, Baron Gottfried
  Wilhelm, 5
von Neumann, John, 11

Wilkes, M. V., 12
Word (*see* Field)
Word mark, 31, 39
Word mark, testing for, 1401, 287,
  288
Work area, 100–103
WRITE A LINE instruction, 52, 53,
  327
WRITE AND BRANCH instruction,
  160, 327
WRITE area, 49, 52, 53

Zone bit, 1401, testing for, 287,
  288
Zone position (bit), 26, 27, 30–32